A GHOST IN THE MACHINES.

During my time in the T.A. Parachute regiment I had been told that we a huge Military excercize in West So I had to go off and protect W Democracy's against the Communist Hordes. The name of the project was called "RED HAMMER" or some other bloody silly name.

We would have to be behind enemy lines for 2 weeks, the enemy being played by The fearsome Scottish Black Watch regiment and the French Canadiens. We were to be parachuted in by night and cause as much havoc and destruction as we could manage. Of course all ammunition would be blanks.

It was still pretty scary stuff.

On night jumps your always told to never drop your guard, because you can't see the ground or anything else for that matter, so keeping your knees bent position was vital to keep both Testicals intact. The thing is after a while, you keep wondering where the ground is and just as you relax, bang!! Found it!!

It was raining and chilly, but we gathered our chutes and equipment and hid them in the woods, our officers and sergeants getting us sorted into our squads.

The other love is I think most peop stunned by the and Gil s, pure sci
many
one,
of my favour
Don and Phil E
Acoustic.

I once had about I've Trimmed it de because I felt being used for th One example was Jazz bass, that Donald Duck D and BLUES BROTHERS He needed a spare Eric Clapton Tour then on Paul McCartne He only h sad reason. When he had Tour the 60s, OTIS READIN The cars and other T pretty tight, OTIS plane and Duck his spare on the the rest is history, again. Duck died of a hea in Japan, he was

---

Angus a year later as album
r me the sun came

Friend
gger Targin Gotch who asked if I would do g to my old Pals nd worked and I , it felt like I belonged son I wanted to speak and he said yes, and I reminded of the visit to his his words had got k at it, theres no easy way"

drain.
t few days in sheer that Billy would talk to my dad and would find out the truth, but nothin happened, both of them probably too proud talk about it. I started realising then that being wasn't that easy.

Contents of an English Salad Circa 1950 - 196
2 leaves of lettuce.
½ BOILED EGG.
2 PICKLED ONIONS.
½ TOMATO.
1 SLICE OF MEAT. HAM, SPAM, OR TOUNGUE = CHILD
2   "   "   "   = ADULT
and lots of Bread spread with MARGARINE OR
also the ubiquitous HEINZ SALAD CRE
The middle class used butter.

The Lives of Brian

The Lives of Brian

A memoir

BRIAN JOHNSON

MICHAEL  JOSEPH

PENGUIN MICHAEL JOSEPH

UK | USA | Canada | Ireland | Australia
India | New Zealand | South Africa

Penguin Michael Joseph is part of the Penguin Random House group of companies
whose addresses can be found at global.penguinrandomhouse.com

First published 2022
001

Set in 13.5/16pt Garamond MT Std
Typeset by Jouve (UK), Milton Keynes
Printed and bound in Great Britain by Clays Ltd, Elcograf S.p.A.

The authorized representative in the EEA is Penguin Random House Ireland,
Morrison Chambers, 32 Nassau Street, Dublin D02 YH68

A CIP catalogue record for this book is available from the British Library

HARDBACK ISBN: 978–0–241–44640–9
TRADE PAPERBACK ISBN: 978–0–241–44642–3

www.greenpenguin.co.uk

Penguin Random House is committed to a
sustainable future for our business, our readers
and our planet. This book is made from Forest
Stewardship Council® certified paper.

To my Great, Great, Great Grandchildren, who I'll never meet. It's nice to know we'll connect through these words. I wish you the very best in life whoever you are.

With Love your Great, Great, Great Grandfather Brian Johnson

Contents

PART THREE

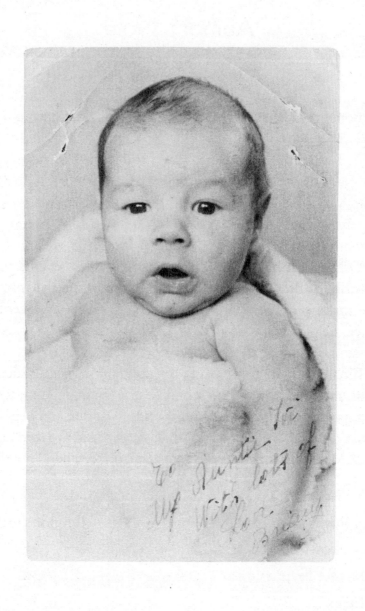

Author's Note

✦

Experience is what you get when you don't get what you want.

This is a book about what happened when I didn't get what I wanted, but never stopped believing, and never gave up. Luck also played its part, of course – but I truly believe that you can achieve just about anything if your dreams are urgent enough, and if you don't just sit around, waiting for something to happen.

Others will have different memories of the events that I describe in these pages. It's been more than forty years since the making of *Back in Black*, after all – and half a century since the glory days of my first band, Geordie. This is just *my* version of how it all went down.

Finally, I'd like to say a big thank you to Angus, Malcolm, Cliff and Phil for rolling the dice and giving me a second chance at a professional music career under some of the most difficult and tragic circumstances that any band could face. Malcolm, if there is another side, mate, when I get there I'll be buying you and Bon a beer.

B. J. – London, 2022

Prologue

⚡

I'd taken some hard blows before. But this time felt different.

This time, barring a miracle, there'd be no getting back up.

The first hint that something was about to go very badly wrong had come in Edmonton, Canada.

It was the end of September 2015, halfway through AC/DC's *Rock or Bust World Tour*, and we were playing Commonwealth Stadium, the biggest outdoor venue in the country – packed to capacity with more than 60,000 people. It was extremely cold and extremely wet, with buckets of rain coming down in front of the stage.

Angus already had a bad fever, and I could feel myself starting to come down with the same thing.

Being Canadian, the crowd didn't seem to have even noticed the weather. But of course, they were bundled up in the kinds of clothes that you can only buy north of the U.S. border, which protect you from everything from raging blizzards to pissed-off polar bears.

As for us, we were just in our usual gear. Me in a black T-shirt and jeans. Angus in his thin white school shirt and shorts. The stage was at least dry, with some warmth from the lights, but Angus and I always like to go out onto the walkway to be with the audience. So, that's where we spent a lot of the show – and after a few songs, we'd worked up such a sweat from all the moving around, we didn't care that we were getting soaked to the bone in near-freezing conditions.

Two hours, nineteen songs and a couple of encores later, we came off stage, feeling great about the gig. The sound on stage had been perfect. The fans had been screaming and cheering and singing along. Angus had played like a man possessed. But there was no time to hang around – we had to get to our next show. So, we said our goodbyes and climbed into our minibuses, which sped us straight to the airport.

As we boarded the jet that would take us to Vancouver, the adrenaline of the show was starting to wear off – and the physical toll that it had taken was starting to become clear.

I couldn't stop shaking.

The thought crossed my mind that for someone just a week away from celebrating his sixty-eighth birthday, maybe all that time in the freezing rain hadn't been such a great idea.

Then again, Angus wasn't faring much better – and he was just a wee nipper of sixty.

Touring is always hard on the body, I reminded myself, no matter what your age. Coming down with the occasional bout of flu between shows is just part of the deal.

I ordered a big shot of whisky, which helped, while Angus had his usual mug of steaming hot tea – and before we knew it, we were wheels-down in Vancouver and heading to our hotel.

But something wasn't right.

It was my ears.

They hadn't popped.

I tried all the old tricks – yawning, swallowing, holding my nose and blowing – but nothing worked. I gave up, thinking that they'd clear themselves during the night.

But when I woke up the next morning . . . oh, shit. I felt like I was wearing a bearskin balaclava.

If anything, my hearing had gotten even worse.

I couldn't bring myself to mention it to anyone at breakfast. When you're the lead singer of a band, your bandmates, the crew, the management, the support staff, the record label and, most important of all, the hundreds of thousands of fans, are all depending on you to get up on stage and do your job, no matter what.

My ears would pop eventually, I told myself.

They always had before.

By the time we got on stage that night at BC Place – another stadium, but this time with a roof – Angus seemed to have shaken off the worst of the fever. But I was still struggling.

Then disaster struck.

About two-thirds of the way through the set, the guitars lost all their tone in my ears, and I found myself searching for the key of the song. It was like driving in fog – all reference points suddenly gone. It was the absolute worst experience that I'd ever had as a singer, made all the more terrifying by the fact that it was happening with several more songs to go . . . in front of tens of thousands of paying fans. But somehow, I made it through – and if anyone noticed, they were too kind to say.

With only two more shows to go on this leg of the tour – AT&T Park in San Francisco and Dodger Stadium in Los Angeles – I convinced myself that I could keep going, that my ears would eventually pop. It seemed impossible to me that they wouldn't.

But the exact same thing happened at both shows. Two-thirds of the way through, I lost the key of the song and couldn't get it back. Worse still, I couldn't hear the conversation in the dressing room afterwards – or later, when we went out to a restaurant for dinner. I just smiled and nodded along, pretending that everything was fine.

But inside, panic was setting in.

Since Angus formed AC/DC with his brother Malcolm in 1973 – first with Dave Evans on vocals, then the great Bon Scott, then yours truly – it's always been an all-or-nothing kind of band.

Just take the giant stack of speakers that we use on stage.

A lot of bands, they use fakes or real cabinets with empty compartments to get the same aggressive, awe-inspiring look. Not AC/DC. With AC/DC, what you see is what you hear – and what you hear as a result is the loudest band on the face of the earth.

Then there's Angus.

The intensity that lad brings to the stage, the whirlwind of energy he can keep up for more than two hours . . . it's frightening. He can't turn it off. When he comes back to the dressing room after a show, he's spent, dead on his feet, gulping down oxygen.

The normal, off-stage Angus is just this nice, softly spoken, five-foot-something guy. But on stage, something happens to him. He transforms. When he goes for a piss before the show, he's still Angus. But when he comes back and he's at the side of the stage, you've lost him. You can't look into his eyes and tell him, 'Have a good one.'

He's gone. Dr. Jekyll has become Mr. Hyde.

And then off he goes, walking out in his schoolboy outfit, Gibson around his neck, lifts his fist to the crowd and 50, 60, maybe 100,000 people lose their fucking minds. He hasn't even played a note. It's just the poise. The growl in his eyes. Who else can do that? Maybe Elvis Presley or Freddie Mercury could do it back in the day. But now it's Angus alone. And the guy can move like the best dancer. The hips. The legs. The whole thing. He out Chuck Berrys Chuck Berry. When you're up close on stage with him, it's the most incredible thing to see.

For most of AC/DC's history, of course, Angus also had his opposite on stage in the form of Malcolm. All of the Young kids – who were born in Glasgow, but emigrated with their parents to Sydney, Australia in the early 1960s – were musical. Another of Angus's brothers, George, was one of the biggest pop stars in Australia with The Easybeats. He also wrote one of the greatest songs of all time, 'Friday on My Mind'.

Malcolm was never any less intense than his younger brother. He just didn't care about being the centre of attention. He'd run up to the mic and sing whatever lines that he had to sing, then he'd walk back to his amp stack and stay out of the way. But make no mistake – Malcolm was the beating heart of the band.

Over the many, many years that I spent with Malcolm on the road, I saw just about every great guitarist you could think of take him aside and ask him how he got those thick-wound strings on his battered Gretsch with a missing pickup to sound that way.

'I just hit 'em hard,' he'd reply with a shrug.

Malcolm also had this uncanny ability to simultaneously watch every single move of every single person in the band, listen to their performance, study the audience's reaction, and at the end of the night, give the kind of feedback that might not have been easy to hear, but made the show better the next night. I've never known any musician to command so much respect from their bandmates and crew.

But even an all-or-nothing band like AC/DC sometimes has to compromise when faced with the setbacks and tragedies that can't be avoided when you spend a lifetime on the road.

A year before the *Rock or Bust World Tour* began, Malcolm had to leave the band to get treatment for early-onset dementia. He'd been suffering from lapses of memory and concentration since the *Black Ice* tour of 2010. So, he stepped back – with his nephew Stevie filling in.

It was the biggest shock to the band since Bon's death, thirty-five years earlier.

And it wasn't the only shock. The master of bass, Cliff Williams – AC/DC's Essex Boy to my Geordie, with the band since 1978 – made it known that *Rock or Bust* would be his last tour. Meanwhile, Phil Rudd had to bow out due to legal problems in New Zealand, with Chris Slade – who'd played on *Razors Edge* – taking over on drums.

And then . . . well, there was me.

It's strange to talk about my own part in AC/DC . . . never mind my own voice. You have to be a pent-up, wound-up animal to hit those notes in 'Back in Black', 'Thunderstruck' and 'For Those about to Rock'. Before a show, I feel like my feet are in the blocks at the start of a gold-medal sprint at the Olympics – because I know that it's going to take every last piece of me to produce that roar of power, rage and attack, and keep it up, for song after song after song. It's like singing with a fixed bayonet.

But without my hearing?

I couldn't escape the feeling that, after thirty-five years with the band, maybe I was nearing the end too.

After the three shows in a row where I couldn't hear the guitars, we had October off, which I hoped would be enough time to rest my body and ears and make everything fine again.

But back home in Sarasota, Florida, it was more obvious than ever that there was something very wrong. It had been six weeks now since my ears hadn't popped.

I needed to get help.

The next leg of the tour was due to start in Sydney, Australia. As it happened, I knew that one of the world's best ear, nose and throat doctors was also there – Dr. Chang. So, after talking to the band's tour manager, Tim Brockman, I decided to fly out ten days early to get my ears properly checked out. I also knew that Malcolm was being treated for his dementia nearby. I hoped that I could pay him a visit.

It was a relief to see Dr. Chang and finally confide in someone about what had been going on. But the relief didn't last very long. After an examination and some tests, he turned deadly serious and said that he would have to put me under and operate.

'After the tour?' I asked.

'No, right now,' he replied.

When I'd contracted the fever in Edmonton, Dr. Chang explained, fluid had built up in my ears. The flight to Vancouver had then caused swelling that had trapped it there. That's why my ears hadn't popped. And because I'd kept touring instead of getting treatment, the fluid had crystallized – and for every minute longer that it stayed in there, the more damage it was doing. So, it had to be removed, immediately.

'Will the operation fix it?' I asked.

'I don't know,' Dr. Chang replied. 'But we can certainly try and stop it from getting worse.'

'But I've got a gig in ten days . . .'

'We'll do everything we can to get you better by then.'

'One more thing, Dr. Chang,' I said, now feeling very nervous. 'How will you get the crystals out?'

'Are you sure you want to know?'

'I mean . . . yeah . . . ?'

'With a chisel.'

He didn't look like he was joking.

PART ONE

I

Alan and Esther

⚡

The soundtrack of my early childhood was the clatter of my mother's sewing machine, followed by the muffled sobs of her crying herself to sleep every night downstairs.

She was Italian, my ma – Esther Maria Victoria Octavia De Luca was her maiden name – and she'd moved to the North East of England with my dad after the war, not realizing that it would be absolutely nothing like her home town of Frascati, just outside Rome.

I can only imagine how much the poor lass's heart sank when she first set eyes on Dunston, the part of Gateshead – just south of the river from Newcastle upon Tyne – where my dad was from. The factories and coal staithes. The back-to-back terraced houses on the steep slope of the Scotswood Road. The soot-faced men trudging home from work. Bombed houses everywhere. The constant wind and rain.

On top of that, of course, there was the rationing, which went on for another nine years after we 'won' the war – the food made worse by the British custom of boiling it until every last atom disintegrated, turning every meal into a plate of grey sludge.

I mean, I've got to hand it to my dad – who served with the Durham Light Infantry in North Africa and then Italy, where he met my ma – that he ever managed to persuade such a beautiful, well-to-do young woman to come home with him.

What made it even more impressive was that my mother was engaged at the time to a tall, handsome Italian dentist who probably had a fabulous name like *Alessandro* or *Giovani* or something, while my dad was a five-foot-two Geordie sergeant called Alan. But my old man's secret weapon was his voice. It was so massive and commanding, he could make you simultaneously stand to attention and shit yourself from a thousand yards. Even when he growled – which he did a lot – he could somehow make the words come out at the same terrifying volume. His secret was he learned to speak Italian and promised my mother he would speak Italian in England. For the rest of his life, he never broke his promise and we kids listened and wondered why no one else spoke like that. It was a little confusing going to school and hearing English.

My dad had joined the army in 1939, just before conscription, to try and get out of working down the pits. But then Hitler invaded Poland, Britain declared war and, all of a sudden, then-Private Johnson found himself shipped off to North Africa, where he fought with the Desert Rats. Now, as any history buff knows, Germany's Afrika Korps were a far superior fighting force to the British in those early days of the war, so the fact my old man survived two blood-soaked years in the Tunisian desert is nothing short of a miracle. But he didn't just survive. He rose all the way to sergeant – not that there was much competition for promotions, given that most candidates were dead before they could be considered for the job.

My dad almost didn't make it back in one piece himself.

His most terrifying near-miss came when he was in the back of a truck that ran straight into the path of a German half-track with a 20mm anti-aircraft cannon on it. After a pause of about two seconds, the truck and anyone still in it were turned to ashes and dust. My dad managed to jump out in time with a few others, and they all piled into a nearby cave for cover. But the Germans just trained their cannon on the cave and let loose until they got bored. When the shelling finally stopped, my dad was the only one left in there alive. He was convinced that the Germans saw him crawl out, but they let him go anyway, probably not wanting the bother of dealing with a shell-shocked prisoner of war who could barely walk.

That didn't mean he was safe, of course.

Once he'd finally limped his way to the nearest Allied position – several miles away – the British sentry panicked and opened fire with his rifle. But luckily my dad was armed with an even more powerful weapon: his voice. 'I'M A BRIT-ISH SERGEANT, YOU IDIOT!!' he roared. 'YOU'RE SUPPOSED TO ASK ME FOR THE WATCHWORD!!'

There was a sheepish pause. Then a little cough. 'Er . . . sorry, Sarge. What's the watchwor—'

'I CAN'T REMEMBER! JUST LET ME IN!'

My dad and his unit made it all the way to Sicily in the end – which earned them an invitation to take part in the near five-month Battle of Anzio. Tens of thousands more men were killed or wounded in that monumental cock-up of an operation, when the hesitation of the U.S. commander, Major General John Lucas, left my dad and his pals stranded on Nettuno beach, where the British had attacked just a few kilometres away.* Once again, however, Sergeant Johnson lived to tell the tale.

By the time it was all over, my dad had seen enough

---

* 'I had hoped that we were hurling a wildcat into the shore,' Winston Churchill later said of the landings, 'but all we got was a stranded whale.'

carnage and misery to make him an atheist for life . . . but he kept that to himself when he got to Rome and realized that there was a city full of gorgeous young Catholic girls waiting to be swept off their feet.

My mother's life before the war could hardly have been any more different than my dad's.

The De Lucas were wealthy and well-connected, for a start. In the photographs taken of them in the 1930s, they look so carefree, happy and tanned they could have all been movie stars. In the North East, people like that just didn't exist.

My ma and her sisters were expected to marry well and they did. One of my Italian aunts landed herself a husband who owned a tile factory. Another married into the family that still owns the Frascati equivalent of Boots the Chemists. Meanwhile, one of my cousins on the De Luca side, Giacomo Christafonelli, served as a member of the Italian parliament for years.

'Love at first sight', was how my mother described meeting my dad in Rome at the end of the war.

She said he looked just like the American movie star George Raft, who starred in the original *Scarface* from the 1930s and, later on, *Some Like It Hot*. I mean, Sergeant Johnson was a bit on the short side, aye, but she was tiny herself, so what did it matter?

Sometimes I wish I'd been able to meet the version of my dad my ma fell in love with – smiley, jokey, everything going his way, the war not just over but *won*, a 'home for heroes' waiting for him in Dunston. It's a side of him that none of his kids ever got to see.

When Rome fell to the Allies, of course, the British army didn't like their men consorting with the female enemy – especially not if they were Catholic. And the top brass would do anything in their power to pour cold water on any romances, so the victorious British soldiers could be saved for the lasses back home. But my dad was a sneaky bugger, and he realized that they would have less to object to if he converted to Catholicism himself. He also thought this would help with my ma's family, who were livid about her calling off her engagement to the handsome dentist.

My dad had barely recovered from the piss-up to celebrate his homecoming when he realized that Sergeant Johnson was surplus to requirements. I mean, the only thing he knew how to do was kill Germans, and there weren't very many of them in Dunston after the war. And while the Americans were printing money to rebuild Europe, they were taking Britain to the cleaners on its debts. To the returning soldiers like my dad – who was sent a medal in the post and discharged from service – it felt more like we'd lost the war than won it. Everything was bombed and broken. There was no money for anything. Britain didn't even get its first stretch of motorway until 1958, after just about every other country in Europe. The only work my dad could find was at the Smith Patterson foundry in Blaydon, County Durham, where they made castings for everything from manhole covers to railway lines. He had to clean out the insides of the furnaces there – a job so disgusting there must have been times he wished he was back in the desert, being shot at by Nazis.

It wasn't even like they provided him with overalls and gloves or eye protection to do the work. Like all the other men, he just wore his everyday jacket with a handkerchief tied around his face. It must have been torture for the poor guy because, as a former sergeant, he couldn't stand it if he didn't look absolutely immaculate.

As for my ma, she'd become pregnant with me before even leaving Italy, and on 5 October 1947, a mother and father were born when I arrived. A year later would come my brother, Maurice, followed another year later by my youngest brother, Victor. The last of the Johnson kids was my little sister Julie, who was born five years after me.

My dad couldn't afford any kind of mortgage on his labourer's wages, of course, and there was a ten-year waiting list for a council house. So, he and my ma had to live with his parents at No. 1 Oak Avenue in Dunston, along with various other family members. These included my unmarried and obnoxious Uncle Norman, who stood at four-foot round and liked to scratch various orifices with his fork at the dinner table. Then there was my Aunt Ethel and her daughter Annette, both of them tough as old boots, and Aunt Ethel's lovely husband, a miner from Scotland whom I came to know as 'Uncle Shughie'. His name wasn't actually Shughie, of course – it just sounded that way when my Aunt Ethel said it. Also living there was my Uncle Billy, who had a tiny moustache, dressed meticulously, and drove a pre-war Vauxhall. At one point, after me and my two brothers and Julie had all arrived, it was a household of *seventeen*. Or, as the neighbours called it, 'a bloody disgrace!'

My mum didn't know much English back then, but even when she started to learn, she almost never spoke it in the house. My dad spoke Italian in a thick Geordie accent, and when my ma didn't understand what he was saying, he'd just repeat himself, but louder. None of which went down very well with the other Johnsons in the house, not least because they'd just been at war with Italy and hated foreigners. Even my grandfather, bless his heart, would refer to his own grand-kids as 'Italian pigs' under his breath.

I mean, this was Dunston in the 1940s, you've got to remember. Other than the French onion sellers with their berets and Gauloises cigarettes, foreign folk were few and far between. I don't think that I saw a single Black or Asian person during my early years growing up – and because it was such a closed society, outsiders were treated with extreme suspicion. Even people from Sunderland were hissed at. The Scots were practically extraterrestrial. I suppose that's why, when I was a kid, I never wanted to learn Italian myself. I just wanted to keep my head down and fit in.

Aunt Ethel was the worst when it came to picking on us for being 'foreign' – which is shocking, given that she was family. One of my first memories is of her taking me with her to the Post Office when I was about four. It was about a three-quarters of a mile walk. And it was winter – and snowing. But Aunt Ethel didn't put any socks or shoes on me. 'You bloody foreigners don't need any of that,' she sniffed.

By the time we got there, I was basically an ice cube in child form. The older lady behind the counter almost had a heart attack when she set eyes on me. 'What are you doing?!!' she screamed at Aunt Ethel, who explained that it was 'Alreet, 'cos he's foreign like.' The older lady grabbed me, found a towel, and wrapped it around my feet – while her husband went to the shop next door to buy me a lollipop. I've no idea how I got home. I just remember the Post Office lady ripping into Aunt Ethel, going, 'You stupid, *stupid* woman – the little lad will catch his death!'

***

THE LIVES OF BRIAN

I dread to think of how alone my mother must have felt after the war. All of the women on our street – who seemed *ancient* to me as a kid but must have been only in their twenties or thirties – would gather every day on the corner with their headscarves and bags, and they'd gossip for what seemed like hours. But my mother could barely understand English, never mind broad Geordie. As the years passed, though, all the neighbours came to realize that she just was the loveliest, kindest, most generous woman, always happy and smiling, always giving away home-cooked food and mending people's clothes. And the way she'd say 'Allo!' was just so infectious.

If anything kept my mother sane during those early years, it was her sewing machine. A foot-powered tabletop thing at first, then a little electric Singer. She'd go at it all day and well into the night – and she really was the most incredible seamstress. In fact, she would eventually build herself a nice little business making wedding dresses for all the local brides. Not to mention stage outfits for a certain young lad after he became a professional singer . . .

My mother loved to knit too. She'd knit *anything*. Balaclavas. Mittens. Tea cosies. Jumpers. One time, when the Johnsons decided they'd have a day out at the seaside – the sea in question being the North Sea, which is only a fraction of a degree warmer than a continental ice sheet – she knitted me and my brothers each a pair of swimming trunks because she couldn't afford to buy real ones. They were dark blue, I remember, and kept up with pieces of old knicker elastic. We'd never set foot in the ocean before, I should add – none of us even knew how to swim – but we were incredibly excited to put on our new kit and start splashing around.

Our excitement about the beach started to wear off pretty quickly as we approached the shore. 'Alright lads, *gerrin!*'

barked my dad. And he pushed us in. The cold water took our breath away.

After maybe fifteen minutes, my father said we were useless and walked off. But that was also the moment when we realized why you never see anyone wearing knitted swimwear. It's because wool has the capacity to take in many, many times its own weight in water – it's like a sponge! – while getting incredibly heavy at the same time.* So, our little willies were on show to everyone. We had to scramble back up the beach red-faced with our hands covering our willies while our backsides were on show with our drenched swimming trunks slapping against the backs of our legs.

Gateshead in those early years of my childhood was a grey and grimy place. During the war, when 'Lord Haw-Haw' made his German propaganda radio broadcasts, he would say things like, 'We shan't be dropping bombs on Gateshead, we shall be dropping bars of soap!' Which, of course, made everyone furious and determined to build the tanks in the Vickers factory at twice the speed. But the truth was, everyone had a 'tidemark' where their clothes met their necks.

The food didn't add much to brighten things up and for my poor ma – who was used to fresh cantaloupe, smoked meats, crusty bread, olive oil and Parmesan – it was torture. The only thing that wasn't boiled was the liver, which was fried – and it was so hard, if you threw it out of the window, you could take out a street light. My ma would just sit there,

* After this revelation, I just assumed that my ma would throw them out. But no, nothing was ever thrown out in our house. Instead, when winter came around, our ma presented us with a set of suspiciously familiar-looking dark blue woollen balaclavas – which smelled of saltwater when you put them on.

sobbing, going, 'I just cannot-a eat-a this!!' And it's not like she could rustle up some Italian home cooking of her own. I mean, you had to go to the chemist to get a bottle of olive oil in post-war Dunston. The only tomato sauce you could get was ketchup. Garlic was probably illegal. Even bacon – an Italian staple – was rationed to eight slices a week, four slices at a time.

My ma's lack of appetite wasn't helped by the fact my grandfather would be sitting there in his waistcoat, pipe in mouth, muttering about the fucking wops in his house, cutting up the previous day's newspaper into pieces so we could use it as toilet paper.

As if all that weren't enough to contend with, my dad fell ill after the war. While he was in that cave in Tunisia, he'd inhaled toxic fumes from the shells and tiny pieces of shrapnel along with all the dust and smoke, and it had basically poisoned him, leaving him with chronic stomach pain. Visibly, he was fine – the only sign of the damage he'd taken was a scar on his thumb. But his stomach kept getting worse and worse, until he couldn't keep down food anymore. And at that point, even for a man as stubborn as he was, he could no longer just keep pretending that everything was fine.

The first I knew about any of this was when I woke up one morning and he was gone. 'Brian, my son, your father . . . he had to go 'ospitale', said my ma, her voice trembling.

A few days later, we went to visit him at a convalescence centre, which was in a beautiful old stately home near Ryton, by the Tyneside Golf Club. I'd never seen such a magnificent place. When we walked in, there was dad, sitting in a comfy chair, doing some needlework to pass the time because he was in too much pain to move. I was like, wow, is *this* where he lives now? He's really gone up in the world . . .

Then I looked around and saw all these other dads sitting around with bandages on their heads and glass eyes and pieces of them missing. Some were even hobbling around on early-NHS prosthetic legs, which were wooden in those days and made horrible creaking noises. So, I realized it was some kind of hospital, but I didn't connect that to the war. I mean, at school, we used to all get in a line and chant, 'We won the war, in 1944!' We had no idea. We devoured all these Eagle comic books about handsome British soldiers with bulging muscles and names like Slogger Smith, who went around shooting Nazis. So, in my kid's mind, there was no reason to think that the war had anything to do with these very ordinary-looking people who'd somehow all managed to suffer the most horrific injuries.

My dad made several long visits to that place, each time after a new operation on his stomach. My ma would take the bus to see him every day, which meant we had to be babysat by Aunt Ethel, who treated us like the prisoners of war she basically thought we were. And by the end of it, our house was full of these beautifully embroidered table covers that my dad had sewn. In another time and another place, he and my ma could have gone into business together and made a killing. But not in those days. The second my dad was released from that beautiful old home, off he went, back to work.

He also worked as a labourer in London for a while, commuting there by steam train and staying all week before returning home for the weekend.

My brother Maurice and I once went with him. It was the most exciting trip that we'd ever made in our lives – not that my dad was living it up in London or anything. When we got off the train at King's Cross, I remember us walking towards a taxi rank, and my heart almost jumping out of my chest at the thought of riding in a black cab.

But when we got to it, my dad just kept on going . . . to the bus stop on the other side of the street.

It wasn't easy for my ma to stay close to her family in Frascati. But when she wrote a postcard to her niece telling her how hard things were in the North East, Ma's sisters wrote back to her asking for her telephone number. All the De Lucas had telephones in their homes, but Ma had to send them the number of the telephone box on our street along with instructions to call it at a certain time, on a certain day. Her sisters then all got together and huddled around the phone while they made their call. And they were so happy to hear each other's voices again – there were a lot of tears and *'Ti voglio benes'* – that many more calls followed, each one lasting no longer than precisely three minutes, because that's as long as you were allowed for an international call in a phone box back then.

When my mother's sisters realized just how difficult my ma's situation was, they were eager to help.

Like my ma, they'd thought that a British sergeant would go home to a country cottage with a manicured lawn and a big garden full of flowers, like something out of a Victorian romance novel – not a council house in Dunston. So, they started to send over supplies. A beautiful set of new pots and pans. A mink coat that had belonged to a great aunt. Scarves and blouses. The essentials of life, in their upper-class minds. But in trying to help, they often just made things worse.

Half of the packages were ripped open at British customs,

with most of the stuff getting 'lost', And whatever made it to Dunston was more often than not intercepted by Uncle Norman or Uncle Colin and pawned for cash. The way they saw it, my mother hadn't *bought* any of this stuff, and they needed money more than she needed expensive gifts from Italy, so what did she have to complain about?

Every time it happened, my ma would just cry and cry.

And this went on and on, week after week, month after month.

And the wind never stopped . . . and the rain kept on falling.

And the food never got better.

And it was always *freezing*.

And my dad was barely earning enough to pay his share of the rent, never mind get his own house.

Then one day, my ma snapped.

I was sitting in the living room, minding my own business, playing with some wooden blocks when it happened. My parents had been arguing about something in the other room – a bit louder than usual, but nothing out of the ordinary – when suddenly my mother grabbed me, put a coat on me, and bundled me out of the door.

'Where do you think you're going?!' my dad roared at her in his Geordie Italian. I didn't understand the words, but you didn't need to with my dad. The volume was enough.

'It's *horrible* here!' she shouted back at him, in tears. 'I'm going home. Your family are –'

She couldn't even think of a bad enough word.

'C'mon, Esther,' snorted my dad. 'You're not going anywhere.'

'I'm leaving!'

'No, you're not.'

'It's horrible here. *Horrible*! I'm going back home!'

And that was that – she was out of the door, pulling me along with her. I don't think it was planned. It was just one of those heat-of-the-moment things. Although she had enough money with her, so I suppose she must have had a secret stash, just in case.

We jumped onto a bus before my dad could catch up, and soon enough it was pulling up outside Newcastle Central Station. And, of course, the drama of that place was just totally overwhelming to me as a kid. All the trains were steam-powered in those days, so they were huffing and puffing and whistling at such a volume I had to clamp my hands over my ears – and on top of that, there were P.A. announcements echoing, the *Evening Chronicle* seller crying out, crowds of people rushing between platforms, and uniformed porters pulling along trolleys piled high with suitcases, cursing whenever a suitcase tumbled off, spilling its contents everywhere.

And there's my poor ma, tugging me this way and that, and I'm trying to ask her what's happening, starting to feel a bit frightened. And her face is all wet and puffy, and she's straining her neck to study this massive paper timetable of departures – about eight feet tall and the length of a double-decker bus – looking for a service to London Victoria. It had to be Victoria, because from there she could take a 'boat train' service to Paris Gare du Nord, where she could change again, headed for Rome.

Eventually, she found the right train and just made a run for it, still pulling me along.

But at the same moment, there was this unmistakable roar behind us, loud enough to drown out the Flying Scotsman at full-throttle. It made everyone in the place stop and stare.

'ESTHER!!!'

Standing there on the platform – just the saddest thing you'd ever seen – was my dad.

He knew what he'd done. What he'd promised his beautiful Italian wife. What he'd failed to deliver.

And, of course, my ma must have seen the pain in his eyes. And she must have known that he was trying as hard as he could, working himself into the ground.

'C'mon, Esther,' he said to her softly, as she began to sob like I'd never seen anyone sob before. 'You can't go. We'll get our own house. I'll call the council. I'll make it better.'

I don't think she believed him.

But it was enough to get her home.

2

Out in the Cold

⚡

It was a winter's day in Dunston, mid-1950s, a few years after my ma's escape attempt. We were now living in a council house of our own on Beech Drive, a ten-minute walk from my grandparents' place on Oak Avenue. We'd started out at No. 106, which had two bedrooms, before my dad, delivering on his promise to my ma, convinced the council to upgrade us to No. 1, which had an extra room in the back. It was still far too small for a family of six – my two brothers and I had to share a double mattress in one room – but with eleven fewer Johnsons than at my grandparents' house, it felt like Buckingham Palace.

Just as we were settling in, though, I did something that made me so ill, I was lucky to ever recover.

It all started with a silent documentary called *Nanook of the North* that I'd watched on our brand-new black-and-white television. The film had been made in the 1920s – you can still find it on the internet today – and it must have been shown on the BBC because the BBC was the only thing that our rooftop aerial could pick up at the time. (The North East didn't get any television at all until six years after the war.)

Now, usually I wasn't interested in the television at all. It was all horticultural programmes and church organ recitals and, if you were lucky, re-runs of Gregory Peck films and Mickey Mouse cartoons – boring, awful stuff that you couldn't have paid me to sit through instead of playing outside with my friends. But *Nanook of the North* was different. It was *gripping*. The star of it was this Inuk guy called Nanook who lived in the Canadian Arctic, and you got to see him building an igloo, hunting for seals and eating the blubber and having a fight with a polar bear – all while a blizzard was raging, ice was cracking under his feet and it was twenty below freezing. And he carried around a big hunting knife and had this stunning Inuk wife and a cute little Inuk baby who wore a little fur hat. And because it was winter in Dunston and snowing, my imagination just ran absolutely wild.

The moment the film was over, I ran outside into the snow and said to myself, 'Right, I'm gonna make an igloo, just like Nanook's.' So, I did. And it was fabulous. About five-foot-wide – same in height – with a little hole in the front for crawling in and out.

But the problem with doing something so incredibly exciting in the late afternoon when you're a kid is that you end up lying in bed, wide awake, mind racing, long after everyone else has gone to sleep. Which is exactly what happened – and why I decided, in the middle of the night, that there'd be no harm in me going outside in the dark to take one more quick look at what I'd built. So, I put a jumper on over my pyjamas, fetched my dad's torch, then snuck out of the back door and into the garden. And as I crawled into my igloo, I stopped being Brian Johnson in the back garden of his council house in Dunston, and became Brianook of the North East, relaxing after a hard day of seal hunting and a feast of blubber pie. Then I yawned just like Nanook would yawn, which was a big mistake because it made me realize just how knackered I was, and I went out like a light.

When my dad got up for work a few hours later – he was

usually out of the house by 6.30 a.m. – he could sense immediately that something was wrong. The house felt like the
North Pole because the back door was open, with snow
blowing in. Then when he checked on the boys' room, it was
one Johnson short.

But in a huge stroke of luck, the noises coming from the
house had woken me up in the igloo, so I rushed back inside
just as my dad was coming downstairs. He thought I'd just
got up early. He had no idea that I'd been out there for most
of the night.

'You daft bugger, you'll catch your death!' he growled at
me. 'Now get yerself dressed . . .'

That was the end of that little adventure, as far as I was
concerned.

But something horrible happened later on that morning at
school when I was trying to practise my writing. All of this
liquid started seeping out of me, like I was a block of ice
starting to melt. It went all over my paper and into my ink-
well, until the teacher, Mrs. Patterson, came over and said,
'Brian Johnson! That's too messy! Start again!'

I was feeling so woozy, I couldn't even answer.

'Wake up!' she barked, clipping me around the ear. 'You've
ruined this piece of paper! What's *wrong* with you! Get yourself home this minute. Is your mother in?'

I managed to grunt a yes, which was all she needed to
know to kick me out into the wind and snow.

Now, being sent home by your teacher was a guarantee of
a massive, belt-whipping bollocking, but I was feeling so
dreadful that wasn't even on my mind. As I followed the
familiar route from school back to Beech Drive, I kept getting slower and slower . . . until my feet wouldn't work
any more. I had no idea what was happening to me. I mean,

usually I ran everywhere at full speed, but now I could barely stand on my own two feet. I ended up just sitting down on the pavement and curling up into a ball. Brianook of the North East was preparing to meet his maker.

That was when I heard the voice of a kindly older lady who'd found me lying there on the street.

'Can ya tell us your name, dear?'

We still didn't have a telephone at that point, never mind a car, so when the Good Samaritan of Dunston dropped me off at home, my mother had to leave me alone in front of the fire and run to the nearest phone box to call our local GP – lovely old Dr. Fairbairn. He told her that he'd be over right away, he just needed to get some lunch first, then finish with his surgery patients, which would take, oh, about five hours.

It was about 5 p.m. when he finally showed up. By which time I was moaning and sweating and freezing cold at the same time, and starting to have trouble breathing. Dr. Fairbairn announced that I was 'gravely ill' and rolled me over to give me an injection in my backside to stabilize me. He stayed with me until well past midnight – which was unheard of. 'I need you to be a strong soldier tonight, okay Brian?' I remember him saying, before giving me another injection. Then he asked me if I liked cars.

Well, I didn't just *like* cars. I was 'car daft', as my dad often said. They were so rare in those days. There was only one on our street – a Morris Minor – which belonged to my dad's boss. I could stare at it for hours, imagining myself driving, lost in my own never-never land. In fact, my dad got so sick of me talking about cars and trying to find new cars to look at on the street that he eventually went to our local garage and asked them if they would give him a steering wheel. (The only stipulation being that it didn't come from a *German* car.) He ended up getting one for sixpence – which was taken out of my pocket money – then he got a large stick, pushed it through our bedhead, attached it to the steering wheel, and piled pillows up around it, like a driving seat. I must have put at least 50,000 miles on that bed.

'Yes, I like cars,' I whimpered to Dr. Fairbairn.

'Well, I'm glad to hear that, son,' he beamed. 'Because, between you and me, I just got myself a new Rover. And if you can stay strong and get better, I'll give you a ride in it.'

Behind him, I could see my parents looking at me and holding hands – which scared the shit out of me because they *never* held hands. The expression on my dad's face, in particular, was something that I'd never seen before. It was, well . . . *love*, I suppose. And fear. Both of which were things that a guy like my dad never let anyone see. There was also a strange kind of resignation. I mean, for my dad's generation, it wasn't that unusual to lose a kid or two to the flu or tuberculosis – even to strep throat. Well, there's the first one to go, he seemed to be thinking.

What my dad should have known, of course, was that a Rover in those days was halfway to a Rolls-Royce. It had chrome dials and a wooden dashboard – with an *AM radio* built into it. What's more, its engine was so powerful it could go from zero to sixty mph in under twenty seconds . . . on its way to a top speed of over eighty mph!

So, obviously, there was no way on earth that I was going to let myself die and miss out on that.

Apart from my near-death experience with the igloo, life on Beech Drive was a massive improvement over Oak Avenue. Just a few days after we arrived – this was at No. 106 – I remember waking up to see these flags up everywhere and tables and chairs on the streets, with all this food and drink and everyone throwing a huge party because we had a new Queen. It pissed it down for most of the day, of course, but no one cared. They even slaughtered a pig and roasted it in Dunston Park. And on top of it all, everyone got a free mug. It's hard to describe just how mind-blowing that was in a time of rationed bacon. I was like, bloody hell, if everyone on our street can get a free mug, then literally *anything* is possible in this place!

Beech Drive was a brand-new development at that time, I should probably mention – the jewel in the crown of North-East council estates. Everything was new and modern, from the freshly laid red tarmac to the brightly coloured front doors. And people were so proud – especially the mothers and wives. Every front step was immaculate. Every net curtain spotless. And everyone's living room had a 'sideboard' and 'bureau' and a fireplace so clean you could have eaten your dinner off it. A lot of mothers even wrapped their settees in plastic to keep them looking new.

The street still had gas lights, mind you, which were lit every night by a guy with a big stick. And we still had a rag-and-bone man – 'the rag man' we called him – who had a little cart pulled by a very sad-looking horse with a balloon tied to its reins. I'll never forget the day when I realized that if you gave the rag man an old jumper or a bedsheet, you got a penny or a balloon. I was like, *why has no one ever told me about this before?* But, of course, as soon as my ma found out what I was doing, she was chasing the rag man halfway up the street, trying to get back a pair of my dad's old socks.

The fun we had in those days was unbelievable. In an age when there were no cars, no traffic, no glowing screens and video games to get hopelessly addicted to – and when everyone looked out for everyone else's kids – we were free in a way that you couldn't imagine today. And because everyone had tiny houses, kids lived outdoors, made their own entertainment and formed their own little gangs. On Beech Drive, for example, there was the Top Gang and the Bottom Gang, depending on which part of the estate you lived on, and within the Top Gang you had the Big ones (me and my friends) and the Little ones (our younger brothers). This was funny because Maurice was a Little one, even though he was taller than me.

Even school – Dunston Hill infants, followed by juniors – wasn't all that bad, all things considered.

The Big ones would walk the Little ones there and back every day, all of us in short trousers – rain, drizzle, sleet, hail, snow, whatever. I would add 'shine', but I could count the times that I glimpsed the sun in Dunston during my childhood on one hand.

Part of the reason why I liked infants' school so much was the classroom, which had a seesaw and a little roundabout in it, both of which would make the kids vomit. Mr. Graham, the caretaker, would always be standing there, mop and bucket at the ready.

When playtime was over, Mrs. Patterson would give us each a little blackboard and a piece of chalk to practise writing our ABCs. Then we'd have music lessons, and all the girls would get recorders, and all the boys would get triangles and tambourines.

That was the beginning of a lifelong love of music for me because I *loved* tingling my triangle. I could do it for hours. And we'd sing songs while Mrs. Patterson played the piano. Awful stuff like 'Underneath the Spreading Chestnut Tree'.

But I didn't care. As long as I could tingle my triangle, I'd sing whatever Mrs. Patterson wanted.

English was my best subject. I loved writing and I always got top marks for my stories and essays – and when I got a gold star, I'd take it home to show my ma and dad.

But it was *after* school when life really began.

Every night, no matter how hard it was raining, we'd put our jumpers in the middle of the street as goalposts and have a game of football. And when it snowed, the street would become a battlefield and we'd have snowball fights that would go on for hours.

I was always at a disadvantage in the snowball fights, though, thanks to the mittens that my mother would knit for me. To make sure that I didn't lose them, she would sew a piece of elastic into one glove, then run the elastic up the arm of my jacket, and down the other arm to the other glove. This worked brilliantly when it came to stopping the gloves falling off. But the problem was that whenever I reached back to throw a snowball, the elastic would yank up my other hand – and I'd end up smacking myself in the mouth. But I'd be so excited, I'd keep forgetting – no matter how many fat lips I gave myself. 'Look! Brian Johnson just punched himself in the face again!' the other kids would shout, as blood ran down my chin and I cried for my ma. 'Dee it again, Brian! *Dee it again*!'

These were also the days when I first *really* discovered football and music.

It was my dad who took me to see my first footie match. It wasn't a Newcastle United game though, because the tickets would have cost an arm and a leg and St. James's Park was at least a thirty-minute bus ride away. Instead, we walked to nearby Redheugh Park to see United's poor relatives, Gateshead AFC, which charged only tuppence at the gate and attracted a crowd of a couple of thousand on a good day.

My dad brought along a 'cracket' – a small wooden stool with wickerwork on top – which he put beside the wall at the side of the pitch so I could stand on it and see over.

What I remember most is staring at all the faded and peeling old adverts from the 1930s that were still on the wall. Things like, 'You know it's wise to use Bovril to keep away pneumonia and chills!' Some of them had been painted onto metal backing, and the paint had slowly chipped away and rust was showing through. But they were the only hints of colour in our otherwise grey world, and that fascinated me.

Beyond the stands, meanwhile, you could see the five massive iron-framed gas holders of the Redheugh Gas Works – the gas in those days was made by heating up coal in a sealed furnace* – and the Dunston flour mill.

I didn't really understand or care what was happening on the pitch. It wasn't like there were any *Match of the Day* moments going on. The Gateshead players weren't even all that fit – and of course they'd light up tabs while eating their orange slices at half-time.

Like most boys, I was just happy to be doing something – anything, really – with my dad.

That didn't apply to listening to our family's record collection, mind you, which had been donated to us by an older couple – Mr. and Mrs. Adams – who lived in one of the 'OAP cottages' up the street. (OAP meaning Old Age Pensioner, of course.)

We had one of those old gramophones back then with a steel needle that you wound up with a crank handle, and every

---

* Many decades later, the IRA would try to blow the place up.

so often my dad would decide to put on one of these ancient 78s – although, to be honest, he never really cared about music. The only one I remember was 'A Bird in a Gilded Cage' by Harry Anthony, who had this ridiculous, warbly, strangled-sounding tenor voice. Not that you could hear much over the wall of hiss. I couldn't abide it. In fact, my brothers and I ended up taking the records and throwing them one by one over the fence in our back garden, which was a lot more fun than it sounds because if you flicked your wrist when you threw them, the 78s would spin around and kind of float for a bit in the air before coming down gently. We basically turned Harry Anthony into a Frisbee, which was pretty impressive since the Frisbee hadn't even been invented yet.

As for my own taste in music, it was being formed entirely by the BBC Radio show *Children's Favourites*, hosted by the very stiff and Victorian-sounding 'Uncle Mac'. Every episode would start with him saying, 'Hello children, everywhere,' followed by one of the greatest BBC theme tunes of all time – 'Puffin' Billy' by the Melodi Light Orchestra.

Every Saturday morning, starting at 9.10 a.m., Uncle Mac would play things like 'The Laughing Policeman' or 'I Taut I Taw a Puddy Tat' by Mel Blanc – the guy who voiced most of the Looney Tunes characters – with a bit of Bing Crosby and Max Bygraves mixed in. And if you were lucky and Uncle Mac was in a daring mood, you might even get to hear one of the tamer hits of Frank Sinatra or Doris Day.

It was the highlight of my week.

Some of my most vivid and magical memories of growing up in Dunston are of our Christmases, even though in the early days we couldn't afford a turkey, never mind proper presents.

My dad, bless his heart, would always take a trip out into the woods somewhere and find us a tree. And because he'd grown up without electricity, and was a man who valued tradition, he'd light up the tree with candles – real candles, with real flames – which he insisted was totally safe because the Johnsons had been doing it for generations, and not a single one of us had ever been lost in a house fire.

Then would come Christmas Eve – the longest night in any kid's life. Every year, without fail, my dad would put out a biscuit and a glass of milk for Santa Claus, and once we were all tucked up in bed, he'd take a bite out of the biscuit and gulp down the milk – making sure to leave sooty finger-prints everywhere from the coal in the fireplace. This just goes to show that for all his toughness, Sergeant Johnson was a gigantic softy at heart. And, of course, my brothers and I would be lying awake for what felt like an eternity, calling out, 'Dad?! Has he been yet!' at fifteen-minute intervals from about 3 a.m. onwards. 'Go to *bed*!' would come the muffled reply . . . until my dad finally broke and led us downstairs at the crack of dawn.

As for the presents, you'd never fail to get an orange covered in tinfoil at the bottom of your stocking (to make it look 'Christmassy') and a bar of Fry's Five Boys milk chocolate or, if you were *really* lucky, a Cadbury's Chocolate Selection Box, which looked incredibly exciting when it was covered in wrapping paper, just because it was so big.

The trick was to make the chocolates last as long as possible, which, in my case, was never beyond noon the next day. My little brother Victor, on the other hand, could make his last for *months*, a feat of self-discipline that seemed almost superhuman to me.

But it wasn't all good. Somewhere amongst the presents

there would always be The Curse of Christmas – a wooden box filled with shrivelled figs that looked like camel's testicles, and a little plastic spoon to eat them with. Every year, one of us would be unlucky enough to get this awful present – and if you got caught throwing out the spoon and feeding the figs to the sparrows, you'd get a bloody good hiding, even though everyone hated the figs – especially my ma, who knew what real ones tasted like.

As the years went by, the presents got better (including a gorgeous, very grown-up Raleigh bicycle) until one Christmas, Santa Claus delivered a 'family present' that changed my life – an Elizabethan reel-to-reel tape recorder with a little plug-in microphone.

It was a game-changer, that tape recorder. All of a sudden, I could put the microphone up against the speaker of the radio and record *Children's Favourites*, so I could listen to the songs whenever I wanted to. As usual, though, there was a problem . . . which came in the form of our pet budgerigar, whose name was either Bobby or Peter, I can't remember which. Everyone had a budgie in those days, and they were all called Bobby or Peter. People loved them because you could teach them to say things like 'Whey aye, man' and 'Alreet pet' and all they ate was seeds, so they were one of the cheapest forms of entertainment that you could get.*

Anyway, this budgie got into the habit of breaking into song every time the radio came on. He loved *Children's Favourites* almost as much as I did. And he was really, *really* loud.

It didn't help that the little microphone could only pick up

* Not that our budgie could talk – because no one ever spoke to him. When he was out of his cage, he'd just knock things over and crap on the sofa.

high tones and had no bass qualities whatsoever. So, when I played back my first recording of Uncle Mac's show, all I could hear was a very distant and muffled James Baskett singing 'Zip-a-Dee-Doo-Dah' with this awful high-pitched whistling over the top.

Moving the budgie to another room didn't help because that just made him upset – and when he was upset, the little fella would start squawking at twice the usual volume.

I gave up after a while and just started singing into the microphone myself, which for some reason didn't set the budgie off in the same way. The only songs I could think to sing at first were the same corny ones we did at school. But recording myself was so much fun, I couldn't stop doing it. Adding to the entertainment, I realized that I could slow the tape down or speed it up, making me sound like a deep-voiced old man or Alvin the Chipmunk. I spent most of that Christmas in the bedroom I shared with my brothers, singing into the microphone while watching the tape reels go around, then rewinding, playing it back, and starting over – or adding something else – until my dad must have started to regret ever buying the bloody thing. 'Like the sound of your own voice, do you?' he huffed at one point.

I turned bright red and mumbled something. But the correct answer – which of course I was far too embarrassed to admit – was *yes, I do.* It was the novelty of it that got me, the feeling of creating something new, of being the first to hear it.

I just never got bored of it.

I'm still not bored of it today.

3

A-Wop Bop A-Loo Bop

⚡

My mother's homesickness finally started to wear off after a few years at No. 1 Beech Drive. Or maybe it was just that she'd found an outlet for it – an Italian food-importing company up in Glasgow, run by a guy named Pietro Fazzi, who'd been thrown in prison with his brothers by the British during the war, then released after VE Day.

The company had started out as a family ice-cream shop and café in the 1920s, but one of Mr. Fazzi's sons realized they could make more money selling raw ingredients directly to restaurants and homesick Italians all over Scotland and the North East. (Quite a few Italian prisoners of war had married in Britain and never returned home.) We're talking things like Mennucci pasta, Bertolli olive oil, proper salami, gallon-tins of tomatoes, Parmigiano Reggiano and doppio zero flour for pizza crusts.

Whatever you wanted – if it was Italian and made your mouth water – Mr. Fazzi could get it.

Once my ma found out this guy existed, she never looked back.

Every Friday afternoon, my ma would call in her order from a phone box up the street, and I'd listen to her babbling away to Mr. Fazzi in Italian for what felt like hours. Then a few days later, a guy would show up on our doorstep to deliver her supplies – and my ma would look as happy as a kid on Christmas morning.

Watching her prepare this food was just the best thing ever. My brother Maurice – a future chef – was especially trans-fixed by it. I mean, although the food in 1950s Britain had a dreadful reputation, the Geordies were rightfully proud of their soups, scones, lamb chops, English bangers, bacon sarnies and Sunday roasts – comfort food that I still cook at home today. But what my mother could do in the kitchen was something else. She used spices that we'd never ever tasted before. Made pastas from scratch that we'd never seen before. Cooking was an outpouring of emotion for her – a way to remind herself of the life that she'd left behind in Italy.

I'll never forget the first time she made her Italian doughnuts – *bomboloni* they're called because they look like lit-tle bombs – on a Sunday afternoon. The entire family sat and watched that dough rise in front of the fire, a damp towel placed carefully over it, like it was a Hollywood film. Then she kneaded it, cut it into little rounds, laid out the doughnuts care-fully on parchment paper, then fried them gently in the very best oil that Mr. Fazzi could get. And then out they came, all warm and soft and insanely delicious-looking, and she cut out the centres as a special treat for the kids, rolled them in sugar, and *ohhhhhhhhh,* you just couldn't believe how good they tasted! My brothers and I could have eaten a thousand of them.

And, of course, the neighbours ended up smelling the *bomboloni* from halfway up the street, and they'd never smelled anything like it before, so they all came running over. And by then my ma was onto her third or fourth batch, so she starts wrapping the doughnuts up in old newspaper and handing them out, and before I know it, I'm taking them into school for Mrs. Patterson and Mr. Graham the caretaker, and everyone has stopped making fun of us for being Italian behind our backs.

From then on, I didn't really mind that we were different. In fact, I started to quite like it.

Every morning, my ma would make proper Italian coffee after my dad left for work. The beans would come from Mr. Fazzi, and she'd grind them herself in one of those wooden box things with a twisty handle on the top. The smell was so good you just wanted to bury your head in the stuff. Then she'd brew one of those Italian pots of coffee on the stove, pour us each a little bowl of it, add a splash of milk, and drop in some little squares of toast. That was our cereal. I mean, were there any other kids in the North East who got to start their school days like that?

She was a wonderful woman, my ma. Always surprising us and delighting us with her recipes – all of which she'd memorized. Always happy and smiling when us kids were around. Always wanting us to see and do the things that she never could.

Every so often, though, the old pain would come back. Like the time I was playing soldiers with the broom and I charged and smashed her pastel pink chandelier in the living room – one of the few things that she'd brought with her from Italy that hadn't ended up being stolen or pawned. It was the first and last time that I was ever scared of my ma. She wasn't just angry, she was absolutely livid.

But as soon as the anger passed, all the sadness came out, and she grabbed me in her arms and cried.

This would probably be a good moment to mention that my mother had another go at taking me back to Italy – only this time with some advance warning, during a school holiday.

I must have been seven or eight.

The only parts of the journey there that I remember are using a toilet on the train that emptied directly onto the tracks – 'the loudest toilet in the world', I named it – and being paralysed with fear when we had to carry our suitcases over these narrow, wobbly planks onto the cross-channel ferry at Dover. I felt absolutely sure that we were both going to die. How my mother finally coaxed me aboard, I've no idea.

But Italy was a revelation.

The station we arrived at – Roma Termini – was this brand-new modern masterpiece with a huge atrium and cantilevered roof, like nothing I'd ever seen before.

I was even more amazed by the Italian trains, which were diesel, not steam, and painted in the most beautiful reds, oranges and greens. And when we got off the train, the terminal smelled of coffee and fresh bread, and there wasn't a single piece of litter blowing around. Nothing could blow around, in fact, because there was no gale blowing in from the North Sea. And it wasn't pissing it down. And I could feel something unusual on my face, something that I'd never felt before . . .

Heat.

From the sun.

I felt like I'd arrived in paradise.

As soon as we got off the train – me dressed in my usual shorts with a pair of open-toed sandals – my ma's sisters and her niece Julianna showed up, and everyone cried for about ten minutes. They were the loveliest, friendliest people I'd ever met, and so incredibly beautiful, I couldn't stop looking at them. None of them wore nylons, because their legs were naturally tanned. Their teeth were straight and white. And their makeup was so subtle, you could barely even tell they were wearing lipstick. One of them even had a car and drove it herself, which I couldn't believe. Cars were rare enough in Dunston. But *women* drivers? I was in shock. My Italian aunties and cousin Julianna just seemed so free, so stylish . . . so happy.

Then off we went to Frascati – which was about forty-five minutes away, up in the hills – and we passed all these burned-out German tanks and artillery pieces on the side of the road.

Next thing I knew, we were pulling up outside an incredibly posh-looking block of flats, where it turned out my Aunty Maria had the whole top floor to herself.

I was in shock at how she lived. I can still picture the silk curtains, which were pale light blue and gold, and the kitchen, which had a long table for cutting and preparing all this fresh and colourful-looking food. There were even vines of grapes just growing naturally in terracotta pots on the balcony, spilling over the side and creeping up the wooden latticework, creating a canopy of shade.

That night, we were treated to the most delicious meal of pasta, fish, meats and cheeses that I'd ever tasted, and I got to sit with Julianna and my other Italian cousins on a special children's table. They gave me a little beaker of red wine. And for the first time, the full weight of what my ma had given up for my dad – for all of us – began to sink in.

If my mother was the soul of the family, my dad was its back-bone. Getting so much as a hint of emotion out of him was like getting blood out of a stone. He grunted. He growled. Sometimes he bellowed. Mostly, he said very little at all. When he spoke to me, it was usually to say, 'Oy, *you*! Stop that!' or, 'Oy, *you*! Gerrover here now!'

For years, I thought my name was 'Hugh'.

It wasn't that he was cruel. He just didn't want to be seen as soft. And that wasn't just a macho thing, either. When you're a sergeant, discipline is everything. If you can't keep your men in line, sooner or later someone is going to get killed.

The first hint I got of what my dad had been through during the war came one Saturday afternoon when I was about ten years old. One of my favourite things to do back then was build Airfix model aircraft and on that particular day, I was putting the finishing touches to an American P-38 Lightning twin-engined fighter bomber (as the Germans called them, 'The Fork-Tailed Devil'). My dad had never taken much of an interest in my creations before, but when he came back from his club and saw the P-38, he stopped, smiled and said, 'That's the most beautiful plane in the world.'

Which kinda shook me because he never usually said anything at all.

'Why's that, Dad?'

He said: 'It saved our lives, that did.'

And that was it. I was expecting a story but talking about the war just wasn't cool. It took another twenty years before I finally got an explanation.

Years later, my brother Maurice and I were in Frascati staying with ma's family, with her and Dad. One afternoon, Dad said, 'I'd like to go to Nettuno', which is not far from Anzio. This is where, on 22 January 1944, the Allies attacked the German-held beachheads. The Americans at Anzio, the British at Nettuno, which is where my dad landed.

So, Maurice and I drove him to Nettuno. The drive from Frascati took about an hour. It took the Allies about five months. When we arrived, we were met by some of my ma's extended family, who had an apartment right on the beach. They welcomed us in, took us up to their balcony and brought out this glorious spread of food. There were salamis, cheese, bread and wine. Perfect. We looked out over the beach drinking wine and taking it all in when, out of the blue, my father said: 'You see that rock?'

About half a mile away, just before the beach met the water, stood a huge rock.

We all looked and nodded.

'We took cover behind that when we got out of our landing craft,' he said. 'There were bodies everywhere. Floating in the water. On the beach. Men were dropping like flies. I told my men to run for that rock and stop for nothing. I don't know how we made it, but we did . . . well, *some* of us did, anyway.'

Maurice and I were stunned. This was the first time we'd ever heard our dad talk about the war.

'Then, out of nowhere, these P-38 Lightnings came swooping down and strafed and bombed the Germans,' my dad said. 'They were the most beautiful things I'd ever seen.'

I suddenly got it, all those years on from that Saturday afternoon.

We then went to the Allied War Cemetery. Thousands of crosses, with a Star of David here and there – it just took your breath away. I'd never seen anything so sad and beautiful at the same time. The flowers, the death all around – young fellas who gave everything they had and two generations later, nobody knew or cared where Nettuno or Anzio was.

I felt quite ashamed when I thought about what I'd wanted when I was their age. A new P.A. system. A motorbike. Those lads never got a chance.

My father's shoulders straightened instinctively as he walked into the cemetery, then he marched determinedly to a row of graves that he must have remembered from when the bodies were buried way back. Maurice and I followed him as he pointed to various headstones. 'Ah, Tommy, he was a good lad, and there's Eric, a funny fella – I went to school with him, y'know – and that's Mickey, he didn't make it five yards.'

We could see none of them had even made it to their twenty-first birthday.

'Give us a couple of minutes, lads,' asked my dad – and we left him there with his fallen pals. We watched as he talked to them all without opening his mouth, smiling now and then, nodding occasionally – the boys back together after so many years of silence. I hope he's with them now. There were tears in his eyes and lumps in our throats. Then he pulled himself up to his full height and gave a proper sergeant's salute, rigid and intense. No trumpets. No last call.

Then he dropped the salute, did an immaculate right turn, and marched towards us.

'I'm done,' he said – and we followed him out.

We looked at our dad in a new light after that.*

For all my dad's cantankerousness, there were only a couple of times when I saw him really lose it. And on the occasion that it was with me, in all honesty, I had it coming.

---

* After I moved in 1989 to Sarasota, Florida, I met one of my very best friends – William Kelley, a world-class artist who counted the late BBC art historian Sister Wendy Beckett amongst his biggest fans. When my dad came over to visit one year, he and Billy – a hard-drinking, fun-loving Irish Bostonian – got on like a house on fire. I'll never forget my dad watching the two of us play golf, shouting, 'You're making a mockery of this game!' – even though my dad had never played a single hole of golf in his life. (When he had a go later on, he *played* like someone who had never played a single hole in his life.) Anyway, during that visit, we realized over a beer that Billy's dad had landed at Anzio on the very same day that my dad had landed at Nettuno. Thus was born The Sons of Anzio, an organization of which Billy and I – along with my brothers Maurice and Victor, and our respective nephews – are still proud members to this day.

I'd come home from school one afternoon and noticed this huge cloud of black smoke billowing out over the top of the house and thought, *what the hell is that*? So, me and a few of the other Big ones ran to find the source and quickly found the railway line, which ran directly behind our street and was separated from our back garden by just a little fence. This gave us the idea to create an incredibly fun new game, which the Little ones also soon eagerly joined in with. The game was called . . . 'steam train chicken'. Which, as you can probably work out for yourself, involved us standing on the line and waiting for a train – while listening to the driver blowing his whistle, and screaming every curse word that he could think of at us – and seeing who could hold their nerve the longest before jumping out of the way.

The closer you came to a horribly violent death, in other words, the better your chances of winning, which, in our kids' minds, seemed like an entirely reasonable gamble to take.

Anyway, this game went on for weeks, providing us with endless hours of entertainment, until my dad looked out of his bedroom window one day and saw what was going on.

Let's just say that his reaction wasn't one of fatherly pride. He didn't open the window and call out, 'Brian, my son! What an exciting game you've invented there! Well done, little fella!'

Instead, as he stormed out of the house, he got the same look in his eye he must have had when he was killing Germans in Tunisia. He pointed at us in turn and roared, 'You!! You!! You!! AGAINST THE FENCE. *Now*!' Then he pulled down a tree branch and started whacking the shit out of us. 'If I *ever* see you doing that again,' – WHACK! – 'I'll call the police' – WHACK! – 'You'll go to prison, *d'you hear*?!' – WHACK!

'Yes, Dad,' we whimpered in turn, tears streaming down our faces, our arses on fire.

Later that night, one of my friend's dads came to the house, all riled up, demanding to know why his son had been beaten with a stick. But when my dad explained that he'd been caught playing chicken with a steam train, the other dad went very quiet and said, 'Well, I'm sorry for doubting you, Alan. If you ever catch him doing that again, please give him another good fucking hiding from me.'

Lettuce

In 1950s Dunston, the stubbornness of the average working-class dad was a constant hazard, and almost impossible to navigate – a prime example being the time my old man asked me to go over to his friend Billy's allotment to pick up a lettuce for my ma.

In the late fifties, in all working-class areas in Britain, there were allotments. These were a throwback from the war. The idea was to grow your own food and usually have a cree for your homing pigeons.

Not far from Beech Drive, where we lived, there were literally hundreds of them. All about forty yards by twenty-five, give or take a turnip. These allotments were rented out by the local council, and all were surrounded by corrugated iron and secured and guarded jealously by the tenants. Especially when prize leeks were involved.

My father's mate had one, and on a beautiful sunny spring day Dad said to me, 'Go to Billy's allotment and pick up a lettuce for your mother.' It was spring and that's when you ate salads because, unlike today, it was a seasonal thing.

He gave me a twopence and off I went. I knocked on the corrugated iron fence, but nothing, so I shouted, because the fence was too high to climb. Billy came and said, 'C'mon son, I've got a nice head of lettuce for your Mam.' It was wrapped in a newspaper and I said to him, 'Here's your twopence from Dad.'

'What?' he said. 'There's no need for that, I have plenty, off you go.'

I went home and proudly announced the lettuce was free, Billy didn't want any money. My father said, 'Take that money back and tell him, I always pay my way.'

A little confused, I ran back to Billy's allotment and said to Billy, 'Dad won't take it for nothing and here's the two-pence.'

Billy laughed and said to tell Dad not to be so daft, 'I don't need the twopence, now go on and bugger off.'

Whilst buggering off, I realized this was a political game I was ill-equipped to deal with. What the hell was my father going to say?

I must point out at this juncture, that at the time in the North East fathers were strict and were not used to being disobeyed, and I was just a pawn in the game of pride.

I went back again to plead with Billy to take the bloody twopence. It was too late, he was gone, panic set in. I couldn't keep the money or I'd be accused of stealing. I couldn't take it back or I'd be doing the allotment shuffle for all eternity, and this was a Saturday and nearly time for the afternoon matinee at the pictures.

So, this was what it was like to have to make a decision. The closest I'd been to that was in a sweet shop, deciding between midget gems or pineapple chunks.

I didn't like this decision-making at all – it was confusing and scary. So, I thought long and hard about what to do. About five minutes later, I had come to a conclusion and threw the money down the drain.

I spent the next few days in sheer terror that Billy would talk to my dad and they would find out the truth, but nothing happened. Both of them were probably too proud to talk about it. I started realizing then that being honest wasn't that easy.

Contents of an English Salad circa 1950–1965
2 leaves of lettuce
½ boiled egg
2 pickled onions
½ tomato
1 slice of meat, ham, spam or tongue for a child
2 " " " for an adult

and lots of bread spread with margarine or dripping or the ubiquitous Heinz Salad Cream (the middle class used butter).

Then the lettuce would disappear for another year, but time moves on and hydroponics changed the lettuce world. We bred them like battery chickens, and both taste nothing like the originals. Just like water.

Nineteen fifty-eight was the year that everything changed for me, in ways both awful and amazing.

The awful part was that I had to take the 'eleven-plus' – a brain-meltingly hard IQ test that also included questions on everything you'd ever been taught in school.

In Britain in those days, it's no exaggeration to say your performance in that one exam – at the grand old age of eleven – decided how the rest of your life would turn out. The high scorers went to grammar schools that prepared them for universities. The rest went to secondary moderns, where the focus was on practical skills like woodwork and metalwork – and you had more chance of walking on the moon than getting a university education. There were also a few 'technical schools' that taught trades, but most trades were learned through on-the-job apprenticeships.

The exam lasted forty-five to sixty minutes. You couldn't retake it. So, the pressure was absolutely horrendous. It didn't help that Britain hadn't built enough grammar schools to handle all the kids born after the war, so every year they made the questions harder.

My dad being my dad, the only kind of encouragement he knew was fear. 'Oy, *you*! You'd better pass that exam or you'll end up sweeping the roads!' he kept saying to me. Sweeping the roads was the worst job imaginable as far as my dad was concerned. For me, though, the fate that scared me the most was becoming a coal miner.

What my dad should have known, of course, is that you can't scare someone into doing well at something that requires preparation and a cool head – on top of whatever natural intelligence you were born with. And I didn't prepare at all for the eleven-plus. But the truth was, I was also just very underdeveloped at that age compared with my friends. I still hadn't grown out of playing Cowboys and Indians. And I suffered from terrible performance anxiety – I still do.

The whole thing was just a total humiliation. I got the exam papers in front of me and froze. I was so nervous my brain wouldn't work and I couldn't make head nor tail of it. The questions might as well have been written in Swedish. It was one of the worst hours of my life. What made it even more painful was that I'd been such a good student at school, always getting gold stars and top marks.

We got the results about a week later. What a day that was. Suddenly everyone was separated into groups. In one group were the future pilots of the world, the doctors, the lawyers. Some of the high-scorers were friends of mine and had always come lower than me in class – but they'd obviously prepared for the exam and been able to hold their nerve when it counted. But when my name was called, I was told to go and stand with the kids who usually got 'D's and 'E's. My heart sank. I'd failed, obviously. I'd be going to a secondary modern. Not that it made any difference in the end. Even the hardest of blows you take in life can be overcome if you just play the hand you're dealt, instead of moping around and feeling sorry for yourself. But I'm not gonna lie to you, when the grammar school kids went one way, and I went the other . . . I couldn't have felt more empty.

A few weeks later, the amazing thing happened.

I was off school on the day in question – I must have been feeling poorly or had a dentist appointment or something – and was out of my mind with boredom, so I switched on the television and started watching this daytime BBC show with the very catchy name of *Farming*. That was it, just *Farming*. Later on, they'd spice it up – no doubt creating a whiff of scandal at Broadcasting House – by renaming it *Farming Today*. Either way, it was just a guy in a suit and tie talking straight to camera – in this particular episode, about the difference between mulch and manure.

Now, at this point you might be asking yourself, why didn't the little lad just change the channel? But in the North East in those days, remember, the BBC was the *only* channel, with

Tyne Tees Television not launching until a year or so later. So, it was either suffer through an episode of *Farming* – in black-and-white, just to add to the thrill – or stare at the wall. And I'd done as much staring at the wall as any eleven-year-old boy could take in one day.

So, there I was, sitting and watching this mind-numbing form of entertainment – eyes glassing over, drool coming out of my mouth – when all of a sudden the credits rolled and this plummy-voiced BBC announcer said, 'and now, for the *interlude* . . .'

I almost certainly groaned. Because if you can believe it, the BBC's 'interludes' were even worse than the awful programming itself. Things like, 'Here's a short film of fish swimming in a pond', or 'Here's an elderly Scottish woman decorating a pot', or 'And now for a church choir singing a hymn . . . *very slowly*'.

But not on this day. Oh no. On this day, the Gods of rock'n'roll had decided that little Brian Johnson at No. 1 Beech Drive was going to get a bolt of lightning up his arse.

Instead of being treated to a short film of fish swimming, I suddenly found myself staring in awe at a black guy with a wafer-thin moustache and a crazy mop of hair. Oh, and he was wearing makeup and a sequinned shirt with a skinny tie, and everything about him was just so obviously, wildly, fabulously gay, but of course gay to me just meant happy, and it would for many more years to come.

'This young American boy goes by the name of Little Richard,' said the announcer, with a hint of mischief in his voice, like he knew this was far too racy for the BBC, 'and here is his most popular song . . . which has been a *terrific* success across the Atlantic!'

With that, Little Richard opened his mouth and let out a

noise at the very top of his lungs that was just pure joy, sex and liberation all rolled into one. 'A-WOP BOP A-LOO BOP, A-WOP BAM BOOM!!'

Many have described that song, 'Tutti Frutti', as the sound of rock'n'roll being born – which is fitting, because my dream of becoming a singer was born in that moment too.

I felt like someone had just plugged me into the mains. Every part of me was suddenly standing on end, from my hair to my nipples to the bits down below that I didn't even know how to use yet. It was like nothing I'd ever seen, heard or felt before . . . and it absolutely blew my mind.

Like all highs, though, 'Tutti Frutti' was very quickly followed by a crushing low. Because I wanted – no, *needed* – to hear those screamed lyrics and those unhinged 'wooooos' and that full-throttle rhythm section again. Immediately. But I was just an eleven-year-old kid in Dunston. I was too young to go to a record shop. I didn't have any money. And even if the single had magically fallen from the sky, I wouldn't have had anything to play it on. Our ancient wind-up gramophone only went at 78 rpm.

It was *agony*!

Then, a few days later, coming home from school, I heard that unmistakable shriek of rock'n'roll ecstasy carried down the street. I ran around, trying to find the source – and when I realized that it was coming out of a neighbour's downstairs window, I jumped the fence and just stood in their front garden listening to it, mesmerized.

Then it stopped – and to this day, I can't believe what I did next. I knocked on their front door.

A lady answered in her curlers. I remember thinking that she seemed far too old to be listening to 'my' kind of music – but she was probably only nineteen or twenty. 'Sorry to bother you, Missus,' I said, feeling my cheeks turn bright red, 'but could you . . . *play that again?*'

The lady looked back at me for a moment, not quite believing what she was hearing.

'Well . . . if you'd like,' she said, with a little smile. Then she went back inside, I heard the crackle and hiss of a needle on vinyl, and then, *oh yes, oh yes, oh yes, oh yes* . . .

'A-WOP BOP A-LOO BOP, A-WOP BAM BOOM!!'

Next thing I knew, the lady was back on the front step with me, doing the hand jive to the music. That just floored me. It was the best thing I'd ever seen. So, of course I joined in, and there we were, this kid who'd just failed his eleven-plus and this fully-grown young woman, on a council estate in Dunston, and we were grinning our faces off to this totally alien-sounding, but unbelievably exciting, new kind of music. It was hands-down the best Tuesday afternoon of my life.

'What's your name, sweetie?' asked the girl, out of breath, when the song ended for the second time.

I told her.

'Well, it was nice to meet you, Brian,' she said. 'I'm Annette.'

Annette, if you're reading this, many thanks for pointing the way.

SCOUT-INK

BOY SCOUT
MEMBERSHIP CARD
AND RECORD OF PROGRESS

5th TYNE SEA SCOUTS

GROUP

Name *Brian Johnson*

Warren Young

SCOUTMASTER

DATE

3: August

NO. B.1   "SCOUT-INK" SERIES. COPYRIGHT   MADE IN ENGLAND

4

Showstopper

⚡

My biggest problem growing up . . . was that I wasn't grow-ing *up*. I was a titch. A short-arse. Vertically challenged, as the condition is probably known today. I'd always been one of the smallest in my class, of course – and my 'little' brother Maurice had always been a few inches taller than me. But by the time I started at Dunston Hill Secondary Modern, most of my friends were five-foot-something and counting . . . while I was stuck in the mid-fours. Even Victor had shot up past me, and the way things were going, I was worried that my little sister Julie would be catching up soon.

With every week and month that passed – without so much as a fraction of an inch in growth to show for it – my situation became more desperate.

Then one day I was skimming through the back pages of a boys' magazine when I came across an advertisement for a 'practical book' that seemed like the answer to all my prayers. *The Morley Method of Scientific Height Development* was the title – written by a world-famous authority on childhood growth named John Morley. So, of course, I rushed down the Post Office, bought myself a postal order for the price of the book, and sent it off to the address in the advertisement.

A week later, the book was waiting for me on the front mat when I got home from school. 'Congratulations!' read the inside cover. 'You are holding in your hands The Famous

Morley Method, with which you can increase your height in just twelve days!'

I almost cried, I was so relieved.

The book turned out to be even more helpful than I'd expected. Within just a few chapters, I'd learned that the best way to grow taller was to harness 'nature's magnetic forces' and sleep with my head pointing north and my feet pointing south. *Why hadn't anyone told me this before?* So off I went to find my dad's compass, and when it was time for bed, I arranged myself on the mattress accordingly. I couldn't get the angle exactly right, mind you, because there were two other Johnsons in the same bed – both of whom seemed to be getting bigger by the day. Maybe that's why it wasn't working, I thought, as Day Twelve came and went.

Then another twelve days passed.

Then another.

And guess what?

I was still four-foot-six.

Now, at this point, as you might expect, I was starting to wonder if John Morley really *was* a world-famous authority on childhood growth. I mean, when I looked in the back of the book at the other titles he'd written, I discovered that he was also a world-famous authority on balding, healthy feet, magnetic super-strength, profitable stamp-dealing, weight-gain, jiu-jitsu, building a powerful chest, strong sight (without glasses), 'scientific boxing' and bashfulness. Meanwhile, he claimed that the most common cause of shortness was 'slouching', which was enough of a leap to make even my gullible pre-pubescent mind go . . . *what*? Surely, whether you were slouching or not, *you were still the same height*. Then I noticed that all of the endorsements on the back were from kids who said they'd risen by several inches after reading the book, which, when I thought about it for a second, was exactly what would have happened anyway *through natural growth.*

But I refused to believe that I'd been conned. So, I kept reading and re-reading each chapter, staying up later and later every night, searching for missed advice, a hidden clue, *anything* . . . until my dad realized what was going on and sat me down for a talk.

'Son,' he growled, 'you've always been a t'arse, and you always will be a t'arse.' (My dad never swore, so 't'arse' was his version of 'short arse'.) 'Now, for God's sake get your nose out of that stupid book and start making the best of what you've got.'

To be fair to my old man, he did give me some helpful advice about my height – mainly because he was worried that in a town full of hard men who liked to pick fights, a kid of my size was a walking liability. I mean, my dad was short too, but he was an absolute pit bull of a guy, which was how he'd managed to survive five years of death and destruction during World War II.

But he was under no illusions about *my* fighting skills. 'You're just not big enough, son,' he told me, 'so, if you find yourself in any trouble, turn around and walk the other way. And if you can't do that, nut them as hard as you can on the nose . . . then *run*.' This tried-and-tested manoeuvre, my dad added, was called 'a Newcastle kiss'.

He'd been right to worry, it turned out, because I soon found myself having to fend off an attacker.

I had a part-time job as a milk delivery boy at the time, which meant getting up at 5 a.m., running up the hill to Youens' Dairy, loading up a little Austin A50 van – they also had a horse and cart – and hanging onto the back of it, delivering bottles to the houses as we passed them. It was a tricky job because there were all kinds of milk – silver top, red top, green top, gold top and, most expensive of all, brown top from Jersey cows, which only went to doctors and headmasters. So, you had to pay attention, and you also had to make sure you didn't fall off the back of the van – and usually you had to do both of those things even when it was raining, sleeting or snowing, and while a North Sea wind was trying to take off your face.

The second my milk round finished, I should add, I had to dash over to the newsagent's and start my paper round. By the time I got to school, I'd already been at work for more than two hours. But I loved my jobs. Especially on Saturdays, when the milk van driver, Lettie, would take me to the baker's after our round, and I'd get a meat square straight out of the oven, which would burn my mouth and tongue, but it didn't matter because I'd wash it down straight after with a half-pint of full-cream milk. Then I'd get paid and I'd go and buy myself a model aeroplane.

Ah, just fantastic stuff.

Anyway, the trouble started with the last milk round before Christmas, when people would come out of their houses and give me tips. I collected £2 in total that morning – which I'd decided to spend on Christmas presents for my ma and dad.

But there was a big, nasty bully of a kid who also worked at the dairy – I won't mention his name – and he must have heard about my tips because he followed me out of the building after my shift, cornered me in a shop doorway, and demanded that I hand over the money. No reason. He just thought he could get away with it.

No.

So, he drew himself up to his full height, pulled me up by the collar so my face met his, and went, 'I'll ask you one more time, you little shit . . . *give me your money.*'

All I could think of were my dad's words about turning around and walking away. But I was up against a door, so there was no escape. And as a matter of principle, I wasn't going to give this guy a single penny. So, without even thinking – as a surge of pure animal rage took over me – I nutted him so hard, right between the eyes, it broke his nose *and* his cheekbone. The scream he let out was awful. Even I was shocked. Then he started to cry, and of course there was blood dripping everywhere. But I didn't feel sorry for him. He'd tried to rob me because I was small, and as my dad would say, *he had it coming.* So, I left him there and legged it home, looking over my shoulder all the way, just in case he'd followed me.

The police were never called. But when I went back to work after Christmas, Lettie's sister tore into me, calling me every name that she could think of. 'You little Italian pig,' she spat. 'you should be ashamed of yourself, fighting like a dirty foreigner.'

Lettie pointed out that it was the older boy who'd started it by trying to steal my tips – and that he had a long history of being lazy and rude and nicking milk from the van.

'Aye, but we cannit sack *him,*' came the reply. 'He's *English.*'

I kept my job, and he didn't. Lettie was a hero to me. She stuck up for me, and that meant everything, at a tough time.

The one shining beacon of light for me during my late childhood and early teenage years was the Fifth Tyne Sea Scouts. If you're not familiar with the various branches of the Scouts, the Sea Scouts are just like the ordinary Scouts, but with a focus on boats and water – and, of course, there are plenty of both in Tyneside, which once stood alongside Glasgow and Belfast as one of the shipbuilding capitals of the world. But the purpose of the little troop I joined was really more to introduce working-class kids like me to the world beyond our grey, polluted and increasingly rundown industrial surroundings. Which is exactly what it did.

Without the Sea Scouts, I'm pretty sure that my life wouldn't have turned out the way it did.

A lot of this was down to our Scoutmaster and my first mentor, a young guy who went by the name of Warren Young . . . because apparently when I was born, the clouds parted, a shaft of light shone down, and God boomed, 'AND LO, EVERY IMPORTANT FIGURE IN THE LIFE OF THIS CHILD BRIAN SHALL BE CALLED "YOUNG".'

I mean, granted, Warren Young was a bit of an oddball – a bachelor who still lived with his mother in a big old house in Gateshead – but he was the loveliest, kindest, most thoughtful man that I'd ever met. He didn't shout at you if you made a mistake. He'd always listen to what you had to say. And he'd always help you if he could.

To understand just how rare that was back then, bear in mind that it was entirely normal in those days – *expected*, even – for figures of authority to treat kids in ways that would get them locked up today. Back at Dunston Hill juniors, for example, I was once reading out loud in front of the class and got it a little wrong, and the teacher came up behind me and smacked me on the side of the head so hard I fell down and couldn't get back up.

It was criminal, the force he used. And he kept screaming

at me to get up, but I couldn't, so he had to ask one of my classmates to get the school nurse. I thought he'd get into trouble for it, but not at all – he was back to knocking kids around the next day.

The point being that Warren Young was halfway to a saint because he was so patient and kind – and we respected him all the more for it. We also loved him because he was always coming up with new games and activities for us, including endless rounds of 'British Bulldog', during which we got to knock the living shit out of each other in the Scout hut for half an hour at a time, even though one of the Little ones would nearly always end up going home with half of his teeth in a paper bag.

But the games weren't my favourite part of the Sea Scouts. Not by a long shot. What I loved the most . . . was the *singing*. Because it wasn't the boring, stodgy singing that we did at school or in church. It was boisterous, sitting-around-a-campfire, bellowing-it-out-at-the-top-of-your-lungs singing – the kind that makes your spine tingle and puts a huge grin on your face, no matter what kind of mood you're in.

Another reason I liked the singing so much was because I was starting to realize that I was good at it.

It's funny, looking back, that I could belt out a tune even though my voice hadn't broken yet and I was still so under-developed. I suppose I just got the 'huge pair of lungs' gene from my dad. Where my pitch came from, though, I've no idea. My dad couldn't hold a tune to save his life. My mother, God bless her, was even worse.

So, there I'd be in the Scout hut every week, and some-times even at the weekends, dressed up in my little neckerchief and woggle, my knees and arms all bruised and grazed from British Bulldog, singing my heart out, imagining myself somewhere on the plains of Africa . . . just loving every second of it. And then one day, Warren Young took me aside and told me something that would change my life forever.

'Brian, son,' he said, 'I want you to come back here on Tuesday afternoon – *for an audition.*'

'An audition?' I said, my face dropping – I wasn't quite sure if this was a good thing or a punishment for something that I'd done wrong. 'What d'you mean . . . *audition* . . . ?'

'Well, the Scout leaders have had a meeting and we've decided it's high time we put on a Gang Show,' he said. 'And with that voice of yours . . . I think you should be in it.'

Of course, the whole Scout troop would be in it, but he said he wanted me to sing a song solo.

That stopped me in my tracks a tadge.

Now, Gang Shows in those days were pretty awful events – like school pantomimes, only worse. But entertainment was hard to come by in the early 1960s, so everyone wanted to pile into the Scout hut to watch two hours of lads cracking jokes, dancing and singing songs that everyone knew by heart.

Gang Shows had started thirty years earlier with the songwriter and producer Ralph Reader, the guy who wrote 'We're Riding Along on the Crest of a Wave'.

So, getting the chance to be a part of this great British institution was a massive honour – and an opportunity that could very well change my life. But first I had to get through my audition with the show's 'musical director', a much older guy named Mr. Tedd Potts, who had greased back hair and a very affected, theatrical manner.

I was so nervous, I barely ate or slept for days.

I shouldn't have worried, though, because it turned out to

be a mass-audition of Scouts from all kinds of different troops, from all around the area – and all we had to do was skip around in a circle while a guy played the piano and Mr. Tedd Potts watched our every move in a slightly unsettling way. Later on, I was told that I'd passed with flying colours and would be getting *four* songs to sing. A chance to sing in front of a live audience for the first time.

And then we were taught very roughly how to dance. It wasn't dancing, it was more marching and waving hands. It was George, Raymond, Carl – all friends of mine from the Scout troop and Beech Drive. My voice wasn't broken, it wasn't anything to shake the world, but I held a note true. There were a lot of warblers, but I seemed to be able to hold onto a note without thinking about it. The songs were 'Stay after School', 'The Morning of My Life', 'Sisters' and one other.

The first dress rehearsal was in the church hall and we were all dressed up, with the piano and lights. Even though there wasn't anybody there, it was quite nerve-wracking. We had to make costume changes, running downstairs to a room buzzing with activity. All the mothers were helping with makeup, and the makeup was bad because of how bad the lights were. We had to have red cheeks and we looked like mannequins. The wonderful thing was the excitement, which I'd never felt before, like I was part of something. People were tripping up, walking off stage and walking into things, and boys were getting a bollocking. It was just a fantastic feeling; I knew this was the life for me.

I was nervous because there was this one song, 'Stay after School', that was quite rocky. I had to wear jeans, but I didn't have any at the time so I was given a pair with a T-shirt. When we went out to do it on the live show, the girls were screaming, which we loved. Our hair was slicked back, and we wore sneakers. I was so wrapped up in our performance that I didn't think about the parents, but my mother thought we were lovely. To me, it was like there were thousands there in that church hall.

The awful thing was that we only had two performances, a Friday night one and a Saturday night one, and then it was over. I felt like I had nothing to do because before the show we would rehearse twice a week and now, nothing.

5

A Ruff Business

⚡

While I was in the Sea Scouts, Warren Young knew I was a Catholic in a Church of England and Catholics Scout Troop, then again, so was he. We were known as left footers in the North East.

He'd produced the Dunston Scout Gang Shows and he'd heard me sing, so he asked me if I would like to sing in The St. Joseph's Church Choir. I really wasn't interested until he mentioned that I would be paid one shilling and sixpence every week.

'I would love to,' I said.

And God had nothing to do with it, this was a cash deal.

He took me along to the choir practice on Wednesday night, and there were around sixteen youngsters like myself, about thirteen years old and upwards, and about twenty adults.

He asked me to sing for him and handed me a hymn sheet. I took a look and realized it was in Latin. Bye-bye one shilling and sixpence.

I said I couldn't understand it and he smiled and said, 'Neither does anyone else.'

Then he handed me a phonetically written one, *ahh, this was better.*

Dominus vobiscum and such, this made you sound really holy. Latin was a language only spoken by public school boys and priests.

It wasn't a hymn I learned first, but something one of the older boys taught me, which goes:

Nil carborundum illegitimi.

Which, roughly translated, means 'Don't let the bastards grind you down.' A very important lesson in later life.

Everything in Latin or Italian sounds dignified and posh. Take, for instance, a Ferrari *Testa Rossa,* which means 'Red Head', but you just can't call a Ferrari that. Or, how about a *Quattroporte.* It's a beautiful name for a car, but it just means 'Four Doors'. See what I mean?

Getting back to the choir practice, I sang 'Oh Come, All Ye Faithful' and the choirmaster must have been impressed because he handed me a hassock or a cassock, which, when you put it on, made you even holier. All I needed was the wings.

After about two weeks of practice, I was ready for my first gig: the eleven o'clock one-hour mass on the coming Sunday.

The Catholic mass was, to me, the most complicated way to worship a deity I had ever witnessed. The priest said things and the audience answered in monotonous drones. There was no joy in it, no one looked happy. Then again, God's not that funny!

Then there were the altar boys who walked around the stage, sorry the altar, doing stuff like dusting the crucifix and polishing things. The priest pulled out this receptacle with a silver chain and tilted it from side to side and back and forward, with this foul-smelling smoke coming out of it. To me, it looked like voodoo but hey, money talks and bullshit is king. Then we sang something, which I think was a bit of a relief, more like a commercial break, so to speak. Then, just when you thought you were safe, the priest gathered his gang from the altar and walked down the aisle, spraying holy water on everyone. I tried to take a food stain off my cassock once with holy water and it didn't work, so there you go.

Back they came to the stage and Pop Gunning brought out the box of crackers. I thought, great, a tea break. Sadly, he held one of them up to the heavens, said something exceptionally holy, and broke it in pieces, then everyone in the audience came for a piece and, while they ate, we sang. It took a while, but it killed some time . . . this was going on forever. I was getting dizzy with boredom, it surely had to end soon. I lost count of how many times people were standing up and sitting down, then kneeling down and then standing up again. It was bloody exhausting.

Somewhere in amongst all the action, Pop climbed into the pulpit to give a sermon, telling us all to be good and not to give in to the temptation of eating meat on a Friday, except spam because that wasn't real meat. He told us of God's wrath being cast upon us and that the badder you were on earth, the longer you would be in this place called purgatory till you were allowed into Heaven. He finished by saying that God loved us all, but he didn't speak of the Holy Ghost. I suppose it's because it's not very unique being a ghost up there. Then he went back to the altar, poured himself a glass of wine and drank it all himself. I was impressed – he'd already done the eight o'clock and nine o'clock masses and was still steady on his feet.

It was his last orders and, with us singing at full volume, Pop and his gang left the stage, though no one applauded, which I think was unfair. I thought he was quite good.

My mother was there and she was very proud. She said I was the best singer there, which is what mothers do. However, two weeks later at practice the choirmaster announced to the whole choir that I would be Head Choir Boy and handed me a golden sash to put about my neck.

I thought, *shit*, that's a lot of responsibility for someone who has no idea what the hell went on in a mass. I just followed everyone else, and now I would have to sing solo now and again. I wasn't ready, and I knew it.

I was told that the Head Choir Boys got two shillings and sixpence. Wow, a promotion and a pay rise, all in the name of God. There was a price to pay, however. When practice was over, the deposed Head Choir Boy was waiting for me outside the church, and he was a big bugger. Let me tell you, there's nothing scarier than an ex-Head Choir Boy whose voice has broken. He jumped me as soon as I got out the door and was systematically trying to knock the shit out of me when the choirmaster came out, kicked him in the arse and pulled him off, then told him that kicking the shit out of people is right out of the question on holy ground (tell the Crusaders that).

My greatest moment as a choir boy was at midnight mass, Christmas 1960. I sang 'Silent Night' solo. All lights in the church were out and it was candlelight only. It really was a beautiful place to be. My mother was there again, and she cried. It was magical. There was no applause, obviously, but there was a lot of sighing and ahhing.*

Not all of Warren Young's ideas had such happy endings.

The example that immediately springs to mind – because it was such an unmitigated disaster – was the boxing tournament he once organized for our troop against the Sea Cadets from across the river in Scotswood. What you've got to bear in mind is that our troop was made up of schoolboys aged

* In practice, the choirmaster kept saying 'no no no, someone is singing through their nose' and we all knew it was himself, but we didn't dare tell him.

from ten to fourteen, while the Sea Cadets – a proper naval reserve force – was composed of sixteen- to eighteen-year-olds with biceps and tattoos. More to the point, they were from Scotswood, which was where young lads from Dunston went on a Friday or Saturday night . . . if they wanted to die. It was the toughest place in Newcastle, if not the entire North of England – home to the terrifying Tams family and various other *Peaky Blinders*-style gangs. Getting into a boxing ring with these lads, in other words, was absolute madness.

But I was a teenager now and up for anything – something Warren Young clearly liked in me – and I was probably feeling a bit tough after my victory over the thief at the dairy. So, I was one of the handful of idiots who raised their hands to volunteer to join our team, even though I'd never donned a pair of boxing gloves in my life.

A rigorous course of training followed . . . which consisted of exactly *one* practice round. Oh, and our troop had only two pairs of gloves, and the ones I got were bigger than my head, which meant I had to stuff them with newspaper to stop them flying off whenever I attempted a jab. Even when they were stuffed with newspaper, though, they still felt all wobbly and loose – and by the end of the round, I hadn't managed to land a single punch. But by then, it was too late to back out.

When the big night finally arrived, the Scout hut was full of spectators, nearly all of them dads, including one Sergeant Johnson, a former boxer himself and connoisseur of the sport. He sat in the front row, scowling, arms folded. But the second I walked into the dressing room and saw those naval boys, I realized I was in very . . . *very* deep shit. The youngest of them couldn't have been a day under sixteen, and they all had that cold, hard look of street-fighters who'd put you in the morgue over a bag of chips. I was so tiny and tender compared with them, in fact, I don't even think it *occurred* to anybody that I'd be one of their opponents.

A few minutes later, in came the referee – a Cadet officer dressed in a Navy-issue white T-shirt – and we were each given a number and the name of the lad we'd be up against.

When my time came to step into the ring, I could barely move my legs I was so intimidated by the whole spectacle. The ropes. The bell. The church hall lights, a muddy moon colour, due to the cigarette smoke hanging from the ceiling. The first-aid man with a bucket in his hand – for what reason I had no idea. It was a vision from hell.

Then I set eyes on my opponent.

He was four years older than me, five-foot-eight, and looked like he was on work-release from prison. And, of course, he was decked out in all the proper gear, with black shorts and boxing shoes and gloves the right size, while I was there in my little school shorts and plimsolls and gloves stuffed with newspaper. Well, I've had a good life, I thought. At least I'll go down swinging . . .

'Oh, c'mon, ref – this is stupid,' snarled the Sea Cadet when he saw me. 'I'll kill this little lad.'

The ref looked at me and hesitated. Oh, thank God, I thought, he's a sensible man, he'll put a stop to this. Then he shrugged and went, 'Nah, he'll be alright.'

'Listen, son,' said the much older kid, leaning in. 'I'll hit you once, then just fucking stay down.'

I nodded back, thinking, I've got to survive at least *one round*. I can't go down with the first punch. I'll be a laughing-stock. My old man will never look me in the eye again.

So, we touch gloves – DING DING! – and off I go, dancing around, Mohammed Ali-style, ducking and diving, using my speed and my featherweight size to my advantage. And I'm starting to think, y'know . . . I'm actually not too bad at this. I mean, maybe I can just waste time, run down the clock . . . wear the guy out.

Not that the Sea Cadet was moving very much.

He was just standing there, looking bored out of his mind, like he was trying to decide when to –

THUMP.

I woke up in the dressing room with a doctor leaning over me, asking how many fingers he was holding up.

'How . . . many . . . rounds . . . did I last?' I croaked.

'Rounds?' snorted the doctor. 'Son, you barely lasted a whole second.'

Later that night, when I got home, my ma called out from the kitchen to ask how it went. Like most of the other Sea Scout mothers, she hadn't wanted to go, because she couldn't bear to see her little pumpkin get his brains rearranged by a sailor from Scotswood. Now she was terrified to come out of the kitchen to survey the damage.

'Coulda been worse,' I said, like I'd been stung on the tongue.

Then my dad walked in behind me and delivered his own verdict.

'He couldn't knock the skin off a rice pudding,' he growled.

Looking back now, it's hard to believe that I was lucky enough to become a teenager in 1960, of all years – the start of the greatest decade in history. I mean, talk about *timing*. If I'd been born just a few years earlier, my teenage years would have been the same as every other generation of Geordies since before the Second World War. It would have been all music hall songs like 'Keep Yer Feet Still Geordie Hinny' and 'Blaydon Races', no sex before marriage, and BBC variety shows. Instead, I was about to get treated to The Beatles and miniskirts and women's liberation and E-Type Jags and missions to the moon. Although, to be fair, we also had to live with the Cold War and the ever-present threat of the atomic bomb.

You could feel the mood of the country change even before the 1960s began. Suddenly, the grinding poverty of the post-war period ended and a new, unfamiliar feeling set in . . .

Optimism.

My life changed too when I got a part as a child actor on Tyne Tees Television, appearing in various segments of the weekly *One O'Clock Show*. (I was small, so could play younger, and I was paid a fortune of five guineas – or just over £5 – per appearance. One of the producers had read about my Gang Show performance, which was how I'd been 'discovered'.) The biggest production that I appeared in was a futuristic drama called *In the Year 2000*, and my one and only line was, 'Daddy, what's a cold?' – because colds were supposed to have been eradicated by then. Aye, that's how bright-eyed and innocent we were . . .

Meanwhile, just before the turn of the decade, my dad did something that would have been unthinkably bold just a few years before. One Saturday morning, he took me and Maurice to Byker, on the other side of Newcastle, and headed straight for a used-car garage called Northern Motors. I was in absolute shock. *We were getting a car.* My dad settled on a dark green Wolseley 6/90 with a long bonnet, six cylinders and the registration plate PBB96. An absolute beauty. The salesman wouldn't even let him take it for a test drive – the most he would do was let him listen to the engine. But that was enough to seal the deal for a bank-breaking £195.

My dad didn't even have a proper driving licence at the time. It was an army one, which qualified him to drive a three-ton truck in the Tunisian desert. He hadn't driven anything since the war, in fact, so he was a bit rusty, to say the least. 'Shurrup!' he kept snapping at us as he attempted to operate the buttons and stalks and wind-up windows and – most troublesome of all – the column-shift gearbox, 'I'm trying to drive!'

Half an hour later, he was sweating heavily and singing, 'I'm lost, I'm lost, I don't know where I am!' at the top of his voice, with a demented look in his eyes. By the time we finally made it home – another hour later – he stumbled out of the car, gasping for breath, then walked the one and a half miles to his social club for a beer.

But we had a car parked outside our house! And it wasn't the doctor's or the rent man's – it was *ours*. The moment my dad was gone, I climbed into the front seat and sat there until dinner time. Then after dinner, I stood in the front room and looked at it through the window. My dad kept it for only a couple of years, mind you – because by then the repairs, insurance, taxes and petrol had become too much.

After that, it was back to walking or buses.

He never owned another car – or drove again – in his life.

No sooner had I become a teenager than my schoolwork started to suffer. For years, I'd been top of the 'A' class. Then they created an 'X' class to stop the top 'A' kids getting bored, and I came top of that too. But then suddenly I lost interest and slid from No. 1 to No. 6 . . . and after that, my education was pretty much a lost cause. Music being the culprit.

It didn't help that the school was bulging at the seams with forty-eight kids to a class, meaning the teachers spent more time trying to keep the peace than helping us learn. Or that secondary-modern kids almost never went on to take A levels anyway – you were out on your ear at the age of fifteen – giving you no reason to try harder.

I even managed to run into a spot of bother at the Sea Scouts, if you can believe it.

The trouble started with a 'field test' that I had to take to reach the highest Sea Scout rank of first class. This involved me and another Scout – my best pal George Beveridge – going to a campsite called Beamish in County Durham, where we were supposed to capture and cook a wood pigeon according to a set of very specific instructions. We had from Friday afternoon after school until Sunday afternoon to get this done, and we had to *walk* the seven miles or so from Dunston to Beamish, because if you took the bus or hitched a lift, you were instantly disqualified.

So, off we went in the beautiful sunshine – just kidding, it was pissing it down – and when finally we got there, we had to spend a miserable hour pitching our tent in the dark.

Neither of us had a sleeping bag – they were far too expensive in those days – so we had to make do with some blankets held together with safety pins. And it was freezing cold and wet – and we hadn't brought enough food – but we were so knackered, we slept.

The next morning, it was time to make our pigeon trap – basically, just leaves, string and twigs with a door held open by another twig and a bit of bread inside as bait. When a hungry wood pigeon wandered in there to have a bit of a nibble, you pulled out the twig, and the bird would be trapped, so you could wring its neck. Cooking the thing was a whole separate operation that involved creating a 'mud oven' in the bank of a river. But, until we'd caught our bird, we weren't going to waste our time worrying about that.

So, we made the trap, set it up . . . then sat there and watched.

And watched.

And watched.

Before we knew it, it was mid-afternoon. By which time we were starting to ask ourselves why any wood pigeon in its right mind would choose to live at a campsite where hungry Sea Scouts in short trousers kept showing up to create wood pigeon traps.

By four o'clock, we were still out of luck, and starting to get worried, because an examiner would be coming at noon the next day to look at our trap and taste our wood pigeon. And we both really, *really* wanted to become first-class Sea Scouts. So, we said, sod this, let's walk to the nearest sign of civilization – which turned out to be an old colliery town called Stanley – and see if we can get any help.

In a massive stroke of luck, right there on the high street in Stanley was a poulterer's shop – like a butcher's shop, but one that deals only in poultry and game. So, we went in and asked the farmer-looking guy in a flat cap behind the counter how much a wood pigeon would cost. He told us the price, we checked to see if we had enough money between us – we did – so we decided right then and there to just buy one.

'Do you want it plucked?' asked the guy. 'Because that'll be an extra tuppence.'

'Nooo!' we cried in unison, knowing that the Sea Scout handbook called for the bird to be cooked with its feathers on. Having a plucked bird would be a dead fucking giveaway.

'. . . are you sure, lads?' asked the poulterer. 'It's messy work, plucking a bird.'

'Oh yes, sir, we're sure.' And off we went, back to the campsite for an early night.

After a good night's kip, we set about cooking the bird we'd 'caught' at the poulterer's shop, making sure to follow the instructions in the Sea Scout handbook to the letter.

First, we had to chop its head off, which wasn't a very pleasant task. Then off came its feet. Then we went down to the bank of the river that ran through the campsite – Beamish Burn it's called – and dug two holes in the mud, one above the other. In the bottom hole, we put some pieces of wood and kindling and created a fire, and in the top one we put our wood pigeon. Then we closed up the top hole with mud, basically creating a kind of makeshift clay oven. The cooking time was about two to three hours, and when that was over, we got our billycans out and filled them with some carrots and potatoes and water and boiled them up over the fire. By this time, our meal was just about ready to be served.

Finally, the examiner turned up to judge our work.

It was a huge moment. If he gave us the thumbs up, we'd officially become first-class Sea Scouts. We'd have reached the very pinnacle of Scouting achievement.

'Patrol Leader Johnson,' barked the examiner, 'show me your pigeon.'

'Aye-aye, sir,' I said, producing this lump of baked mud with a dead bird inside it.

'Hmm,' he said, peering at it sceptically, '. . . and your side dishes?'

'Here you go, sir,' said George, showing him a little tin plate with our veggies on it. Naturally, we'd boiled the living shit out of them until they'd turned to a greyish mush.

'Very nicely prepared,' nodded the examiner. Then he took the mud lump from me and cracked it open with his field knife, like you'd crack open a coconut. And what do you know … there inside was some beautifully cooked wood pigeon breast – red and gamey, almost like lamb – with the feathers and skin separated naturally thanks to the heat of the oven, just like the handbook had said they would be.

I couldn't believe it.

'We did it!' I mouthed to George. He nodded and made the thumbs-up sign in reply.

So, the guy sits down on a log, cuts out the meat, puts it on the tin plate with the boiled veggies, and starts wolfing it down. And judging by the noises he's making, *he's loving it.*

'Do you have any salt?' he asked, his mouth full of veggies and pigeon.

'Excuse me?' replied George.

'Salt,' he said, making a little salt-shaker motion.

'Oh yes, sir! Here you go, sir!' said George, doing the honours. But the guy had already just about cleaned his plate. I looked at George, grinning, and he grinned back at me, then –
CRACK.

Suddenly the examiner was holding his jaw and howling in pain, in a state of great distress, trying to pull something out of his mouth, something he'd just bitten down on, hard. Then he spat his mouthful out onto the plate and started poking around in it with his finger until he found what he was looking for. He held it up for us to see.

George and I squinted at the tiny black speck in his hand.

It was … ah … this could be a problem.

A shotgun pellet.

'Was it *hard* to catch this pigeon, eh, lads?' hissed the examiner, seething with rage.

'How did *that* get in there?' spluttered George.

'The bird must have been shot . . . right before it walked into the trap!' I gasped. 'What are the odds?!'

'Enough!!' bellowed the examiner. 'You *cheated* on this test! You've let down your troop . . . and you've let down the Scouts! You should be *ashamed* of yourselves! I'll be recommending to your Scoutmaster that you're both dishonourably discharged!'

This was a serious business.

We returned to Dunston with knots in our stomachs, feeling very sorry for ourselves. I hated the thought of letting Warren Young down after everything he'd done for me. And I certainly didn't want a dishonourable discharge from the Sea Scouts on my record when the time came to start looking for a job. I mean, who the fuck ever gets thrown out of the Sea Scouts? I could already hear my dad's voice echoing in my head – 'You'll end up sweeping the roads!'

At our next troop meeting, we had to go and explain ourselves to our Commodore, a retired naval captain in his seventies who, for some murky reason, lived in a room above a pub in Birtley.

But the strange thing was . . . he didn't really seem to care.

Neither did Warren Young.

'Don't worry, lads, no one in the history of that test has ever caught a wood pigeon,' he told us. 'You're the first ones who at least showed a bit of initiative. We're always telling you to be prepared . . . and you were. I mean, aye, you should have been honest with the examiner . . . he's going to need a fair bit of dental work. But as I said to him myself, a Sea Scout can't learn without making mistakes!'

George and I just stood there in silence. Surely, we weren't going to get off this easily?

'So, er . . . we won't be dishonourably discharged, then?' ventured George.

'No, of course not!' snorted Warren Young. 'The examiner was just very cross.'

'So . . . we'll be, er . . . *honourably* discharged?' I asked.

'Noooo, no, no, no, no,' said Warren Young, laughing. 'We wouldn't discharge a Sea Scout over something as silly as that! And I think you've learned your lesson, right lads?'

We both nodded vigorously.

'Good,' said Warren Young, suddenly growing serious, 'because the decision's been made to put on another Gang Show – and I'm going to be needing both of your services . . .'

A few weeks later, Warren Young did me his last and biggest favour.

I knew that he worked as a draughtsman at C. A. Parsons & Co., which was based over the river on Shields Road in Heaton. It was a huge place, covering a hundred acres, with a railway terminal next to it and tracks running straight into the factory buildings. The only way you could really appreciate the scale of it was to see it for yourself. It's what people meant when they called Britain the 'workshop of the world'.

I'd always assumed that getting any kind of job there would be impossible. It was well known that they took on only sixty or so apprentices a year – from all over the North East – so the only way to get in through the door was to be the best of the best.

But Warren Young insisted that I apply, and he promised that he'd put in a good word for me.

'Brian, son,' he said, 'you might not have got into grammar school, but you're a bright lad, you're full of energy, and you're a hard worker and, most important of all, you're always willing to try new things – whether it's stepping into a boxing ring, catching a wood pigeon or dressing up as a Beverley Sister at the Gang Show. And don't worry . . . I won't mention any of those things in your reference letter.'

So, I took his advice and applied, expecting to hear nothing back. Then I got called in for an interview . . . and a few weeks later, a letter arrived that made my ma burst into tears.

I'd been invited to become a Parsons apprentice, which meant five years of technical school and on-the-job training, followed by a union-protected job for life – as long as I didn't fuck anything up. Even my old man was over the moon. Or at least, when I told him the news, he grunted a bit more enthusiastically than he usually did.

6

The Apprentice

The offer from Parsons should have set me up for life. For the next five years, I was going to get the benefit of one of the most advanced and rigorous technical apprenticeships anywhere in the world. After that, I'd become the first Johnson to wear a shirt to work . . . to join the *middle-class*. And if I kept at it and worked hard, the sky was the limit. A car. Holidays abroad. Me own three-bedroom house. All of the things that my dad could only have dreamed about in 1945.

It wasn't like Parsons was a boring company to work for either.

I felt like a little kid when I first walked into the main building in Heaton – 'the light machine shop' they called it – which took up the space of twenty football fields, churning out steam turbines that were shipped to navies and power plants all over the world. The toolmakers, the fitters, the turners, the pattern makers, the panel beaters – what those guys did in there was incredible. To me, the blades, valves and bearing cases they made weren't just parts, they were things of beauty.

It was Sir Charles Parsons' nephew, Norman, who was running the place by then.

He was a bit of a legend, in fact, was Mr. Parsons because he knew every nut and bolt on every machine, and he didn't mind getting his hands dirty.

He had a bone-dry sense of humour too.

My favourite story about him was when he was showing a turbine – a massive thing, the size of a double-decker bus – to some students from Oxford University.

One of the students pointed to a steel rod poking out of it and asked what it was for.

'Well, that's an emergency stop pin,' explained Mr. Parsons. 'We use it as a kind of brake if the turbine ever spins too fast – so it doesn't come off its mountings.'

'And if it fails,' asked the student, 'what steps do you take?'

'Well, there's a second pin,' Mr. Parsons went on, 'although we almost *never* have to use that one. And in the extremely unlikely event that also fails, there's even a third pin – much, *much* bigger than the others – which rams itself into the rotor, basically destroying the turbine, but preventing a potentially fatal accident.'

There was a long pause while the student scribbled in his notebook. Then he looked up again and frowned. 'And what steps do you take if *that* doesn't work?'

'Fucking big ones.'

I could tell you all about how I started as a dogsbody in the Parsons general drawing office, delivering plans to the shop floor – or about my time at 'apprentice school' (right there in the factory), followed by my night and day classes at 'apprentice college' in Gateshead, where I eventually passed my City & Guilds exams and got my Tech Three certificate, going on to become a brown-coated trainee inspector, then a trainee marker-off, drawing lines for the drillers and borers. I could even tell you about my first time on a freehand lathe, which could rotate a part any way you wanted, so you could cut it, sand it, knurl it, turn it, whatever your heart desired, just so long as every measurement and angle was absolutely perfect, or else the highly skilled foremen overseeing your work would tell you to start again.

But the truth was, there was only one thing on my mind in those days – and it wasn't steam turbines.

What I was obsessed with – what I just could not get enough of – was music.

This was the beginning of Beatlemania and the British Invasion, after all, with the blues and rockabilly styles of the 1950s rapidly evolving into something harder and louder. An absolutely electrifying time to be alive. And, of course, one of the most exciting bands in the charts was from right there in Newcastle – The Animals. In fact, the Animals' bass player, Bryan James 'Chas' Chandler, had once worked on the very same lathe that I was using at Parsons, which made becoming a rock star feel like something that might actually be possible, rather than something that just happened to people in London or Liverpool. I even flirted for a while with the idea that the lathe might have magical powers that could be bestowed upon me. Years later, I mentioned that to my great friend Jimmy Nail – another ex-Parsons apprentice – and he used it as the storyline in his 1990s BBC drama *Crocodile Shoes*. I got a massive kick out of his character in the show mentioning my name.

Adding to the excitement was just how forbidden and dangerous this new type of music felt at the time. Until Radio One launched, the BBC refused to play any kind of rock'n'roll for fear of corrupting the nation's youth. If you wanted to hear it, you had to hunt around the medium-wave frequencies on your parents' wireless set to find the 'pirate stations', like Radio Caroline – the latter broadcast from various ships with military-style transmitters in international waters.

Not that you could really listen to pirate radio as far north as Newcastle.* The reception was so bad that for every two seconds of music you heard, you got another minute of *interference*.

As strange as it is to admit, the music of the 1960s that I first became obsessed with wasn't even rock'n'roll. Instead, it was the work of a sensitive, curly-haired young folk singer from the other side of the pond.

And I'd discovered Dylan completely by accident.

There was a girl I was sort of going out with at the time – her name escapes me, I'm sorry to say – and she was working at a record shop on Clayton Street in Newcastle. I'd pop in there on a Saturday morning to say hello and, of course, it was torture because I wanted to buy everything in the place, but records were far beyond my means. My apprentice's wage was just £1, 17 shillings and sixpence a week, and about a third of that went to my ma for room and board, with the rest going to bus fares and the odd bag of chips. I didn't even have my own record player. If I wanted to listen to an LP, I had to go over to my cousin Stuart's house and listen to his records.

Anyway, I was in there one day, flirting away with this girl by the cash till – getting my end away was pretty high up on my list of priorities – when she pointed to a stack of albums and said, 'Look – these came in last month but no one's buying them . . . they'll be sent back to the record company first thing on Monday.'

* All broadcast signals were terrible in Dunston because it's a low-lying area, surrounded by hills. Luckily for us, a company called Rediffusion – which had started in Hull – eventually dug up the streets and laid cables, so our radios could be hardwired.

And there it was: Bob Dylan's *Freewheelin'* – his first album of mostly original songs before 'The Times They Are a-Changin'' turned him into an icon – with the man himself on the cover, standing moodily on a street corner in New York's Greenwich Village, shoulders hunched in the cold, a beautiful long-haired lass in a long coat and boots clinging onto his arm. It was just the coolest thing I'd ever seen in my life.

'Who's *Bob Dylan*?'

'No idea,' she shrugged. Then she grabbed the record and stuffed it up my jumper, making me look like I had two very pointy square nipples. 'Now quick, bugger off!'

For a minute, I was paralysed. I wasn't a thief and I hated stealing of any kind – something I'd got from my dad. But this girl was a stunner and I wasn't going to do anything that might stand in the way of a snog – or better yet, a shag. So I went, 'Right, er, okay, thanks!' and legged it.

An hour or two later, I was sitting on my cousin Stuart's living room floor next to his turntable, ready to put on the album that I'd just been gifted. He was a strange lad, was Stuart, with a love of Dusty Springfield and a poster of Marlene Dietrich on his wall. (Like I said before, we knew nothing of gay people in those days.) But from the first line of the first song – 'Blowin' in the Wind', of course – we were both in a trance. Every chord, every word, every breath just felt so heady and dangerous – like one man and his guitar really could change the world.

I soon diversified from Dylan thanks to my sort-of-girlfriend on Clayton Street. It wasn't just unsold stock she'd slip me. She'd also give me the samples she got from record label reps. The one I listened to the most was the album by The Paul Butterfield Blues Band. There was no title – the band name was all you got – and it had 'PLAY AT FULL

VOLUME FOR THE BEST EFFECT' written on the back cover. The music was just sensational. 'I Got My Mojo Working', 'Shake Your Money-Maker', 'Look Over Yonders Wall', 'Born in Chicago' . . . 'Mystery Train'. They were mostly covers of traditional black Chicago blues songs, of course, but Butterfield and his band turned up their amps so loud, you could imagine the lights dimming across the entire state of Illinois when they started to play.

Every time I put it on, I'd grin from ear to ear.

It didn't take long before I'd found a few other apprentices at Parsons who liked the same music that I did.

And, of course, one thing led to another – and before I knew it, I was in my first band.

We were a quartet called Section 5. And if you think that's a stupid name, you should have heard some of the other suggestions. Everyone's band had a stupid name in those days. One of the biggest acts on the North East club gig circuit at the time was called Mr. Poobah's Chicago Line – and no one ever batted an eyelid at that.

Admittedly, calling ourselves a band was a bit of a stretch.

We didn't have any gigs. We didn't have any fans. And we didn't know any songs. Other than that, though . . . we were all set for a glittering career of chart-topping success.

On bass was a wonderful young lad named Steve Chance, who'd managed to get himself this gorgeous Rosetti guitar, along with a matching 50-Watt amp, on a hire-purchase agreement. Handily, Steve also had an older brother, Les, who'd taught himself to play lead guitar on a Hofner Very-thin semi-acoustic. (Les was the only member of the band who wasn't an apprentice at Parsons.) On drums, meanwhile, was a guy named Robert Conlin, a solid addition to the line-up in every way but one – he couldn't actually play the drums. He did have an amazing kit though – all brand-new Rogers gear – because he was an only child and his parents spoiled him rotten. During his short time in the band, Rob seemed to be firmly of the opinion that it was physically impossible to use one foot to play the bass drum while the other controlled the hi-hats, *especially* if he was also using his arms.

Not that it mattered – Steve's amp was so loud you really couldn't hear anything else.

As for me . . . I'd flirted with playing an instrument myself. Paul Butterfield's harmonica, in particular, was an inspiration. I wished I could play like him. But I tried and tried and couldn't get the hang of it. It was the same with every other instrument – I just didn't have the concentration. I couldn't even master the guitar in a conventional sense, playing one chord after the other. My fingers felt like sausages. So, I stuck with what I'd been born with: my voice and a lot of balls.

With Steve's amp to compete with, I soon realized that I couldn't just scream at the top of my voice. I needed some equipment of my own. But I was earning a pittance as an apprentice, which left me with no choice but to go cap in hand to my old man.

'Dad,' I said, taking a deep breath. 'I need a P.A. system.'

'What?'

'Y'know . . . like a microphone and speakers. With a little amp. For playing shows like. Because I've decided I want to be a professional singer.'

That got his attention. 'A professional *what*?!' A sudden look of panic in his eyes.

'A professional *singer*, Dad.'

'Yes, I heard you the first time and I still think you're daft. Now, Johnny Cash is a real singer and you're no Johnny Cash, so forget about it.'

'Dad . . . I'm *serious.*'

To be fair to my old man, of course, no Johnson in history had ever been in the entertainment business. So, all this was completely alien to him.

After enough nagging, though, he finally came around. So off we went on the No. 66 bus via Marlborough Crescent – the good old Dunston circular – to Millers Music, which was in a basement just off Pink Lane in Newcastle. It was heaven to me, that place, with all the shiny new guitars, amps, keyboards and drums.

Once my dad had signed the hire-purchase agreement – there was a £3 and 10 shillings deposit, followed by weekly payments of 10 shillings and sixpence, which had to be made in person at the counter – I walked out with a brand-new Crystal handheld mic and 10-Watt Watkins amplifier, 'Made in England' stamped on the back.

I couldn't have been happier. And my dad couldn't have been more sceptical.

'If you miss *one* payment, son,' he snapped, 'it's gannin' back!'

Band rehearsals were every Saturday afternoon at the Chances' house in Walker.

I was so excited, I'd take the 11.30 a.m. bus and get there just before lunch.

I loved the looks I got when I carried my P.A. system onto the bus and people realized that I must be a musician, which felt dead cool in mid-1960s Gateshead. But the feeling soon disappeared when I realized that I'd have to lug the same gear from the bus stop in Walker to the Chances' house – a good half-a-mile walk.

The Chances' house wasn't a normal semi-detached like ours. It was a steel-framed prefabricated bungalow that had been built in a factory and transported by road to the estate in Walker where they lived. All the houses on the estate were prefabs. They'd built tens of thousands of the things after the war to try and end the housing shortage caused by the Blitz and the baby boom. Unless you were the rent man, you'd always use the back door, which took you straight into a tiny kitchen. Beyond that were the living room and a narrow hallway that led to the two small bedrooms. Of course, the living room was Mrs. Chance's pride and joy, complete with sideboard, TV and best china, rounded off by Peter the Budgie, the family pet.

The only place for us to set up our gear and rehearse was in Steve and Les's bedroom. I'd stand at the foot of the bed – my little 10-Watt Watkins amp on the mattress itself – with Steve and Les on either side. Meanwhile, Rob would set up his kit in the doorway, his arse sticking out into the hall. And even though the entire house was the size of only three or four parking spaces, Steve's mum and dad – God bless them both – didn't mind at all. They were the most wonderful people you could ever imagine, they really were. Always so smiley and proud (Steve's mum was gorgeous too). Every week, we'd take over that room and make the most terrible racket for hours on end, and they never once told us to stop. It's so rare to find people like that, who encourage you at the time of life when you need it most.

Looking back, those Saturdays in the Chances' prefab were some of the happiest of my life. And exciting too. Because it seemed like we could do anything if we just tried.

The first songs we learned were straight off The Stones' first album. Dead-easy stuff to play. 'Route 66', 'Mona', 'I Just Want to Make Love to You' and, best of all, 'I'm a King Bee', The Stones' cover of the classic Muddy Waters track. We knew we weren't very good, of course. But with every Saturday that went by, we got closer to touching something that we couldn't have dreamed of touching before, something otherwise completely unattainable in our industrial, working-class world – a sense of glamour and excitement and sex and adventure, I suppose. And when we finally made it through a song without stopping, it just felt absolutely magical.

But I also got bored quickly.

'Right,' I'd say, after I'd sung the last line, 'why don't we try something else, eh?'

'No, no, no,' Steve would reply, 'we've got to do this again until we get it right.'

'But we just did it *twice*!'

'Aye, and it still sounds like shite. We've got to practise, man!'

'Oh, for fuck's sake . . .'

I'd love to tell you that I've since become more of a patient man.

But I'd be lying, so I won't.

In the early days of those Saturday afternoon rehearsals – I must have been sixteen or seventeen – the decision was made to celebrate our mastery of a new Rolling Stones' number by going out for a pint. My first ever pint, as it so happened. Or at least the first one that I would ever order for myself in a pub. So, we took the bus to a Walker institution called The Scrogg, a name that manages to sum up everything about the place, from the walking in mud to the cigarette tar that dripped from the ceiling.*

When I say we took the bus, I mean the bus stopped *right outside* the front door, because in the North East it's written in stone somewhere that a bus stop can't ever be more than three paces from a pint. Then it was time to take a deep breath and make our entrance . . . which we did, only to be almost knocked unconscious by the fog of sweat, beer fumes and disinfectant that hung in the air, along with the plumes of smoke from the overflowing ashtrays and our fellow patrons' blackened lungs.

We almost walked straight out again. But everyone else was breathing the same air . . . and *they* were all still alive, well barely. Movement was not a common sight.

It was obvious that we were underage, but The Scrogg wasn't the kind of place where people asked questions, a question being too close to a conversation for anyone's liking.

I had no idea what to drink. I just knew the word 'beer'. But Les told me to order a 'black velvet' instead. This was half a pint of stout mixed with half a pint of strong cider and I was like . . . mmm, this tastes *gooooood* . . . so down it went and up went my confidence, then it was, 'Let's have another one' . . . three or four more times. The only interruption being a quick trip outside to piss against the wall – pint still in hand, tab still in mouth – because the only way you could have survived the toilets was with a gas mask and an oxygen tank, and I hadn't brought either.

Now, I probably don't need to explain to you what happens to a five-foot-six teenager when he drinks four pints of

* It's still there today – 125 Scrogg Road, next to Walker Park – if you're feeling brave.

beer without food in his stomach, having never smelled the proverbial barmaid's apron before. I became suddenly, fabulously, paralytically drunk. As did Steve, Les and Rob. Only they were quite a bit bigger than me, so they at least retained a few basic functions. Such as the ability to talk.

I, on the other hand, was just one big vowel movement.

'Let's get the bus home,' slurred Steve. 'I know where my dad hides his whisky.'

'Yeesshh!' the others cried, before we set out on the long, treacherous voyage back outside.

What I remember next is waiting on the pavement for the bus with a very neatly trimmed privet hedge behind me, and a full moon overhead. Then suddenly the moon moved, and not just a little bit, but across the entire universe, before disappearing completely. Wow, that must have been a *shooting moon*, I thought, before realizing that I'd lost my balance, fallen backwards and was now lying face-up in the hedge, hands still in pockets. A strange sensation, like being in handcuffs.

'Where's Brian?' I heard Steve ask Les. 'He was standing right there a moment ago . . .'

Then somebody noticed my feet sticking out from the privet – and a great deal of merriment ensued.

When the bus arrived, I somehow managed to unfall out of the hedge and get myself upright, before making my way to the upper deck. The main topic of conversation, I seem to remember, was my state of drunkenness, and how very funny that was.

Then a strange feeling came over me – or rather, came over my stomach. I wasn't sure what it was, but it felt like . . . *something trying to get out*. Then I started to make a series of strange noises. At which point, it seemed like a good idea to open the window next to me. But the upper decks of buses had very small windows, about four inches across – and they opened sideways. Which was a problem, because a great deal of liquid and whatever remained of my lunch and breakfast was now coming up my throat with the velocity of a mortar shell.

I had no choice. Even though I knew that puking at a ninety-degree angle out of a four-inch window while travelling at forty mph would be impossible, I tried it anyway.

When I was done, all the laughing had stopped, and a lot of screaming had started because everyone around me was now covered in the contents of my stomach.

When we finally got back to the Chances' house, Mrs. Chance declared that I was in no state to go back to Dunston and should sleep with Steve and Les, three of us in a bed.

So that's what happened.

And, of course, I vomited again, but this time, luckily, there was something there to catch it – Steve's new state-of-the-art Chelsea boots. Oh aye, this was the kind of night of which legends are made.

I'd love to tell you that I learned something important from the experience of drinking too much. But, most of all, I just wanted to do it again.

And we did.

Many other adventures at The Scrogg followed – and one tragedy. The latter occurred when we came back to Steve's with a little too much loudmouth soup in our bellies. Steve slumped himself down on the sofa and we followed.

Mrs. Chance said, 'I'll make you all a nice cup of tea.' She went to the kitchen and said, 'Where's Peter? C'mon Peter my little boy, come to Mam.'

But Peter the budgerigar – a much-loved member of the

family who used to sit on people's shoulders, sip tea, peck on biscuits and watch the BBC News – was nowhere to be seen.

'Oh my,' Mrs. Chance said. 'He must have flown out when you came in. The cats will get him!' So, Mr. and Mrs. Chance went out in the street calling for little Peter.

We didn't move. Steve was farting professionally and we smiled, nodding our approval, then the horror when the stink hit at half the speed of smell.

Mrs. Chance was distraught when she came back in, dabbing her eyes, when Steve suddenly got up and it was then we realized where Peter had been: dying a horrible death under the dancing buttocks of Steve Chance. Mr. Chance tried to resuscitate him, but no luck. The crossed eyes were definitely the result of broken wind. A sad end to the night and to Peter's life.

As a punishment, Steve got no breakfast and the stink-eye from Mrs. Chance the next day.

As for me, I made myself sick from alcohol a few more times after The Scrogg, but not too many. I'm lucky, I suppose, that I have this alarm bell in my brain that says, 'That's enough, Brian', and I stop before things get out of control. If any of my friends are reading this, of course, they're probably thinking, Brian, you're a lying bastard.

But that's my story – and I'm sticking to it.

7

Eine Kleine Rockmusik

My first ever show wasn't what I expected. It wasn't even with Section 5. I was just minding my own business at Parsons one day when these two older lads came up to me and said they had a band and they'd heard I was a bit of a singer, so would I be interested in playing with them at Sunniside Working Men's Club the following week.

These were boom times for working men's clubs, of course, with the demand for live music far exceeding the supply, which meant the bar for getting a gig wasn't exactly high. But I didn't know that at the time. As far as I was concerned, it was incredible that anyone could get themselves a real paid gig anywhere – and my heart almost leapt out of my chest at the very mention of it. Also, Sunniside was only a few miles up the road from Dunston, so getting there wouldn't be a problem.

'What kind of stuff do you play then?' I asked, trying to sound like this was no big deal.

'We're a folk band.'

'What, like Bob Dylan?'

'Bob *who*?'

My heart sank. How could they be a folk band if they'd never heard of Bob Dylan? 'Look, I'm sorry lads,' I said, 'but I don't know any folk songs, and I'm already in a band, so I can't –'

'Here you go,' they said, handing me a book of lyrics. 'We'll see you next Tuesday, eh?'

We were billed as ... I can hardly bear to write this down ... The Toasty Folk Trio.

As for our set, it consisted of six songs, the lyrics to which I wrote out in longhand to help me learn them by heart. It wasn't *folk* music, as such. More like country and western. The stuff that Gene Autry used to sing. One of the older lads played guitar and the other had a stand-up snare drum. Well, Brian, you've got to start somewhere, I said to myself as we waited to go on. Then the club's emcee introduced us by saying, 'Aalreet, so the lad coming oot to sing tonight might look a bit young, but divvant boo him or hoy anything at him, just give the bairn a chance, eh?'

The whole place groaned. Then about half the room got up and went out for a piss.

This is gonna be a long night, I thought.

The first song was 'Red River Valley', a traditional number that originates from Canada.

That was also the last song – because we were so fucking awful, the emcee jumped back on stage and said he would pay us ten bob each to pack up our stuff and go home.

I felt terrible. Totally humiliated. But as I collected my book of lyrics, the emcee grabbed me and said, 'Not *you*, sunshine – you stay right here.' Then a big fat woman came out and invited me to sit down next to her at the club's Hammond organ so we could belt out a few songs together. And it turned out she was brilliant. She could play that organ like no one's business, and she had this absolutely terrific, almost gospel-like voice ... She also kept trying to give me cuddles between songs, which wasn't exactly how I'd imagined my professional debut. But still, a gig was a gig ...

The last song we did was 'House of the Rising Sun', which the lady introduced as a 'good old Geordie song' – but of course it wasn't, really, apart from the fact that The Animals had just released a version of it. But we did it proud . . . so much so, in fact, that many years later I would cover it again in my band Geordie, and we'd record a version that I'm very proud of to this day. (It would later be used in the Al Pacino film *Hangman*.)

We walked off stage to a standing ovation. Well . . . either that or the tickets to the bingo had just gone on sale. Whatever the case, the club's manager was so pleased he gave me £5 – *five pounds!* – in addition to the ten bob that I'd already got for the Toasty Folk Trio to fuck off. I couldn't believe it. Five pounds was three times as much as I was getting for a weekly wage at Parsons! The two lads from the Toasty Folk Trio couldn't believe it, either. In fact, the moment I walked out of the door, they jumped on me and told me I owed them two-thirds of it. 'What?' I said. '*Why?*'

'That's our management fee,' they said.

'But I don't have managers!'

'You do tonight, son.'

The first show that started it all for me, and it was important for the rest of my life, was Section 5's first gig, which was a few weeks later at Walker Boys' Club. It was more of a church hall than anything else, but it was a start and I'll never forget it.

Seeing as we were too young to drive – not that we could have afforded a van, anyway – we had no choice but to take the trolleybus and stow our gear under the stairs. If I'd once felt like a rock star hauling my little P.A. around by myself, I felt like an even bigger deal with an entire band and their instruments in tow. It was brilliant. Not that the conductor or the other passengers were too happy about the time it took for us to carry all our gear from the pavement onto the bus. Especially since we just went one stop – then had to do it all again in reverse.

The only reason we'd got the gig was because Steve and Les had been members of the club when they were kids – at the same time, they claimed, that one of The Animals had been on the boxing team. (Which Animal, no one seemed too sure about.) That had been many years before, however, and when we walked in, it was obvious that the place had gone to the dogs. I mean, it was basically just an empty room with bare floorboards. A total shithole. Then again, Section 5 weren't exactly ready for Wembley Stadium just yet.

All we played that night, I'm pretty sure, was Chuck Berry. Or at least the kind of Chuck Berry songs that The Rolling Stones had made their own. Tracks like 'Come On' and 'Carol'. I think we also did 'Walking the Dog', another Stones number.

It was a moment of truth for us, really. Because we'd been rehearsing and rehearsing and rehearsing for this moment . . . and we were still shite. We'd told Rob, the drummer, 'Just do what they do on the record', but he either wouldn't or couldn't, and on stage, he just froze. The guitars were too loud. Les broke a string. I forgot the words . . . to everything. Our worst number was the Manfred Mann song '5-4-3-2-1' – instantly recognizable back then as the theme of the hit ITV show *Ready Steady Go!* It was a hard enough song to begin with, with a lot of harmonica in it – which no one could play – and some group shouts of '5,4,3,2,1', which none of the other lads wanted to do because they couldn't sing and they didn't have microphones. So, our version of it was miss-ing two-thirds of what made it worth playing in the first place. And the third that remained was a dog's fucking dinner.

For the sake of a good story, I'd love to tell you that the audience booed us off stage.

But the reality was, they'd barely noticed us to begin with.

They deeply and truthfully could not give a fuck.

The few people who *were* paying attention just stood against the wall, looking depressed, not moving an inch. There was no booze. Not even pop. Nothing. The only reason they were there was because it cost only a shilling to get in – about £1.80 in today's money – and there was nothing else to do and nowhere else to go in Walker. When we were finished, there was just complete silence, not even a smattering of polite applause. Everyone just buggered off to the chippie next door.

But the night was a roaring success in another way. In the audience that evening happened to be a flaxen-haired young German bird of about nineteen or twenty years old – her dad must have worked on a merchant ship or something – and when I walked out of the club for a tab, there she was on the pavement, waiting for me with some friends. I've no idea if she enjoyed the show. All I know is that her tongue ended up in my ear, and before I knew it, she was beckoning me to follow her to a romantic hideaway around the back of the club – the hideaway in question being a brick alleyway filled with nettles, tab-ends and general rubbish. Then she pulled down my jeans, pushed me to the ground, and I felt nettles stinging me all over my arse and down the back of my legs. But it didn't seem to hurt at the time. Especially not after she'd hitched up her skirt and started to lower herself on top of me.

And lo, it came to pass that on that evening – after Section

5's first-ever show to a near-empty room at Walker Boys' Club – I lost my virginity to this quite unbelievably sexy older German girl, who jumped up and down on top of me like she was riding a horse, all the while still wearing her coat and jumper, smoking a cigarette, using my stomach as an ashtray and looking around furtively to see if anyone was coming. Which, as it so happened . . . I just had.

'You're finished *already*?' she asked.

'More?!' was all I managed to reply – those being the days when once you were up, you were up for the night.

'Where did *you* go?' asked Steve, when I returned to pack up my gear, feeling ten-feet tall. 'And why are you walking funny?'

'I sat on some nettles,' I explained.

'There's toilets in here, y'know,' he said, looking confused. 'You didn't need to crap in the bushes . . .'

But I wasn't really listening, because I couldn't stop thinking, why *me* – and why on *this* night, of all nights? It's got to be the singing, I concluded. Which led me to another thought. If I get better at this singing business – and eventually join a better band – maybe this will happen to me every night . . . for the rest of my life.

Such are the moments when Important Career Decisions are made.

8

Crashing and Burning

⚡

It was summer 1966, and we were driving down the A1 to Dover to go on our first international holiday, to my Italian side of the family's house in Frascati, near Rome. By 'we', I mean George Beveridge, Robert Conlin and me. England were beating Germany 4–2 in the World Cup at Wembley. What a day! We gave two fingers to every German car we saw. This was the life: three nineteen-year-old lads in a quite new Renault 4 – it was Rob Conlin's (he was an only child, lucky git). We were going where our fathers had been twenty years earlier, but we weren't going to get shot at.

We boarded the ferry at Dover, and the cars were just unbelievable: Aston Martin 4s and 5s, Bentley Continentals, Facel Vegas, Ferraris, even a Gullwing Mercedes, all on one ship. We couldn't believe there were so many rich people in the world.

This was a time when you were really proud to be British. Honest. The Beatles and The Stones ruled the world, Minis were selling everywhere, though in Italy they were made under licence and called Innocenti. British bikes still ruled the roost: Norton, Triumph, BSA, Ariel, James.

We were off. The ferry left the port, and for the first time in my life I saw what the White Cliffs of Dover fuss was all about. The drive through France, Switzerland, then Northern Italy, then, on the well-named Autostrada Sud, to Frascati was just wonderful. We had a great time, and suddenly realized that cars were everything to the Italians. The beautiful Alfas, Giuliettas, Lancias. They were a little different.

When we left, after two great weeks, little did we know what was about to happen to us. The family loaded us up with cardboard boxes full of wine and hams and salamis. We were hemmed in pretty good. Off we set, late as usual, and got lost a few times trying to find the road out of Frascati.

After driving through the night, Robert Conlin was pretty tired by about 4 a.m. He wouldn't let George or myself help him drive, in case 'we broke the gears'. I swear that's what he said. So we slept as best we could in the car. We were about a third of the way through France, on the dreaded N7 autoroute, notorious in motoring fraternities for death and destruction. We had to get to Calais for the ferry or we'd miss work in Newcastle on Monday. The day was Saturday, and the ferry ticket said 4.30 p.m. departure. If we kept going, only stopping for petrol, we'd be okay.

Rob didn't look that good, so we volunteered our driving services, but we were denied yet again. George Beveridge said to me, 'Hey, how about a swap, Brian? I'm sick of sitting in the back.' The back did look like a mobile grocer's, but it was my turn, so we swapped. That was the best swap I ever did in my life.

One hour later, on the N7, there was a family of four having a picnic at the side of the road, by their Peugeot Estate. We had just passed a car full of English nurses, and we'd waved to each other. Rob Conlin fell fast asleep at the wheel doing seventy mph, and before we could do anything, he hit the Peugeot full on. Everything turned black and white; I mysteriously went completely deaf; and it's true, it was all in slow motion: HOLY SHIT, is this thing ever gonna stop rolling? It went over seven times, according to witnesses. The roof of the car was flattened to the door-handle level. There was complete silence.

Then the screaming started. Rob Conlin was the screamer: the steering wheel had collapsed and the ignition key had gone through his ribcage. George had been catapulted out of the front seat into a field. I was trapped. This car was rear-engined. There was no way out. I took deep breaths and checked for blood. None – that's not possible. Ooh, you jammy git, I thought. The bloody awful French sirens were getting closer. Voices surrounded the car, English voices, girls' voices, nurses' voices. I sat and waited to be rescued, but the problem was they didn't know I was there. They couldn't see me.

I must admit to a smidgen of panic, because the car was on its side, petrol was leaking everywhere and the engine was hot. I started shouting, but I was told later that everybody was looking after Rob or in the field with George, who had horrendous injuries.

I decided to try to get out through the engine bay, daft bugger. I pulled the seat away – not difficult in 1960s Renaults – put my hand through and promptly burned myself. I screamed, 'OOYAH!' Just then a *pompier* saw me and shouted, '*Cet git anglais entre l'auto est FUCKAYED!*' (I think.)

They got me out and laid me down. Shock was setting in now, and the enormity of the swap I did with George. There was my best pal on a stretcher, lookin' so dead, being rushed into an ambulance. Oh, George, don't die . . .

Everybody was looking at me kinda weird, I couldn't understand it. I'd just survived a major prang and they were looking at me like it was my fault. Then the policeman asked if we'd been drinking, and that's when I realized I was drenched in Italy's finest wine. The only reason we weren't done for that was because I pointed out that all the corks were still in the bottle necks. And that's when the pain in my chest kicked in. So I hadn't got away with it; it was an inside job – three broken ribs.

I was put in a village B&B. They were so nice to me. The others were in hospital; I'll never forget that night. I was alive, but I didn't know if George was. Next day, I went to the hospital. The lads were alive. A little battered, but that didn't matter. We had no money at all, so all we worried about was getting out of there. George had stitches all over his face and was still bleeding. What we did was, I rubbed some of his blood on my face, jumped into bed and pretended to be George, while George, with Rob's help, dressed in a cupboard. We then proceeded to the train station to catch the train to Paris, with hospital staff chasing us to pay the bill.

A wonderful guy from the British Embassy had got us tickets to England on the boat train, but it was to London only. We had no money for food and, God, we were hungry. When we got to King's Cross, after walking through London with our clothes in cardboard boxes, we got three tickets home by promising to pay the people who'd lent us the money back within a month.

Finally, on Sunday afternoon, we arrived in Newcastle. What must we have looked like – George like a young Frankenstein, and me with blood all over my trousers? That's when Rob Conlin pulled out his wallet and said he was getting a cab home. The bugger had had money all the time! George and I dragged our sorry asses to Dunston, our home village, about four miles away.

At 7.25 on Monday morning, I clocked on at C. A. Parsons & Co. Ltd, broken ribs and all. George went to hospital to get more glass out of his face. He still has a piece in his head to this day.

A few weeks later, my apprenticeship over, Parsons came good and offered me a permanent position.

I was a proper grown-up now.

And no . . . I didn't much like the sound of that either.

Mum and Dad. First days in Dunston after Italy.

The photo you never want your mother to show every person who comes to the house.

Our first own home. 106 Beech Drive.

Oak Avenue. Look, I can run!

The dreaded knitted swimming trunks.
That's me on the right, pre-swim.

The family on a day visit to Durham City.

Programme from the Gang Show.

Getting ready for the Sea Scouts.

With lifelong pal George Beveridge.
(His dad was always betting on the horses,
thus the jumper decision . . .)

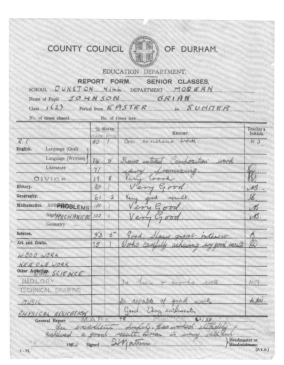

I like the music report. 'Is capable of good work.'
Is that good or bad?

Umberto, George, me and Rob on the beach in Frascati.

Parsons pass, which allowed access to the
different workshops – the equivalent of a
backstage pass.

This is the second gig I ever played in my life and it still gets me every time I see it. A great memory. The venue was the Playhouse Theatre in Jesmond.

No 2
SCROGG INN
125 Scrogg Road, Walker, Newcastle NE6 2PR Tel: 659917

Scottish & Newcastle Inns

The Scrogg.

My wedding party.
North Shields, 1968.
Not a lot of smiles!!

Carol and Joanne.

First promo shot. We're sitting on the top
of a Commer van.

At last, our name on a ticket.

The Jasper Hart Band van with
Ken Brown at the window.

The Jasper Hart Band in 1970. I wouldn't say we were successful.
Just very happy!

Our first press conference. Looking bored.

The 'Red Bus' red bus.

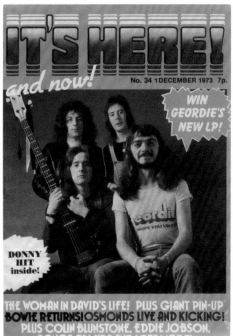

This is the pop crap I was talking about!

Only a mother could make this outfit.
Desperate times.

On tour in Japan.

Those bloody boots keep coming back to haunt me.

Ride 'em cowboy. Tom Hill in the saddle.

We rented a boat for a week. Kala and Joanne life-vested up.

On tour: life on the road didn't go hand in hand with family life.

PART TWO

9

Oops

⚡

New Year's Eve, 1966.

I'm young, free and single – or unmarried, anyway – and things could not be going better.

I've moved on from Section 5, for a start, and I'm the singer in a new, much-better band, with a far more sensible name. Okay, that last part isn't true. We're called The Gobi Desert Kanoe Klub, which we saw written on a novelty T-shirt advertised in the back of the *New Musical Express*, next to an offer for stick-on sideburns . . . which we ordered, without thinking to check the colour.* As for our musical style, let's just say that I go on stage equipped with maracas and tambourine. Oh, and we don't play 'gigs'. We play 'happenings' – and even better, 'love-ins'.

Did I mention I've got a new girlfriend? Aye, and she's a stunner. Flaming red hair. Big blue eyes. Carol is her name, and we can't keep our hands off each other.

And now here we are, just before midnight, at a party to celebrate 1966 turning to 1967, at the home of The Gobi Desert Kanoe Klub's rhythm guitarist, Dave Yarwood, a man bravely sporting a bowl cut paired with a floral shirt and tight white trousers.

* Reddish-orange.

Like everyone else in the room that night, Dave is that most wonderful and unlikely of creatures – a hippie in New-castle. There are hundreds of us in the North East of 1966, if not thousands. Our God is the sweet-voiced Scott McKen-zie, and our anthem is 'San Francisco' – even though San Francisco is a very, very long way away from Dave's house here on the Scotswood Road.

Now, New Year's Eve – or Old Year's Night as some call it – is a big deal in Newcastle, and not just because Geordies will embrace any excuse for a piss-up. When the clock strikes midnight, every ship on the Tyne blasts its horn, and the whole city vibrates to this eerie, stirring sound, which carries for miles through the fog and the rain. Then it's time for 'first-footing', when the first person to enter a house on 1 January carries with them a lump of coal for good luck and is greeted on the other side with a glass of whisky and a rous-ing chorus of 'Auld Lang Syne' . . . unless the first-footer is a woman, or a redhead, in which case a curse will be upon you for the next twelve months. A strange superstition, given the number of lasses and gingers in these parts – but don't blame me, I'm half-Italian, I had nothing to do with it.

To this day, neither Carol nor I can remember a single detail between the clock striking midnight and us waking up in each other's arms the following morning on Dave's living room floor.

All I can tell you for sure is that we both got very drunk . . .

And one of us ended up very pregnant.

In the race to find fame and fortune as a rock'n'roll singer, knocking up your girlfriend at the age of nineteen while work-ing full-time in a factory was not performance enhancing.

It's not that I regret it. You can't regret it. The little girl who was born nine months later – my beautiful Joanne – has brought me more joy and love than I could ever put into words.

But my timing . . . well, it could have been better.

It certainly couldn't have been much worse.

I mean, for a wannabe rock'n'roll musician, Britain in early 1967 was about as good as it was ever going to get. It was like being an explorer in Portugal in the age of Christopher Columbus. Or a painter in Italy at the height of the Renaissance. When you think of what was going on at the time, it's just staggering. The Rolling Stones had just released the double A-side of 'Let's Spend the Night Together' and 'Ruby Tuesday'. *Sgt. Pepper's Lonely Hearts Club Band* by The Beatles was about to come out . . . as was *Are You Experienced* by the Jimi Hendrix Experience and the single of 'Waterloo Sunset' by The Kinks. Then a few months after that, the BBC would launch Radio One.

Radio One alone would be a truly life-changing development. Before it went on the air, all BBC Radio offered was the awful crap of the Light Programme or, even worse, the Home Service, with its shipping forecasts that seemed to go on for days at a time, describing every last gust of wind and drop of rain in places that only a handful of fishermen knew existed. 'Holmsgarth, northwest, two to four . . . mainly fair, occasionally poor . . . Lochmaddy, intermittent slight rain, falling slowly . . .'

Yet somehow, they went from that to playing 'Flowers in the Rain' by The Move – the first song Radio One ever broadcast. I missed a quarter of an hour's wages that morning because I couldn't tear myself away from the Rediffusion radio in the kitchen.

And when I got to work, all I could think about was getting home again, so I could listen to it some more.

To be fair, I'd felt as though the 1960s were passing me by
even before I became an accidental dad. After all, it wasn't
like my job at Parsons was just nine-to-five. I was devastated
when I realized there would be entire weeks when I'd have to
work the 9 p.m. to 7.30 a.m. shift – even after it was explained
to me that it meant double pay and a four-day week. But I
didn't give a shit about the extra money, even though I needed
every penny that I could get. I just wanted to be out at night,
playing with the band.

I remember my first night shift like it was yesterday. I was
walking to the factory gate with two lads who were fellow
apprentices, and when I looked up, I noticed the most breath-
taking sunset. Now, for all the shit I give the North East
about its weather, I can tell you, hand on heart, it does sunsets like nowhere else. The wind becomes God's paintbrush,
and the rain clouds His palette, and the sky just explodes into
these incredible swirls of pinks, oranges and reds, especially
in summer, because you're so far north it never gets fully
dark.

'Jesus Christ . . . just take a look at that,' I said, straining
my neck as I tried to take it all in.

'Look at what?' came the reply.

'The sky, man, the fucking *sky*.'

The lads glanced up . . . then looked at each other and
shrugged. They'd seen sunsets before.

'Just think of all that's happening in the rest of the world
under that same sun,' I marvelled. 'All those brilliant places.
All those brilliant people. All those adventures just waiting to
be had.' Then I looked over at the light machine shop – a

gaping black hole with train tracks running into it. 'And here's us,' I said, 'going in *there*.'

The lads looked at me as though I'd just landed from another planet.

'You're weird, you. You know that, don't you? You're fucking weird.'

My frustration wasn't helped by the fact that I'd started going to see a lot of big-name acts, giving me a glimpse of the kind of life that I could have if I ever made it as a professional singer.

The earliest show I remember going to was at the Odeon Cinema on Pilgrim Street in Newcastle. Admission was free because it was sponsored by a cigarette company, which was okay in those days, because cigarettes were good for you – according to the doctors who endorsed them, at least. The headliner was Julie London. I remember them giving us each a pack of twenty at the door, which was like Christmas come early for me and George Beveridge, who'd gone with me. Usually, we were so skint we had to buy them in packs of ten. Apart from the main attraction, there was also a line-up of bands who played two songs each. The Bachelors, The Four-most, then The Pretty Things came on and just about blew the doors off the place with 'Don't Bring Me Down'.

I would have given my right arm to trade places with any of those guys on the stage, especially The Pretty Things.

One of the reasons the top acts all came to Newcastle was because of the Club a'Gogo, run by the notorious Cockney music manager Mike Jeffery. It quickly became the North East's answer to the Marquee in London – mainly because Jeffery had hired a brilliant young singer named Eric Burdon to front the house band.

The band, of course, was The Animals.

Everyone played the Club a'Gogo. The Rolling Stones. The Who. Ike and Tina Turner. Howlin' Wolf. The Animals even dedicated a song to the place, which they released on the B-side of 'Don't Let Me Be Misunderstood'. That's how red hot the place was. But there were plenty of other booming venues in town. There was La Dolce Vita, then there were The Downbeat, Change Is, The Oxford, The Majestic, The Cavendish and, of course, The Mayfair, which had a fabulous revolving stage.

Aye, Newcastle really was a hopping place in those days.

The Mayfair was where I went most often because it had the best sound system and a 'rock night' when DJs played the latest heavy rock and blues at the kind of volume that felt like a punch in the gut. The track we most wanted to hear was 'My Generation' by The Who. We'd all wait for the line that Roger Daltrey sang so brilliantly and with such menace – 'Why don't you all . . . f-f-f-*fade away*?' – and we'd mime along, throwing ourselves around the dance floor, heads back, doing Pete Townshend windmills on our air guitars as Keith Moon beat the shit out of his drums.

I loved that song so much, we later tried to cover it in The Gobi Desert Kanoe Klub . . .

But we ran out of talent in the first verse.

The show that really brought home just how fast the future was coming at us was The Jimi Hendrix Experience. I can even tell you the date: Friday, 10 March 1967. At the Club a'Gogo, of course. It must have been one of Hendrix's first shows in Britain – no surprise, given that he was managed by Mike Jeffery and The Animals' Chas Chandler.

The moment I heard that he was coming to town, I knew it would be something else. The guy had blown up even before anyone had really heard his stuff, with the *Record Mirror* writing a profile of him entitled 'Mr. Phenomenon'. Then *Are You Experienced* came out – the opening track, 'Foxy Lady', was said to be about Roger Daltrey's girlfriend – and I remember listening to it and going, *what the fuck is this*? It was as though the guy had somehow beamed himself in from another dimension . . . and brought with him a whole new set of musical frequencies.

Louder ones.

I didn't have the money for a ticket, of course. Not that it mattered, because they sold out in a second. So, I did what any other enterprising young lad would do under the same circumstances. I got down on my hands and knees and crawled in under the admissions box when the bouncers weren't looking.

By the time someone spotted me, I was already bolting up the stairs and into the crowd.

The place was beyond packed. We're talking double, triple capacity. You could barely breathe. I've since found out that at the same gig was one Gordon Sumner, a.k.a. Sting, who was just a wee lad of fifteen at the time. The Club a'Gogo had two rooms, I should probably mention. One of them was marked 'The Young Set' because it was for under-18s, and the other was 'The Jazz Lounge' – for an older, more sophisticated crowd. On this night we were in The Young Set, because the show in the Jazz Lounge didn't start until the ungodly hour of 2 a.m.

Even Sting remembers there being a bit of trouble as the management tried to find the kid who'd snuck in. ('That was *you*?!' he said, when I told him, years later.) But I managed to find a spot near the back where I could stand camouflagi-lently, if that's a word, and listen. And that's all I could do, listen, because I couldn't see a thing . . . other than a bit of headband, the top of a guitar and some ribbon. But then Hendrix swung his guitar and got it stuck in the false ceiling – not hard to do in such a ridiculously claustrophobic space. Most guitarists would have stopped the show, but he just kept on playing it as it hung there.

At one point, if memory serves, with his teeth.

The place went absolutely fucking nuts.

The world will never see the likes of Hendrix again. Just the aura of the guy. The charisma. Words can't begin to do him justice. Although, if I'm being honest – the sound was awful. I mean, *really* bad. I couldn't even see a road crew. There was just Mitch Mitchell doing his thing on the drums, Noel Redding banging away on bass. There was no mixing desk, no sound guy, just the three lads on stage and this incredible, totally overwhelming noise, everything cranked up beyond its limit, fuses glowing, sparks flying, the air fizz-ing and crackling with high-voltage current. The truth is it was Jimi Hendrix's brilliant fingers that shaped and sculpted the whole thing. He opened his soul through his guitar.

The band might have called themselves an experience, but really, they were an assault. When you came out, you knew the world had changed, that *you'd* changed. I see the same effect when Angus Young lets loose, completely lost to him-self and using the guitar to translate what he's feeling.

Needless to say, I was instantly hooked.

My ears were still ringing from the Hendrix show when The Gobi Desert Kanoe Klub got together.

Line up – yours truly on vocals, Dave Yarwood of New

Year's Eve party fame on guitar, and another pretty handy guitarist called Ken Brown. (I'd met Ken at Parsons – he had long hair, a moustache, and later took a shine to Carol's sister, Jen, eventually becoming my brother-in-law.) On bass, meanwhile, was my old pal Steve Chance, and on drums there was a lad with the fabulous Monte Carlo name of Fred Smith.

There's a photograph somewhere of us all sitting on the back steps of Dave's house, trying to look groovy.

If I remember correctly, Ken had wanted us to be called Half Past Thirteen. But we all thought that was a stupid idea.

We had big plans, of course. But our iffy covers of tracks by John Mayall & The Bluesbreakers and the Paul Butterfield Blues Band – my little 10-Watt Watkins P.A. system completely drowned out by Dave and Ken's guitars – were never going to get us far.

But the band did provide me with one of the major rites-of-passage of any musician's career.

I was at my parents' house when it happened, looking out of the front window.

First, came the horrible squealing sound. Then the deafening clatter. Then in a haze of exhaust smoke, it appeared – an Austin J2 van with 'Gobi Desert Kanoe Klub' on the side.

For the first time in my life, I was in a *band with transport*.

Somewhere up above, God's Fender was playing the 'Hallelujah Chorus'.

I mean, okay . . . the van was a piece of shit. But it was *our* piece of shit. We didn't care that the cable connecting the gear lever on the steering column to the transmission kept snapping, meaning we had to change gear on occasion with a pair of pliers. Or that the thing drove almost sideways because the tyres were worn down to the sidewalls and there was something profoundly wrong with the alignment. To us, that funny-looking little van was freedom. Never again would we have to lug our gear onto a public bus – or worse, have to beg any of our friends for a ride. I have no recollection of who sold us such a death-trap. All I know is that we pooled our money, someone's dad chipped in the rest, and that we paid about £20 for it, which was about £20 too much.

The world went into slow-motion when that van pulled up outside No. 1 Beech Drive.

Curtains twitched.

Heads popped up.

There were gasps and whispers.

And as I left the house and walked up the front path, I imagined flashbulbs popping, girls calling my name, fans screaming. Then the side door of the van slid open, I climbed in and it slammed shut behind me. The street suddenly realized that I was a musician. Boy, it felt good.

It was just the most wonderful sense of belonging . . .

Until reality set in.

For all the talk of us playing 'love-ins' and 'happenings' – there was only ever one love-in, an outdoor event put together by Newcastle University students to raise money for 'rag week' – the only places that would book us were the grimmest of North East pubs. As for the working men's clubs – which hadn't yet achieved their total dominance of the 1970s – we just weren't mainstream enough. They preferred to book comedians, jugglers and magicians.

'Can yers not dee nowt from the charts?' the audience would shout, the few times we were booked in those places. Then we'd do another Paul Butterfield number and the people who weren't flicking their tab ends at us in disgust would just leave.

Even less successful was our attempt to branch out into 'events' – which boiled down to one booking from Steve Chance's uncle, who'd just opened the first motel in Northumberland, up the Roman road on the way to Carlisle, in the absolute middle of nowhere. But what a beautiful nowhere.

And this was where Steve Chance's uncle, aspiring tycoon that he was, had decided to build his motel. This was groundbreaking stuff, to go where no Northumbrian had gone before, because they didn't know what a motel was.

It wasn't until we got there – which was a miracle in its own right given the state of the van – that we realized we'd be playing for a local fire brigade's Christmas party. This meant the crowd would be composed mostly of big lads in their 40s and 50s, and their wives, and they'd be tucking into a cigarette ash-sprinkled buffet of ham and peas pudding sandwiches and pies as we played.

'Are you sure it's a good idea?' I asked Steve nervously, as I peered in through the window.

'It's a paying gig!' said Steve. 'What more do you want?'

It was when we were unpacking our gear that the fire captain came over and dropped the bombshell. 'Alreet lads,' he said, 'when you're ready, I'll get on the mic and introduce you, and then – as discussed – you'll open up with "Fire Brigade" by The Move.'

We looked back at him blankly.

'I'm not sure I understand,' I said, as politely as I could. 'We never discussed that with anyone.'

'Well, I made it very clear to the motel manager. "Fire Brigade" is our theme song.'

All eyes turned to Steve – whose uncle was presumably the manager in question. Steve just shrugged.

'I'm very sorry,' I said, 'but we don't know "Fire Brigade".
We thought we'd start with some Chuck Berry.'

'Of course you know it!' laughed the fire captain, before
launching into a rendition of it himself. 'Run-and-get-the-fie-
uh-bruh-gaade, get-the-fie-uh-bruh-gaade, get-the-fie-uh –'

'I mean, aye, we *know* it,' I interrupted, 'what I mean is, we
don't know how to *play* it.'

'It's at No. 1 in the charts! How hard can it be?'

I was starting to feel a bit desperate now. 'Can we please
just do Chuck Berry?' I asked.

'Look, son, the only reason we booked yers was to play
"Fire Brigade". So can you just give it a shot, eh?'

Oh, fucking hell . . .

Once our gear was set up, we huddled for an emergency
rehearsal. Dave, Ken and Steve tried to work out the chords, I
tried to remember the lyrics and Smithy tapped out the
rhythm. (This was 1968 – you couldn't just open your music
app and have a listen.) Still feeling totally unprepared, we then
got up on stage and tried our best to get through the song. I
was just making shit up during the verse, but the chorus was
easy enough, the gist of it being that Roy Wood wanted someone to 'run-and-get-the-fie-uh-bruh-gaade' because the lass
he sat next to at school was so gorgeous. And the audience
didn't care, they just wanted to sing along.

When we finally made it to the end, I'd never felt so
relieved in all my life.

'And now,' I panted, sweat pouring down my forehead,
'for some Chuck Berry . . .'

Which went down like a lead balloon. Followed by, 'Dee
"Fire Brigade" again! Dee "Fire Brigade" again!'

'We don't fucking know it!' I said into the mic, causing a
squeal of feedback.

'JUST FUCKING DEE IT AGAIN, MAN!'

We must have played it five times. Then some smart arse called out and asked for 'Penny Lane'. It took a moment for that one to click. Then I remembered the lyrics about the fire-man keeping his fire engine clean. But we had to try and play it. You don't argue with a room full of pissed-up firemen.

Whether it was the fire brigade gig that killed us, or the fact I was about to become a new dad – or our inability to get into the bigger venues where our kind of music was played – I'm not sure.

Whatever the case, the van crapped out at about the same time that we did. I was driving it back to North Shields one night – after dropping everyone off at their houses – when I saw blue lights behind me. *Oh, shit.* I was being pulled over by the cops. Which was a problem . . . not least because the van's brakes didn't work, so the only way to stop it was to force it into first gear with the pliers, while yanking up the handbrake and hoping that it wouldn't cause some kind of catastrophic mechanical failure.

'Out of the van, son!' snapped the copper once I'd bounced and rolled to a halt. 'I can't let you drive this, it's a danger.'

Then he noticed the tax disc . . . which was, of course, a Brown Ale label. Any van owned by anyone under the age of twenty-five in the North East had a Brown Ale label instead of a tax disc (well I did, anyway). It was as though Scottish & Newcastle Breweries had deliberately made it almost the exact same shape and size. 'I'm gonna pretend I didn't see that,' said the copper. 'And to make both of our lives a bit easier, I'm not even going to ask if you've got insurance, because I'm pretty sure I already know the answer to that question. But I am going to insist that you follow me – *slowly* – to the police station, where I'm going to take possession of this van and put it out of its misery. At the scrap heap.'

My heart sank.

No transport meant no gigs – which meant no band.

But the truth was, I had bigger things to worry about.

I got married to Carol on 1 June, 1968 – by which time she had a very obvious bump. Everyone had tried to talk us out of tying the knot. Carol's ma had offered to look after the baby. My dad had kept telling me I still had my whole life ahead of me, that I had *no idea* what I was getting myself into. But like every other teenager before me, I didn't listen. Marrying the girl I'd got pregnant just seemed like the right thing to do.

The venue was a church in North Shields, the town on the coast where my bride-to-be had grown up – which was a bit awkward, because North Shields is a fishing town and Dunston is a coal village and, historically speaking, fishermen looked down their noses at coal miners, and would never let their daughters marry into coal-mining families. I mean, it was proper Romeo and Juliet shit. But thankfully none of Carol's family were in fishing any more, and the tension had eased over the years.

The service went by in a blur. We were just kids. We had absolutely no idea how to handle ourselves on such an occasion. All I can tell you is that Dave Yarwood was the best man, and that my ma made the wedding dress.

Once the vows had been exchanged, my dad looked at me and went, 'You happy?'

'I'll be alright, Dad,' I said, but the fear was written all over my face. How was this going to work? How was I going to hold down a full-time job and do extra half-shifts and look after a wife and baby and still play in a rock'n'roll band? I already knew the answer, of course. I couldn't. Something would have to give. And it wasn't going to be the job or the extra half-shifts or looking after a wife and baby.

The reception was in a hall just by the church. The whole family was there, including my granddad and grandma. All the women got a sherry, all the men got a whisky. Then we sat down to this very inexpensive but tasty hot buffet. By which time everyone was getting on like a house on fire because we were all half-cut.

The honeymoon – such as it was – consisted of one night at Carol's uncle's house in Belmont, near Chester-le-Street. I had a second-hand Cortina Mark I at the time with a dodgy powder-blue paint job – it had bubbled within ten days of coming out of the shop. It would later develop a nasty habit of losing its bonnet in high winds – the thing would literally just fly off down the street, like a big metal kite – so I suppose we were lucky that the fourteen-mile journey went without incident.

Then suddenly we were at this house, which was small and semi-detached, with a fridge filled with food for us to eat. I remember us looking at each other and thinking, *now what?*

'I could kill a sausage sandwich,' said Carol, who by then was having all kinds of pregnancy cravings.

I ended up trying to cook – and failing miserably. On my wedding night.

When we got back to North Shields the next day, I moved into Carol's bedroom at her parents' house – 'living in' it was called, something most newly-weds did back then. It was so awkward, especially when I came down for breakfast the next morning. Not to mention crowded, given that they had two other kids in the house.

I don't know how we did it, looking back, I really don't.

My musical career, meanwhile, was going nowhere. If anything, in fact, it was going backwards because I'd stopped gigging entirely. The Gobi Desert Kanoe Klub was now history, and none of the bigger bands around town would employ a singer with a measly 10-Watt P.A. system. For good reason too. For your voice to be heard over a rock band at a theatre or nightclub – or even at one of the bigger working men's clubs – you needed a far bigger amp with a proper Shure microphone to go with it. But that was well beyond my means, even with a hire-purchase agreement.

Then Carol's dad, Bill, did something brilliant that took a huge weight off all our shoulders. He'd got some insurance money from an accident at work, so he bought a nearby downstairs flat for £600 – 61 Chirton West View was the address – and he let us move in there as tenants, paying next-to-nothing in rent. It was the first house that he'd ever owned. (He rented his own from the council.)

It was such a relief when he told us, I could have cried.

I mean, yes, the place had been built in 1910 and there was damp on the walls and the toilet was outside, right at the back of the yard, in an outhouse so cold there was a hammer hanging on the wall to break the ice on frozen mornings. But at least we had a place to call our own. And it had a coal fire in the bedroom and another in the front room, so we could have heated the place if we'd had any money, of course. But a small bag of coal from the corner shop cost two shillings and seven pence, and it lasted just a couple of hours. So, we chose to shiver and save our money for food instead.

A few weeks after we moved in, the woman upstairs phoned Bill and told him that her roof was leaking. 'Well, I'm sorry to hear that,' he replied, 'but what's it got to do with me?' That's when he found out that he hadn't just bought the downstairs flat – he'd bought the *whole house*! And now he was on the hook for all the repairs, which were going to cost far more than the pittance he was getting in rent.

Mind you, he soon got his mates over there with some tiles and fixed the place up.

Carol wasn't loving life any more than I was. The poor lass was just sixteen and should have been out having a good time. But she had to stay home and look after a baby. Looking back now, I feel terribly sorry for her. But our little Joanne was a constant joy – as was her sister Kala when she arrived a few years later. The love that both of our daughters brought us, you can't put into words. It's why I wouldn't change a thing.

Rock bottom arrived when I went back to my parents' house one night and found my dad on the street outside, red in the face, shouting in his loudest sergeant's voice at my sister Julie and some guy she was seeing. Julie must have been about fifteen or sixteen at the time.

Poor Julie was in floods of tears and her boyfriend was so scared, he turned tail and ran. But my dad kept on shouting – and I just snapped. I felt like he was always shouting at someone, usually my ma, and it was so embarrassing and so unnecessary. But the truth was, of course, I was wound up to breaking point myself.

'Dad, that's enough!' I screamed at him, in a voice almost as loud as his. 'What's this all about?'

But my dad was in a blind rage. 'Don't you talk to me like that, or I'll take your head off!' he roared.

'I don't think so, Dad,' I said. 'You lay a finger on me and I'll –'

My dad went for me like I was still a ten-year-old boy. But

I was a grown man and strong from all my factory work – and I was on a hair trigger. So, I whacked him. Harder than I meant to. And when he went down, I jumped on him, and I told him that if he ever bullied anyone in my family again, I wouldn't be responsible for my actions. He was all flustered and frustrated, and I couldn't tell if he was proud of me for standing up for myself, or shocked and disgusted.

It didn't matter in the end. I felt so terrible, I went back the next day to apologize.

I just got the usual grunts in return. But I think that he felt bad too, because everything was fine again after that. But the shock of it woke me up and made me realize that I couldn't go on like this, just hoping for a miracle.

It was time that I actually *did* something.

10

A Horrible Shower of Shit

⚡

The answer to my problems came in the unlikely form of a lad named Jimmy Shane, who burst into the light machine shop at Parsons one morning, very excited, because he'd just signed up to join the Territorial Army – Britain's answer to the U.S. National Guard.

'All you have to dee is march aroond on a Wednesday, and every odd weekend you get to gan up the range and fire a gun!' he told me, speaking so quickly, I could barely understand him. 'And if you stick it oot for a year, they give you a £200 bounty!'

'What?' I said, barely able to believe what I thought I'd just heard.

'I said . . . all you have to dee is march aroond on a –'

'No, no, no – the last part.'

'If you stick it oot for a year, they'll give you a £200 bounty!'

Holy shit, I thought – *this is it*. This is how I can buy a bigger P.A. system! This is how I can get back on stage . . . but this time with a bigger, better band. (I also loved the idea of earning a 'bounty'.)

I ran down to the T.A. recruitment office that same day and filled out an application form. Then I was taken to a separate room for a rigorous medical exam.

Doctor: 'Name and address?'

Me: '61 Chirton West View, North Shields.'
Doctor: 'Is there anything wrong with you?'
Me: 'Well, er –'
Doctor: 'You're in.'

Now, I should explain at this point that there was a choice of divisions that you could join, but the parachute regiment – the one that Jimmy Shane had signed up for – was the only one that paid you the almost unimaginable sum of £200. If you joined the engineers, for example, you got 'only' £125. What's more, in the paras you were promised an £8 bonus for every time you jumped out of a plane – not that I thought for a second that I'd ever be doing that. I mean, the British government didn't have money for *anything* in those days. And this was peacetime. And the North East. So, the idea that they'd be sending lads like me up on joyrides in the skies seemed laughable. The paras would be just one step up from the Sea Scouts, in my mind. We'd wear our uniforms, do some drills, maybe go on a camping trip, and at the end of the year, I'd be £200 richer, thanks very much.

Next thing I knew, I was reporting for duty after work at a drill hall in Gosforth, a well-to-do suburb just north of Newcastle. I'd even managed to talk George Beveridge into coming with me. Not that he needed much persuading after hearing about the bounty.

A shiver went down my spine as we approached the drill hall and heard the shouts of command and the thud of marching feet. And that part of me was going, *oh, fuck yeah*. I mean, I was also a bit nervous – the T.A. lads looked hard men – but when they took a break and started talking to us, they couldn't have been more friendly.

The same could not be said of the drill sergeants. Every other word out of their mouths was 'fuck', and when they called out your name – or rather, screamed it in your face – it was nearly always followed by, '*You horrible shower of shit.*'

The first thing I had to do was sign the Official Secrets Act, which seemed a bit much, but also quite exciting.

Then I got my first order: '*YOU!* YOU HORRIBLE SHOWER OF SHIT! GET YOUR FUCKIN' HAIR CUT!'

Oh, crap. I'd forgotten you needed a short-back-and-sides to join the military. I should have remembered the footage of Elvis getting his head shaved and being flown to West Germany so he could sit on a tank. My hair was kind of long and curly, and it looked just the part on stage. But it was useless to me without a P.A. system. And if Jimi Hendrix had been a U.S. Marine – who was I to object?

I was issued my second-hand uniform, which smelled of old battlefields and old hookers – not to mention old stains. We were given new boots – brand new and shiny black, with khaki puttees, or leg-bindings – followed by the coveted crowning glory, my red beret. Only the beret had no wings on it. You had to earn them.

We were then told to make arrangements for two weeks of leave from our workplaces for Basic Training. This was another thing I wasn't planning on. What the fuck was Basic Training all about? I was about to find out.

Basic Training took place at a fucking huge place – Catterick Garrison on the edge of the Yorkshire Dales.

The group of lads I found myself with had been put under the command of a short, stout and incredibly noisy Glaswegian drill sergeant who we nicknamed The Pig.

When The Pig screamed an order, the word 'you' would exit his throat as 'YEEEEEEOOOWW!' – the same sound you might make if someone was trying to insert a cheese grater up your rectum. And when The Pig marched us up and down the parade ground – which was pretty much all of the time – his 'lefts' would come out as 'EFFs!' and his 'rights' as 'HAIGHTs!' As in – 'EFF-HAIGHT! EFF-HAIGHT! EFF-HAIGHT!'

Aye, The Pig's love of misery was legendary. As was his generosity in spreading it around.

Our quarters at Catterick were World War II-era Nissen huts – basically sheets of corrugated iron that had been bent into half cylinders, with a breeze block wall and a door at each end. There was a stove pipe for heating, but we didn't use it, otherwise we would have had to clean it out every night to pass The Pig's morning inspection – The Pig would drop a sixpence on your bedsheets, and if the coin didn't bounce, that meant you hadn't pulled the sheets tight enough, and you'd have to face his wrath.

Our days would begin at the crack of dawn, when The Pig would walk around bashing two dustbin lids together, right next to our heads.

After that, it was breakfast at the Naafi* – a.k.a. the canteen – followed by non-stop marches, drills, lectures on breaking down your gun, then visits to the firing range, until it was time to eat, then hit the sack. By which time you'd be so knackered, you'd be fast asleep the second your head hit the pillow.

The firing range should have been the best part. But we were too worried about failing the test to have much fun. There were no telescopic sights or any of that shit. And the

* Named after The Navy, Army and Air Force Institutes, for you trainspotters out there.

targets were about 200 to 300 yards away, with some as far away as 600 yards, and, of course, The Pig would be breathing down your neck, screaming things like, 'No, no, *no*! *Not like that*! Steady your hand!' just as you were about to pull the trigger. I qualified as average, which meant I missed as many as I hit – enough to pass the test.

The upside of all the adversity was how deeply it made you bond with your fellow recruits.

Within a couple of days, I'd become fast friends with the likes of Jimmy Shane – the guy who'd given me the idea to join the T.A. – along with another lad named Jimmy Smith and a huge fella we knew only as The Dane. But, of course, the more comfortable we got in each other's company, the more we started to mess around . . .

Never a good idea in the military.

One morning, for example, we turned out for parade and The Pig was nowhere to be seen, so I thought that I would do my best impression of him in front of the lads. I must have been doing a good job because the lads were howling with laughter – but then suddenly they stopped and stood to attention. I thought, boy, I'm good at this. Then I heard heavy breathing from behind and a voice filled with unconcealed hatred. '*I hate you, Johnson, and I'm going tae make your life misery.*'

Oh, shit . . . The Pig.

I was *dead*.

He made me run around the parade ground holding my rifle above my head until morning parade was over.

We had a twenty-mile route march with the full kit, then we returned to camp, the lads went to the Naafi, but not me. Sergeant Pig had other ideas, like running round the parade ground again with that fucking heavy rifle getting heavier. After that, I cleaned out a huge coal bunker till he thought it satisfactory. My arms were knackered, the P.A. system seemed a long way off. Needless to say, spanking the monkey was right out of the question for the next couple of days.

Having finished Basic training, I was basically a very basic part-time soldier. But to be the complete parachute package, I had to jump out of a perfectly good aircraft, at 800–1,000 feet, and to do that, we had to go to parachute-training school at RAF Abingdon in Oxfordshire.

There were about forty guys, all wondering what they'd let themselves in for. Laughter was way too loud, and bravado was bouncing off the walls, meaning we were all shit scared.

The first thing you notice at a Royal Air Force base is the absence of parade ground shouting. Everyone was so nice and polite, the sergeant, who greeted us, was so charming.

'Hello lads, I hope you had a good journey, now follow me and I'll take you to your quarters, and you can get settled in. I'll be back in an hour and I'll show you where you'll have lunch.'

Oh, this was great. I liked this nice polite sergeant, and then lunch, brilliant. The canteen was better than I'd dreamed of. This is where the bomber crews had bacon and eggs after a night raid over enemy territory, magic stuff.

The food was good too. After dessert, the lovely sergeant fella said, 'Right boys, we'll now go to the lecture hall and tell you what the next two weeks of training consists of and introduce you to your jump sergeants (masters).'

I had this feeling that someone had just walked over my grave, but I put it down to an errant bowel movement. Into the lecture hall we walked, and there, with a glint in his eye, was the dreaded Pig. *Oh, shit! I'm dead*, and he must have read my mind because he gave me a microscopic nod.

This time he had brought his friends with him, and they all looked eager to get started on the jumping from a great height bit. My dreams of singing in a band in front of an adoring audience disintegrated, along with thoughts of a long life. Still, I was determined to see it through.

The next morning started with the usual parade and inspection, then breakfast, then learning how to fall from varying heights. The sergeants would always shout 'GO!' right in your ear, and when they did, you went.

The most frightening thing was climbing up The Tower. It was basically an electric pylon, and when you got to the top it swayed with the wind. The fear factor was sphincter-rattlingly catastrophic. Then they put a harness round your waist and shoulders, which was attached to a wire. This was attached to a pulley, which when you jumped would spin a two-foot square board, and that was your brake as it were.

The jump sergeant was having the time of his life watching wide-eyed recruits pissing their pants as they realized just how high up they were. I tried to be civil to him, and he smiled and said 'GO!', so I did.

You must realize, at the start of this course we were told that if you hesitated or refused to jump, you would be out of camp within thirty minutes, baggage and all, so you couldn't talk to anyone else of your fear.

That afternoon, we were told that our first real parachute jump would be tomorrow morning. One kid whooped and cheered, but we beat the shit out of him.

The next morning was a beautiful blue-sky day. Nobody ate much breakfast. We lined up for our parachutes and, as we put them on, belting them up around crotch, waist and shoulders, you immediately wondered if yours was okay. We'd been told of the dreaded 'roman candle', which means the chute doesn't open, and the song we sang when drunk was the old parachute ditty.

They jumped from 20,000 feet without a parachute
They jumped from 20,000 feet without a parachute
And he ain't gonna jump no more.

Glory, glory, what a hell of a way to die
Glory, glory, what a hell of a way to die.
And he ain't gonna jump no more.

They scraped him off the runway like
A pound of strawberry jam. . . .

I think you get my drift.

'Right gentlemen, check your reserve chute is properly fixed in position on your chest, and the red handle is facing up and if you lose the handle in any way, we shall take 10 shillings and sixpence out of your pay. Follow me.'

I thought, *bollocks*! All I wanted was a P.A. system. The Beatles and The Stones never did this. They were on the road, shagging birds and getting high, but not as fucking high as me!

We followed the jump masters to our transport to the skies. It was a basket hanging from a balloon, just like the Montgolfier brothers. The sergeant major shouted, 'This is not a fucking balloon, it is a dirigible, and that underneath is not a basket, it's a gondola. Call it anything else and you will face my ire!'

I can't really remember what was going through my mind, but it resembled a white cross with a poppy on it. We were to jump in groups of five. I was number four.

'Right, you lot, your turn, follow me.'

And we did. We walked into this basket, sorry gondola, hanging onto the sides for grim death. Then it started to ascend, the J.M. shouted 'HOOK UP!' and we hooked our chutes to the static line. Up and up, we went. God, this was proper stuff. As usual, my arse was doing its impression of a squirrel's nose. But the scariest of all, was the sheer and absolute silence. So quiet, you could hear birds breaking wind.

'Right lads, here we are, 800 feet. Do exactly as I say.' There was a doorway that remained open at all times. We were still gripping the rail of the basket for dear life.

'What are you holding that for, you'll all be jumping in a minute.'

And that's when it hit me, sod the P.A., sod music, I wanna live.

'Number one, to the door, hand on the door, GO!' And he went, then two, then three . . . 'Number four, to the door, GO!'

And I did, and I fell and kept falling, till a big hand pulled me up and I was floating down and I started to laugh at the same time as steering down my chute. I landed and it didn't hurt, it was an explosive feeling of relief, and I wanted to do it again, because I'd just earned £8.

We did one more that day, £16.

To get your wings as a para, you had to complete seven jumps, two from a dirigible and five out of an aircraft, and that was next and very different.

The next morning, we assembled in the hangar and were shown our 60lb kit bags. These were tied to your right leg, and from that a fifteen-foot lanyard type thing was attached to your waist strap, with a quick-release catch. Once you had jumped and your chute was fully opened, you had to let the bag go, and it hung from your waist. Meaning when you landed, your gear was right beside you.

The trouble was these things started to oscillate, which means swinging like a pendulum, and they can really fuck with your genitalia. On top of all that, if you got scared and jettisoned it, you would be neck deep in shit from everyone who mattered. Basically, because it was very dangerous for those below you.

The whole experience of jumping from an aircraft is bewildering to men or boys. You are hardly able to walk with 60lb strapped to you and there is the noise of the aircraft engines (it was my first time on a plane ever). Climbing into the fuselage; finding the netting; which was your seat. Checking your helmet was secure; no smiles from anyone, no jokes, just rigid looks on everyone's face.

The plane takes off, climbing slowly. It was a Blackburn Beverley, as old and tired as a pit pony.

We circle, then the jump master stands. He looks down the plane and lifts both hands. That means 'stand up'. We do, and face him.

'HOOK UP!'

We can't hear him, but he crooks his forefinger, and we do.

'CHECK EQUIPMENT!'

That means, check the man in front's straps, and that he is safe to go. Meanwhile, hoping the guy behind you is doing the same. And then you're ready. The red light is on, bloody hell, what the fuck am I doing here? I keep getting myself in these situations. *'Dear Mrs. Johnson, here's a bucket of PVT Johnson's remains.'* Stop thinking, Brian.

Green light, and the first man is gone. You can't see anything until you get to the door, and there's the earth.

A long way down and moving fast, go, and I was gone. Almost horizontal for a few seconds and then that lovely chute opens, phew!

Oh shit, I forgot the quick release. I release it, and down my kit bag drops and hangs there, and down we go. I land with a slight roll and pull in the chute. I'm safe, I made it (£24).

We did another four, all exciting as hell and as scary, but I had fucking done it.

BRIAN GIBSON   TOM HILL   BRIAN JOHNSON   VIC MALCOM

 red bus records   Geordie

11

Geordie Boy

⚡

I bought the P.A. system from a music shop called Windows in Newcastle's Central Arcade, a beautiful glass-roofed indoor market that dates back to Edwardian times. What I paid for it, I've no idea. All I remember is that when the salesman asked if I was interested in a hire-purchase agreement, I uttered a phrase that I *never* thought I'd hear coming out of my own mouth – 'No thank you, I'll pay cash.'

The P.A. was a WEM system with a 100-Watt amp and two columns of four eight-inch speakers – less powerful than the stereo in the average South Korean hatchback today, but the absolute dog's bollocks back then. I even had some money left over for an echo machine. Boy, did it sound professional. I was careful not to overdo it, though – you could always tell the terrible singers by how much they turned up their echo machines.

The P.A. system wasn't the only boost to my self-confidence. Now that I'd completed my seven parachute jumps, I was also officially awarded my 'wings' at a special Territorial Army presentation ceremony – and it was one of the greatest moments of my life. Even better, I got to go home in my full uniform of red beret, combat smock and jump boots. That was the best thing about the Paras – the uniform looked so tough. There were no shiny buttons or sashes or any of that shit. You dressed like you were about to jump out of a plane over enemy territory, then crawl through twenty miles of mud to blow up a bridge. I swear my dad shed a tear of pride when he first set eyes on me – before rushing me straight down to his social club to show me off to his friends. It made me so happy to see that look on his face.

Meanwhile, now that I had the right musical equipment, it was time to get back to more important business than fighting the Cold War. I needed to join a new band and start playing some shows.

Before we get to that, I should probably rewind a bit and explain that I hadn't *completely* left the music scene after leaving The Gobi Desert Kanoe Klub and getting married.

For a while, I'd messed around with a couple of lads from Seaton Delaval and a keyboard player who I only ever knew as 'Shrimp'. They'd previously been in a band called Hannibal Kemp – where they got that name, I've no idea – and they wanted to form a new band but under the same name, so they'd keep their old fans. The only problem with that plan being that they'd never actually *had* any fans, so when we booked our first show, no one showed up. An emergency band meeting followed, but after several hours of chin-stroking and heated debate over what we should call ourselves, inspiration still hadn't struck. 'We just need something . . . *fresh!*' I said. And that was that. From then on, we were called 'Fresh'.

It was actually a great little band, was Fresh, because we did stuff that was more chart-y and mainstream than the heavy blues of The Gobi Desert Kanoe Klub. We covered songs like 'Magic Carpet Ride' by Steppenwolf, and 'Back in the USSR' by The Beatles – a great rocky number, with that hard-driving piano riff. Not that I looked much like a rocker. I was still in paratrooper training, preparing to save the world from the Communist hoards, so my hair was short. If it had been a few years later, I could have at least pretended to be a punk. As it was, I just looked very out of place.

Even if we rarely played though, I still loved that sense of belonging that came with being in a band.

We'd walk around town as a band. We'd go to the pub as a band. We'd hang around outside Windows in the Central Arcade as a band, waiting for the hot-off-the-press sheet music to arrive for new songs that had just entered that week's charts.

Fresh reached its creative peak when we hired a sax player. He was one of the top turbine engineers at Parsons, as it happened, an absolutely brilliant guy. Just not so brilliant on the sax. Technically speaking, he couldn't actually play the sax at all. But he could do a few chords.

But our sax player's greatest achievement was building this ingenious, almost Pink Floyd-esque lighting rig. The guts of it were made from an old record player, which he modified by putting ten microswitches on the turntable, so that when it was spinning, the switches would hit different contacts in a pre-set sequence. The contacts would then send electrical signals to an old floorboard with ten light sockets attached to it, each one with a different-coloured bulb – not the kind of bulbs you'd use at home, but big, floodlight-type things. When he gave us a demonstration, our jaws dropped. It was like a strobe, but in colour. Absolutely stunning.

After another band meeting, the decision was made to deploy this secret weapon at our next gig – during the guitar solo in 'Magic Carpet Ride'. We were so excited, we played all the songs before it at about twice the usual speed. Then the big moment arrived. As the guitar solo began, the stage lights went down, the jerry-rigged turntable started to spin, the microswitches were activated in sequence, then . . .

As each giant light bulb lit up, it exploded, sending shards of coloured glass flying everywhere.

I'd always wanted to play to a screaming audience.

But without the wounds and blood . . .

I still miss the boys from Fresh. They were great times.

Then another opportunity came along from an unlikely source – a big, black and very sassy young comic and singer called Ruth Saxon, who was known for going on stage wearing platinum blonde wigs.

Originally from London, Ruth was a breath of fresh air on the working men's club circuit – and she was constantly booked. What's more, she carried herself like a star. She put on a little bit of an American accent, she had a big rented house, she even had a manager. This being the 1970s, I'm sure she must have suffered some racial abuse, but she was such a force of nature, no one dared to give her any stick when she was on stage.

Now, what you need to bear in mind is that this was the time when the hippie rock-musical *Hair* was still very much all the rage. It was just this huge phenomenon. And, of course, the fact that the cast got their kit off halfway through the show didn't harm when it came to selling tickets.

Anyway, *Hair* had given Ruth an idea. Not to perform stark naked, I'm pleased to say, but to write and star in a cabaret act that would tour the country, but with a *Hair*-style rock'n'roll band.

That was where I came in . . . along with some of my old pals from The Gobi Desert Kanoe Klub.

After I'd bought my new P.A. system, the band had basically re-formed under the new name of The Jasper Hart Band. (Once again, I'm afraid to say that I've got no idea where this came from.) On guitar was Ken Brown. On bass was Steve Chance. And on drums again was Fred Smith. The only problem being that we all had full-time jobs – and a wife and a baby, in my case – so the only time we had to practise was at gigs.

We were at least *getting* gigs, which was in part thanks to my P.A. system, but also down to the fact that we'd expanded our repertoire to include songs that didn't all have fifteen-minute blues solos. Even the working men's clubs were starting to ask us back.

It was after one such gig that Ruth's manager approached us and told us about her idea. None of us were really into *Hair*, of course, musicals were for tarts and twats, but hey! Where there's cash, there's a will. To play covers from hell.

But the offer came with conditions. First, we needed to hire a keyboard player so that we could play a wider variety of material. Second, we needed to book ourselves into Studio One on Clayton Street for rehearsals, because Ruth had noticed our lack of practice and wanted us to be (in her words) 'as tight as shit'. Ruth wanted us to get ourselves some proper stage gear, so we looked the part.

It was all incredibly exciting . . . but pretty stressful too. Exciting because we found a keyboard player – a guy named Alan Taylorson – making us a five-piece. (Alan had previously played with Ken, Steve and Fred in another offshoot called Crusade.) But it was stressful because when we booked ourselves into the rehearsal studio and started traipsing around for clothes that would pass muster with Ruth, the bills racked up fast. We even had to drive all the way to Manchester because that's where Ruth wanted us to do our promotional photo shoot. And we really didn't have the money.

Still, we were about to go on tour.

When we got back from Manchester, we were told that our first show had been booked at a cabaret club in

Newcastle – a trial run, to see if we were ready to go full-time on the road.

On the day of the show, Ruth burst in and announced with great excitement that the stars of the travelling production of *Hair* – which was at the Theatre Royal that week – would be stopping by that night to hear 'all the songs that we'd learned'.

'What songs that we've learned?' I asked, genuinely confused.

'The songs from *Hair*!' replied Ruth.

'But we haven't learned any songs from –'

'Here's the sheet music,' she said, handing me a binder. The shame was, no one in the band could read music . . .

We all looked at each other and groaned. On top of the set we'd already rehearsed, we'd now have to spend the hours before our first show rushing through new material like 'Aquarius' and 'Good Morning Starshine'. Not to mention songs with titles like 'Sodomy', 'Hashish' and . . . worse. (You *really* couldn't do some of that stuff today.)

In the end, almost the entire cast of the musical turned up to the gig. Which was a good job, because no one else did. The male actors had the big fluffy things over their shoulders. The girls took their tops off. Peak late-1960s shit – even though this was by now the spring of 1970. So there we were, playing this music that we didn't much like, to a near-empty room, with all these actors jumping and dancing around us.

What a waste of time.

Ruth didn't even seem to *like* heavy rock – whereas the stuff that I was listening to was getting heavier by the day. The big eye-opener for me had been going to see Status Quo play at Blaydon's Central Youth Club, of all places, in October of 1969.

I can't remember who I went with, but I wasn't going to miss it.

So, on Friday night, I set off for Blaydon, about three-and-a-half miles away. My transport was the 89 double-decker bus right into the heart of Blaydon. I bought my ticket at the hall and went into a dark place with not many people in – most people went to Newcastle on Friday. But still, I was excited. The stage lights got a little brighter, then people were moving about on stage. Hang on, these weren't people, they were musicians, and right in the middle was an unbelievable kit of drums, with more cymbals than I'd ever seen before. The amps looked enormous. To my eyes, it was everything I thought it should be.

Then, out of nowhere, Rick Parfitt, one of the guitarists, walked up to the mic and barked 'WE PLAY FUCKING LOUD, SO IF YOU DON'T LIKE IT, FUCK OFF NOW, AND WE WON'T BE PLAYING FUCKING "PICTURES OF MATCHSTICK MEN".'

Wow, he said the F-word in a town hall, out fucking loud.

Then they hammered straight in to 'Down the Dustpipe' . . . oh, that harmonica, it was electrifying. If there was a moment in my life after Little Richard that sparks, then that was it.

Whilst being out of the public eye for a while, they had metamorphosed into a Rock'n'Roll Monster. I can't remember how long they played. It was fucking good, and it was fucking loud and, lo and behold, I was fucking hooked. I was transfixed. It ended too soon, and they left the stage with no encore. They were probably wondering how to get their hands on the moron who'd booked them there.

We left the hall, got a pint at the pub next door and hung around outside. After about an hour, this six-wheeler transit van came round the corner and we could see some of the band sitting in the front, then watched them disappear down the road. I wanted to be a part of that, whatever it was.

While I was preparing for the tour with Ruth, meanwhile, an even harder, louder band came along – Black Sabbath. I can't even begin to put into words just how revolutionary those guys sounded in early 1970 – especially their first big single, 'Paranoid'. Every day at Parsons, I'd volunteer to get lunch for everyone from the café next door – The Paddock, I'm pretty sure the place was called – for the sole reason that they'd just added 'Paranoid' to their jukebox because it was at No. 4 in the charts. All the older guys in the queue for meat pies must have hated me, because I'd dump every coin in my pocket into that jukebox and play the song, over and over again. We even added 'Paranoid' to Jasper Hart's set list for a while – even though Ruth didn't like it. In fact, I was starting to have serious second thoughts about the whole idea of turning professional just to sing songs from *Hair* in half-empty cabaret clubs.

I shouldn't have worried though.

Before the tour started, Ruth disappeared from the face of the earth. Just vanished. We never heard a thing from her again – even though we were all now deep in debt after buying our stage gear and all the equipment for the show. I've since learned that she became ITV's first black presenter at around that time. We had no idea.

It was a lucky escape, really.

During my time in the T.A. Parachute regiment, I had been told that we were to go on a huge military exercise in West Germany. So, I had to go off and protect Western democracies against the Communist hordes. The name of the exercise was Red Hammer, or some other bloody silly name.

We would have to be behind enemy lines for two weeks. The enemy being played by the fearsome Scottish Black Watch regiment and French Canadians.

We were to be parachuted in by night and cause as much havoc and destruction as we could manage. Of course, all ammunition would be blanks, but it was still pretty scary stuff.

To parachute at night is never a good idea, but they always find a way to measure the size of your balls. I believe I was a size $7^{3/4}$.

The inside of the aircraft at night was a ghostly, smog-like colour – the colour of a really bad dream. It's like being in a tube of noise. The smell of bloody hell. The weather was bad, it was cloudy, and we were bouncing around. I felt my last meal reach my Adam's apple, then oof! Home again. And there is no toilet!

This night, we had a guy who was a very experienced jumper, and his designation was 'Pathfinder'. He would jump and make sure it wasn't too rough. If he made it safely to the ground, he would signal the aircraft. If he didn't, it meant he was dead or seriously injured. Brave lad.

The jump master signalled to us, we went through the usual routine, then off we went into the black.

On night jumps you're always told to never drop your guard, because you can't see the ground, or anything else for that matter. So, keeping your knees in the bent position was vital to keep both testicles intact.

The thing is, after a while, you keep wondering where the ground is and just as you relax, bang, found it!

It was raining and chilly, but we gathered our chutes and equipment and went into the woods, our officers and sergeants getting us sorted into our squads. Someone at the front must have known where to go, because we kept walking deeper into the forest.

When we stopped, Corporal Stirling said, 'Right, make your bivouacs, get something to eat and get some shut eye.'

Now, that's easier said than done. First, you have to find branches, stick four of them into the ground, hang on, I'll draw a picture, it's easier. Then put leaves and such underneath as a kind of mattress and your waterproof poncho over the top of it all. They were only about eighteen inches tall, so it was pretty hard to crawl in and, either way, you still got wet.

When I'd finished my built-in-the-dark craphouse, I decided to see what was for dinner. So, I opened my backpack and pulled out my field rations, mmm! That agony of choice: a small tin of sausage and beans and hard biscuits or stewed unknown-to-mankind meat, or how about a tube of cheese, or a tube of jam, and finish it off with a nice piece of blood chocolate. Then again, I did have some packets of soup – now that took heating up. To do that we had these small white blocks of something that smelled vaguely of urinal tablets. The idea was to light them, fill your mug with water from your canteen and sit it on the flames, which you had to keep covered. It took for fucking ever to heat up. Eventually, it was hot enough to absorb the powdered soup or a brew of tea.

The next few days saw us walking and hiding from the enemy, then setting ambushes for convoys of trucks, which never came. And it kept raining. I was singing in a band one week and the next I was in Germany with a rifle. Being my dad twenty-five years earlier, without nearly being killed.

Then one black night in a forest, somewhere and nowhere all at the same time, we stopped. We'd had a long, exhausting day and I just wanted sleep. No cigarettes allowed, no lights allowed, it was pitch black and the trees hid the sky.

'Johnson,' the sergeant whispered, 'follow me, I'm putting you on first sentry duty.'

Oh, bollocks, I was just dropping off.

We stumbled along for a while and he said, 'This'll do. Keep your eyes peeled and your ears sharp, I'll be back in two hours with your replacement.'

'Yes, Sarge,' I said.

I lay on my belly looking at nothing and, after about thirty minutes or so, I started to drift off and then, out in the dark, I could see something. What the hell was it? It looked like a milky-white soldier with a First World War helmet on. With an outstretched hand, it felt like it was asking for water or help or . . . Holy shit, was this a ghost? I turned away and splashed some water over my face to clear my mind and eyes. I turned back again, oh shit, it was still there. That's when I turned into a girl and ran as fast as I could, back in the direction of the squad. The sergeant was a little pissed off. He said, 'What the fuck are you doing here?'

I told him I had just seen a ghost. He grabbed me by the armpit, and we went back to the scene of the haunting. There was nothing there, and probably never was, but I still had another ninety minutes by myself waiting for my new friend to come back. I still don't believe in ghosts.

Footnote: it all ended, thankfully, courtesy of a big, hairy Scotsman who was with the Black Watch, who had been watching us and attacked suddenly. He was no more than two feet away when he fired his rifle right at my stomach. Thank God it was a blank, but bloody hell, the percussive power knocked me over and left me winded. That's when the umpire said, 'You're dead', and gave me a little ribbon to stick on my uniform. We, the dead that is, were put in the back of a three-ton truck and driven to the P.O.W. camp. It was there

I was given a cup of tea and a sandwich. After ten days of sleeping in the woods and the rain, it was luxury. No more sleeping rough. I wish I had been killed sooner.

Back home, the disappointment and financial hit of the aborted cabaret tour with Ruth Saxon were too much for Steve Chance and Alan Taylorson. They both left The Jasper Hart Band soon afterwards. (I'm told that Alan went on to manage a DIY chain store in Sunderland.) But the rest of us weren't ready to give up yet. So, we put the word out that we were hiring, and quickly found two very talented guys, Tom Hill and Brian Gibson, to take over on bass and drums respectively. Both of them were well known locally, having previously played in a band called Sneeze, and we all hit it off immediately.

Soon enough, we'd become the 'tight' band that I'd always wanted to be in, playing two or three shows a week at working men's clubs and nightclubs – sometimes two shows in one night. That was good money to earn on top of a draughtsman's salary. Better yet, we didn't have to play a single song from *Hair* . . .

Then another opportunity came along.

This time, the offer was from a guy called Mike Forster – a manager, songwriter and aspiring music mogul – who'd started a company called Circa 2000 Records. After seeing us play, he wanted us to record three songs that he'd written, with the aim of shopping them around and getting a record deal. So off we went back to Clayton Street – this time to the recording studio next to the rehearsal room – and laid down these okay but rather middle-of-the-road tracks. It was the first time that I'd ever sung in a studio with the big microphone in front of me and the tape going around – and it felt fabulous. Ken still has the master copies today, and you can find a snippet of one of the songs – 'Down by the River' – on the internet somewhere. When you listen to it, though, you can tell how wanting we still were as a band. It's just so empty in places. We were *almost* there . . . but not quite.

In the end, we never got the chance to take our demo tape to any record companies because over the following weeks, The Jasper Hart Band lost all but one of its members.

It wasn't that people left.

We were *poached.*

The poacher in question was Vic Malcolm, a guitarist from South Shields, and about as much of a legend as you could be in the North East without being an actual rock star. He'd been in a band called The Influence with the singer John Miles, later known for his epic song 'Music', and the drummer Paul Thompson, later to join Roxy Music. They'd even released a single in 1969 called 'I Want to Live'. Vic had also been in a couple of other bands with Paul Thompson – Yellow and Smoke Stack Crumble – and both of them had released singles too. He'd even played a two-week residency at the famous Top 10 Club on the Reeperbahn in Hamburg.

Vic was the real deal – there was absolutely no doubt about it.

Anyway, the first I knew that something was up was when Tom Hill told me that he'd been asked to try out for Vic's new band, called U.S.A. – and had been offered the job.

Then Brian Gibson told me that he'd also tried out . . . and had also been offered a position.

I was gutted. Tom and Brian had only just joined The Jasper Hart Band, and we were better than ever. And with the songs we'd just recorded, it seemed like we could go all the way.

'We can't turn down Vic Malcolm,' sighed Tom. 'The guy could be the next Pete Townshend.'

'Aye, I know, I know,' I admitted sadly. 'I'd probably do the same in your shoes.'

'Well, that's good to hear,' grinned Tom. 'Because Vic wants you to try out for the band too.'

The audition was in a scout hut, of all places, in the middle of a council estate in South Shields. It was a pretty low-key thing. On the phone, Vic had just said, 'Come and have a sing.'

From the moment I walked in, though, I could tell that this was going to be next-level stuff.

Vic was in another league as a guitarist. He could have joined pretty much any of the biggest bands in the world and fitted right in. But the riffs and songs that he was playing were *his own*. And they were good. So instantly catchy that you felt like you already knew them from the radio. He looked the part too, with his Fender, hair and low-necked T-shirt, not to mention all his Keith Richards-style jewellery.

Whatever you do, Brian, I told myself, *don't fuck this up*.

Vic had three or four of his songs written out for me, amongst them 'Don't Do That' and 'Keep on Rockin''.

Before I started, I hadn't even thought about what it would be like to sing completely new material. But the feeling of exclusivity – of having a potentially chartworthy single that no one else had – was magical. In the back of my mind, of course, I was also thinking that the clubs would never let us play this stuff, because they wanted covers. But Vic didn't care. He had his sights set far higher than the clubs. Besides, if you didn't have your own songs, you were never going to get a record deal.

'You're in,' said Vic once I'd got through the songs. 'If you want to be, of course . . .'

He added that his plan was to get U.S.A. out on the

GEORDIE BOY

working men's club circuit, get the band nice and tight, then make a demo, take the demo to some of his record company contacts in London, get a record deal, turn professional, and release some singles that would get us on *Top of the Pops*. It sounded almost easy, the way he said it.

There was only one problem – Ken. The poor guy was the only one who hadn't been offered a place in Vic's band. He was a guitarist, after all, and Vic didn't need a guitarist, given that he was one of the best guitarists in the North East. It was especially awkward because Ken was going out with my sister-in-law. But the truth was, The Jasper Hart Band had run its course. It was cruel – especially after everything we'd been through with Ruth Saxon. But that's the music business for you.

It was early 1972 when U.S.A. played its first gig.

I believe it was in the town of Peterlee, County Durham. It was one of those 'new towns' created in Britain, which meant it was a nightmare to navigate because it was split into zones, with each zone sharing the same street names, and all the red brick houses looking identical. Meanwhile, the venue was a working men's club, but there were about a half dozen of the bloody things, also identical, with just *slightly* different names. By the time we found the right one we were seriously late, and the club's 'concert chairman' – that was the grand title these union men liked to give themselves – was none too happy. Not the best way to start our first gig, especially given how nervous I was about singing original material.

But our jitters disappeared within a few minutes of getting into our set. Vic's songs were so good the crowd barely noticed they weren't covers. By the time we got to our encore of 'Don't Do That', a few people were even singing along. I was stunned.

Next thing I knew, we were playing the same clubs and dance halls that had previously refused to give The Jasper Hart Band the time of day – and within six months, we were headlining a show at Croft Park, home of the Blyth Spartans football club, with a capacity of 5,000. We even had two *supporting* acts that night – a band called Lyght Plynth and a rock outfit that went by the name of Brass Alley. The lead singer of Brass Alley was a local star called Dave Ditchburn (and he's still one of my favourite singers to this day), who'd previously been in a band with Vic called Vince King and The Stormers ... whose main claim to fame was that in 1963 they'd won a competition to play at Middlesbrough's Astoria Ballroom with a hot new band from Liverpool.

That's right: Vic had once opened for The Beatles.

And now I was standing on stage next to him.

We had a demo tape ready within just a couple of months. Then it was time for Vic and Tom to take it down to London to see if they could drum up any interest from the record companies down there. They literally just drove the band's six-wheeler Ford Transit straight to Soho and parked it on Wardour Street, which you could do back then because wheel clamps and £10-a-hour parking meters hadn't been invented yet.

I would have gone with them, but it was in the middle of the week, so that was out of the question.

No sooner had Vic and Tom parked the van than the power went out all across London, which was just so typical of 1970s Britain. So, the first few record companies they went to had no way of playing the demo. Whether the lads left tapes behind or not, I've no idea – and Vic's memory of it isn't any clearer. What's not in doubt is that the power came back on just as they got to a company called Red Bus Records, which was new on the scene, but had just signed a deal with EMI Records so were looking for new acts. The timing couldn't have been better.

Vic and Tom were met by a guy called Ellis Elias, a very right-on and groovy showbusiness-type. He owned Red Bus with another guy, Eliot Cohen.

'Well boys, this is great stuff, yeah, alright, I like it,' said Ellis, once he'd listened to the tape.

'So, er . . . you'll have a think . . . and give us a call?' asked Vic.

'Oh, I don't think that'll be necessary,' said Ellis.

Later that night, I got a knock on the door. It was Tom, just back from London. Shell-shocked.

'We fucking did it,' he said.

'You delivered the tape?' I asked.

'No. *We did it.*'

'I don't understand,' I said. 'You *didn't* deliver the tape?'

'We got a *record contract*!'

That was when I remembered that I was married with a kid and a full-time office job. So, I was delighted. But at the same time, I was like . . . what the fuck am I going to do now?

I had all of forty-eight hours to make a decision. Red Bus wanted U.S.A. to get down to London as soon as possible and record our first single – two songs in total, an A and a B side – with an album to follow. Not that there were any guarantees. If the single flopped, who knew if there'd ever be an album. We'd just have to take our chances.

Carol was worried, of course. She hated the thought of it all going wrong and us ending up even more broke than we already were. My draughtsman's job might not have been very lucrative, but it was steady. Having a regular job also meant that I could help around the house. If I went out on the road playing rock'n'roll, on the other hand, Carol would be left at home by herself to look after Joanne, who was now four. Not only that, but Joanne's little sister Kala would also be along soon, adding a newborn baby to the mix. So, it was a pretty bad deal for her, unless of course U.S.A. went all the way and we ended up living a life of luxury.

So, this was it.

One of those moments in life. Do you take the path well-travelled . . . or do you grab the chance with both hands?

What worried me the most, surprisingly enough, was the thought of telling the lads at work that I was quitting to become a professional musician. They'd piss themselves laughing. They'd think I'd completely lost the plot. Then again, the company was offering redundancies because business was drying up, so I had the perfect excuse – and it looked like there'd be more redundancies to come. The workforce had become so expensive in Newcastle and the Japanese were making the same product for a fraction of the price. Parsons would tell its customers, 'We make the Rolls-Royce of turbines, they'll last forever.' But the customers knew that if they bought a Japanese turbine and had to replace it after twenty years, it would *still* be cheaper.

Another reason to leave was my shop steward, Harry Blair – a proud and stubborn man who spoke in war metaphors and was a member of the Communist Party.

I mean, I liked Harry a lot, but we were always butting heads because I couldn't abide his politics. He even once 'sent me to Coventry' – a real thing in 1970s Britain, not just a turn of phrase – when I refused to support changing the name of our union from the Draughtsmen's and Allied Technicians' Association, or DATA, to the Technical, Administrative and Supervisory Section, or TASS. My objection being that TASS was also the name of the notorious Soviet propaganda news agency.

'Exactly!' said Harry, when I pointed this out. 'We're showing solidarity with our brothers!'

It was when I told him how I felt about that – especially as a member of the armed forces, trained to protect him from those same Communists – that he sent me to Coventry by refusing to speak to me for a week. He even announced it to the entire office.

Harry could also be very entertaining company, mind you – especially with a few beers in him.

Every Christmas, for example, there was a big 'do' for all the Parsons draughtsmen, and we each had to stand up and do a party piece. Harry's contribution was a traditional New-castle song called 'Geordie's Lost His Liggie', about a little lad who loses his 'liggie' (or penka, or marble) and goes to extreme lengths to try and find it, including poking a broom handle down the toilet, then blowing up the toilet with dyna-mite, only to eventually discover that the liggie in question was 'in his bloody pocket, aal alang'. Harry's version of the song brought the house down – and I'll always be grateful to him for introducing me to it, because I later recorded a ver-sion with Vic and the lads and I've had a great time performing it ever since.

The redundancy was a godsend because I got a one-off pay-ment of £800 – a massive wedge of cash for someone who was earning £36 a week. If the record deal went south, I thought, I could always live on that money while applying for a draughtsman's job somewhere else. That was wishful think-ing, of course – heavy industry was dying all across the North East, and those kinds of jobs were disappearing as fast as the turbine orders were drying up. But it made me feel better about taking the risk.

A few days later, U.S.A. was being photographed by the *Evening Chronicle* for a feature entitled 'Stars of the Future' – then we were on our way to London in the Transit, which was packed with every piece of equipment that we owned. Tom drove, with Brian riding shotgun – me and Vic in the back, fending off an avalanche of amplifiers every time the van braked. Not exactly a relaxing journey – especially since we set off in the middle of the night to get to London for 9 a.m. – but we couldn't have cared less. We were grinning so much.

Next thing we knew, we were walking triumphantly through the front doors of Red Bus Records.

Which was also when we came crashing back down to earth.

What happened next went something like this:

'About the name, boys,' said Ellis, frowning sympathetically. 'We're not sure "U.S.A." hits *quite* the right buttons . . . I mean, it rather suggests you're from the other side of the pond, no?'

'No . . . I don't think so,' replied Vic. 'It just means we play American-style rock'n'roll.'

'Hmm,' said Ellis.

'I like the name U.S.A.,' I chimed in, trying to be helpful.

'Me too,' added Tom, as the other Brian nodded in support.

'Hmm,' said Ellis again. 'We were thinking of a name that . . . speaks more to your roots?'

'Well . . . I suppose . . . that makes sense,' shrugged Vic.

'I mean, we are a pretty rootsy band,' agreed Tom.

'Excellent!' said Ellis, clapping his hands. 'So that's it then. We'll change the name to . . . Geordie.'

An awful silence.

We all looked at each other in horror, too scared to say what was on our minds. I mean, Geordie just seemed so, well, fucking obvious – and it would make no sense at all to anyone outside of Britain, who'd have no idea that a Geordie was someone from Newcastle, or that the four lads in the band were all Geordies. Not to mention the fact that there were a few parts of Britain where Geordies weren't exactly popular. Sunderland, for example. If we pulled up outside the Sunderland Boilermakers' Club driving a van with 'Geordie' written on the side, we'd be lucky to get out alive. But Ellis didn't seem concerned about any of that – probably because the guy had never set foot outside of Golders Green, other than on his way to the airport.

Maybe we should have said something. But the truth was, we could hardly believe that we were actually *getting paid* to make a record – something that we would have jumped at the chance to do for free. This wasn't the time to kick up a fuss.

So, with that, the meeting was over.

And Geordie it was.

12

Wardour Street

In the history of terrible band names, Geordie really wasn't that bad. I mean, spare a thought for Showaddywaddy. Or the guys in Kajagoogoo. And our misgivings about the new name disappeared when we got the first taste of our new-found success.

No sooner had we left Ellis's office than we were escorted out of the building and around the corner to an emporium on Carnaby Street, where a battalion of shop assistants with pound signs in their eyes were waiting. When we walked into that place, we still looked like four regular guys from the North East. When we came out, Vic was wearing stack-heeled boots with a knee-length coat made of shiny metal discs, Tom was decked out in a black silk hat with matching puffy-sleeved bomber jacket, and I was sporting a pair of hillbilly-style dungarees and the same boots as Vic, only with lightning bolts on the side. (The boots were later stolen . . . thank God.) Only the other Brian refused to get tarted up, sticking with a boring T-shirt and jeans – until we manhandled him into a white sequinned jumpsuit.

I couldn't believe that it was all happening. I mean, this was real rock star stuff. It wasn't a dream, it wasn't a rumour, it was us and them making a fuss over everything we tried on. It was just silly.

After the shopping trip, it was time for a photo shoot.

Then it was back to Red Bus, where we signed some paper-work and found out that our 'salaries' would be £45 per week.

I remember us just walking up and down Wardour Street for the rest of that afternoon in a daze.

Ellis was going to take us out for dinner that night, so we had time to kill, and as we walked, we saw a large, very luxuri-ous car pull up next to us, and these really hip-looking guys got out and swaggered into this little Italian restaurant. They were the Small Faces – or just the Faces, as they'd become known after Rod Stewart became their lead singer. I could have sworn that I also caught a glimpse of Steve Marriott, one of my all-time favourite singers, who'd left by then to form Humble Pie.

It was an incredible moment because although we'd just signed a record deal of our own, we were still just these star-struck kids from Newcastle. I remember us standing on the pavement outside, our faces pressed against the glass, watch-ing as one of the coolest bands ever talked and laughed with the manager.

Guess where Ellis took us out to dinner that night? Yup, that very same place – and we also talked and laughed with the manager, who knew all of our names. But with us it felt a bit fake because the only reason anyone knew who we were was because they'd been told in advance by one of the secre-taries in Ellis's office. It was one of many moments in Geordie when I realized that although we were *this* close to being cool, we weren't there just yet. We never would be, of course.

As far as we knew, Ellis and his business partners were pay-ing for our meals out and everything else. Being working-class lads from Newcastle, the thought never occurred to us that it would all be taken out of future royalties and ticket sales – and that our £45 a week salaries would be a fraction of what we were *actually* earning, and that our salaries would be suspended if we weren't gigging. Not that it would have stopped us from signing the deal, of course. As long as we were having this kind of fun, we weren't asking questions. We'd have signed anything they put in front of us.*

Likewise, when we were booked to play at the Marquee Club – the same venue where The Rolling Stones had played their first-ever gig, a decade earlier – we were delighted when they said we could borrow their in-house P.A. system instead of lugging ours all the way down from Newcastle. We thought they were just being nice. But, of course, they ended up charging us an astronomical sum for 'P.A. rental' and deducting it from our fee, leaving us with almost nothing.

But again, we were playing *The Marquee Club* – the gig was even advertised in the *New Musical Express*! – so falling victim to that racket seemed like a small price to pay.

When we did the Marquee show, of course, it wasn't exactly buzzing – the hip kids were never going to queue up to see a band called Geordie from Newcastle. But I did my best to liven things up, crouching down and telling Tom Hill to get on my shoulders. Then I got up and ran around the stage like a maniac with a fully-grown bass player on my back. That certainly got people's attention. And the Marquee liked us enough to invite us back a few more times – although it was a hell of a commute all the way from Newcastle. Some nights, we'd finish our set, have a beer, get in the Transit, find the

---

* Ten pages into the contract was a red-stamped sign stating that the artist would never receive more than 10 per cent of all earnings, but we never read that far . . .

A1 – which runs right into the middle of London – then follow it for 300 miles back home. A treacherous journey in the middle of the night, when you're exhausted (and drunk) after a show, driving a knackered old van.

One night, there was such bad fog when we left Soho that we couldn't find the A1 and ended up having to pull over somewhere in deepest north London. And right there in front of us – barely visible through these rolls of mist – was a crazy-looking restaurant with a logo over the door of an old bearded guy in a white suit. Stranger still, the place was *open*, even though it was 10 or 11 o'clock at night.

We'd somehow managed to stumble upon one of the first Kentucky Fried Chicken outlets to open in Britain. (McDonald's wouldn't arrive until the end of 1974.)

Out of pure curiosity, we went in and ordered a 'bucket' of chicken, then took it back to the van, so we could wash it down with some Brown Ales, expecting it to taste as disgusting as anything served in a bucket surely would. But oh my God . . . this was good shit. We couldn't get it in our mouths fast enough. We must have ended up getting another two or three buckets. It was a revelation. And of course, we didn't give a shit about the calories or the saturated fats, not because we were young and fancy-free – we just didn't know what the fuck calories or saturated fats *were*.

Ignorance really was bliss in those days.

The big moment for us, the moment that made even Vic jump up and down like an overgrown kid, came when we were in the Transit waiting to cross the Severn Bridge on our way to a show.

By now it was mid-September 1972, and our first single – 'Don't Do That' – was about to be released.

We'd already recorded an entire album's worth of material at Pye Studios in Marble Arch and Lansdowne Studios in Holland Park – including our version of the song that Harry Blair had introduced me to, 'Geordie's Lost His Liggie'. Ellis had acted as producer, along with a fabulous Italian guy called Roberto Danova – long black hair, big black moustache, everything dripping from him the right way. (He'd done a lot of work with Tom Jones, which made perfect sense.)* Due for release early the following year, the album would be called *Hope You Like It* – with the LP cover made to look like a present, wrapped up with ribbon and bow, the title printed on the tag. A bit corny, yes, but Red Bus wanted to market us as a rock band with a cheeky, fun-loving attitude that would appeal to kids and younger teenagers.

'Don't Do That' summed up all of those qualities perfectly. It was an all-out, hard-rocking, foot-stomping track, but with band shouts and hand claps and a country music-style break in the middle that went, 'Grab your partner by the hand/C'mon down to Geordie land/Everybody have a go/ Get your Brown Ale and do-si-do'. As for the B-side of 'Don't Do That', it was a heavier, more stripped-down number called 'Francis Was a Rocker', based around yet another of Vic's riffs.

So, there we were, sitting in the van in heavy traffic by the Severn Bridge, and as always we were listening to Radio One. Noel Edmonds was on at the time – I'm pretty sure this was a Friday afternoon – and part of his show back then was that

---

* All I remember of the process was Roberto taking us to a church hall to rehearse, and asking Vic if he had any more songs. 'I've got shit loads,' he replied – and it went on from there. Great times that neither Vic nor I can remember, which pisses me off. Like most young musicians, we were loud, confident and wrong – but innocent enough to be not-guilty of all the charges.

he'd play a selection of new singles that he thought were good, but hadn't been released yet. Often, just being picked was enough to get you into the following week's Top 40.

'And now for our next track, which is from a new band all the way from Newcastle,' said Noel, as our jaws collectively dropped, 'and I have to say, it really makes me smile . . .'

Was there *another* band from Newcastle that we didn't know about . . . ?

Surely, he couldn't mean . . . ?

'If you can't tap your foot to this, you're not human,' Noel went on. 'So here they are – *Geordie*!!'

We couldn't hear the rest of it because we were all screaming so loud.

It was just . . . I mean, how do you even *begin* to explain the thrill of being on Radio One in 1972?

I almost cried.

Actually, forget that – tears were streaming down all our cheeks. We'd done it. *We'd fucking done it.*

Anyone outside the van must have wondered what the hell was going on, with these four lads inside cheering and bawling and jumping around so much that the vehicle was rocking back and forth on its springs. Then a police officer started to wave us across the bridge, but we had to pull over because we were in no state to operate a vehicle. Then we just sat there, staring at the radio, listening to our own song.

We did get lucky with Noel, though, because he clearly genuinely liked what we were doing. When Tony Blackburn played 'Don't Do That' a few days later, on the other hand, he began by saying, 'Sometimes you don't like what you play, but you've got to play it anyway, so here you go . . .' Yeah, cheers Tony. But Noel's endorsement was enough to get our first-ever single straight into the Top 40 at No. 32 that week, which in turn scored us an appearance on something even bigger than Radio One.

We were going to be on *Top of the Pops*.

The thing to remember about *Top of the Pops* in the 1970s is that it wasn't just a pre-recorded television show broadcast on BBC One at 7.30 p.m. every Thursday night. It was a cultural institution, an integral part of growing up, and grade-A BBC Crap! But pretty much every kid in Britain would be watching it after eating their tea – when they should have been doing their homework – and the audience figures were astronomical, something like 15 million per week. So, the pressure of performing on the show – or rather, lip-syncing on it, which is what everyone had to do – was overwhelming.

The first big question was what to wear.

I'd already worn the clothes that we bought on Carnaby Street in about a hundred different photo shoots, so I needed something new. But Red Bus weren't going to take us on any more shopping trips (when I'd seen the bill from the last one, I'd almost had a heart attack).

It was my ma who ended up saving the day. She had one spare roll of white fabric, for weddings, and another of black fabric, for evening wear. So, she sewed them together to make a kind of rock'n'roll Newcastle United strip, which I wore with my dungarees and the lightning bolt stack-heeled boots – which sadly hadn't been stolen yet. I looked like a walking sandwich board, but my mother was so proud. 'My son is-a so famous, so famous,' she bragged to anyone who'd listen. 'And I make-a special costume for him, so he can top-a the pops.'

I've still got the outfit somewhere – I've never been able to bring myself to throw it out.

Top of the Pops was recorded in those days at BBC Television Centre in White City, just north of Shepherd's Bush. So off we went in the van, all of us by now very familiar with the trip down the A1. We could barely contain our excitement. In our imaginations, of course, we were thinking that everyone would be hanging around before and after the show, swapping stories from the road, jamming together, shooting pool, having a few beers. By the end of the night, I thought, I'd be singing impromptu duets with fourteen-year-old Michael Jackson, while Vic and the lads played drinking games.

Needless to say, I was in for a disappointment.

The weirdest part of it all was the racket that the BBC had going on with the Musicians' Union that forced you to re-record your song in a union-approved studio – from scratch – before the programme. You could use only union members for the re-recording, of course. And even though you were starting again with a different production team, the song had to sound *identical* to the one that was already in the charts. Oh, and the whole process had to be overseen by a union official, who would be paid to just stand there and watch. It was ridiculous – and a total scam (and, of course, it was run by the unions).

What happened in reality was, the second you got into the studio, a guy from your record company would meet the union representative, then take him off for a long and boozy lunch somewhere in Soho or Covent Garden. Meanwhile, you'd just sit around, twiddling your thumbs. Then when the record company guy and the union official finally got back – by now three or four sheets to the wind – the engineer would hand over a copy of the original master tape, and the union official would pretend to believe that it was a newly recorded one, even though he knew fine well that it wasn't. I mean, there was no way on earth that any record company would risk making an entirely new recording of a song that was already a hit. And the BBC would never accept that, either – the reason why they made everyone mime was because they were scared the acts would mess up their own songs if they played them live. (That wasn't the *official* reason, mind you – if you asked to play live, you were told that the noise from the guitar amps and the vibrations from the drums would make the cameras shake during the close-up shots.)

Once the faked re-recording of 'Don't Do That' was over, it was time to head over to Television Centre for the rehearsal, which was when I realized that for a rock'n'roll singer like me, who really belts out a tune, it's *incredibly* difficult to mime. And you really did have to mime – not sing along – otherwise what came out of your mouth could be picked up by the microphones in the studio and clash with the recording. I'd also been expecting a big, exciting, nightclub-type sound from the Television Centre P.A. system – but when we went through the song a couple of times to prepare our moves, it was more like listening to someone playing the record at home. The whole thing was turning out to be a pretty massive letdown.

Finally, at about five or six o'clock in the evening, the 'live' audience was allowed in, and the taping began. Which was when we discovered that the DJ that week was the same guy who'd just complained on-air about playing our record – Tony Blackburn. In fact, most of the taping seemed to revolve around Blackburn, with the crew moving him between various pieces of scaffolding and groups of dancing girls, so he could deliver his intros and links with all the sincerity of a £4 note. He was all white teeth and rollnecks in those days, with hair that looked like a stick-on LEGO piece. Meanwhile, the girls in the audience seemed to be mostly regulars, and really couldn't have cared less about the bands.

Or at least not *our* band.

We just fixed our grins in place and got on with it.

Then suddenly it was all over, and off we went to the green room. On the way there, I saw Blackburn and stopped to give him a piece of my mind. 'You're a DJ, not a music critic, so maybe keep your opinion to yourself,' I said to him – or that's the printable version, anyway – to which he just mumbled something and fuddled off in his rollneck down the corridor.

The vibe in the green room was very cold and jaded. I vaguely remember some Jackson 5 members dropping in for a minute, but it was mostly just old-hands from the programme.

As unfriendly as it was in there, we were all set to stay for the night, have a few beers, savour the moment. But after a couple of drinks, the barman closed down the bar and ushered us out. And as soon as we were out, he opened it back up again.

The message was clear. We might have got into the charts, but we still hadn't made it yet.

The programme aired three days later. It's been lost to history – probably just as well, given how unnatural miming felt to me, which you could tell by the penis-in-a-meatgrinder look in my eyes. The BBC had a policy then of wiping its tapes, so they could be reused. Most *Top of the Pops* footage from its launch in 1964 to the mid-1970s has been erased, including The Beatles' one and only live performance on the show.

As deflating as the whole experience was, it was still a thrill to be on the television.

'I fuckin' saw ya!' people shouted out to me on the street back home. 'It was canny like. Mind, you should get your hair cut, you looked like a fuckin' puff!'

My ma was bursting with pride, of course. Especially since I'd worn the outfit that she'd made. But my dad was unmoved. On the night of the broadcast, he just buggered off to his club at 7 p.m. for a pint, like he always did. 'I've never watched *Top of the Pops* in my life,' he said, 'and I'm not starting now, just 'cos you're on it.'

Geordie's first tour, such as it was, began in late 1972, just before the *Hope You Like It* album was released. For the U.K. leg, we were travelling between venues in a big red double-decker bus that the record company had rented from some hippie guy who lived on the top floor. Then on we went to Belgium, Holland, Scandinavia and Germany. We supported and were supported by some unbelievable bands. In Manchester, we shared a billing with the incredible Suzi Quatro.

There was even better news at the other end of the M62. One day out of the blue, we saw our gig list for the next couple of weeks, and there it was, THE CAVERN – LIVERPOOL. I couldn't quite believe it. This was the hole in the ground where it all started, The Mersey sound, The Beatles, Gerry and the Pacemakers, the whole lot of them. There was our name 'Geordie'. We were going to play there in the Vatican of rock'n'roll.

It was exactly how I had imagined it, a complete shithole, a dump, a cellar of memories and not much else really. The stage couldn't be seen, unless you were right in front of it, because of the convoluted staircases and the passageways. So The Beatles it seems to me could only play in front of about fifty-three people at a time. But none of that mattered – to a musician, that was paradise. I remember the show in detail, we really played our hearts out and if I remember correctly we did pretty good.

The *Liverpool Echo* reported it for posterity, 'Geordie were good, but really are a poor man's Slade'. Ouch, that hurt a bit, but critics are there to be critical and this guy was good. I'm so happy the audience were there to critique us, as non-journalists, and everyone lived happily ever after.

We actually supported Slade in London at the Palladium – and I had the pleasure of meeting Noddy Holder, who couldn't have been friendlier.

Late that month, on 27 January, we were due to start a German tour at the Festhalle in Frankfurt, opening up for Chuck Berry. Unfortunately, this show was cancelled and we had to wait a further five days to share the stage with the legendary guitarist. The moment finally arrived and on 1 February 1973, at the Niedersachsenhalle in Hanover, exactly one year after our Peterlee debut, we shared a bill with one of my heroes. Each night, Chuck would show up, demand payment upfront – which he promptly deposited in his jacket pocket for safekeeping – and then go onstage and plug into our equipment.

At Philipshalle in Düsseldorf, on 2 February, I was sitting on a flight case at the side of the stage, next to Vic Malcolm. Chuck Berry and his band were in full flow but the drum riser hadn't been secured properly and as the drummer thrashed away, the drum riser began to move sideways.

We were watching this, and told our roadies, Charlie and Alan, to get on there quick and fix it. It was hilarious, watching them crawl along the stage on their bellies like two commandos with nails in their teeth and a hammer in hand, thinking they couldn't be seen on a lit stage, with a full house watching. As they were hammering in the nails, Chuck stopped mid-song. He turned to the roadies and said, 'What are you doing?'

They quickly explained the problem and his reply was, 'Well could you at least hammer in time to the music!'

At the end of the song he said thank you, and then, 'There is one man who made it possible – give this boy a big hand.' And he pointed to Charlie. 'Come on, come here.' Charlie reluctantly went on and received his own standing ovation.

After the final show, at the Friedrich-Ebert-Halle in Ludwigshafen, I took the opportunity to approach Chuck Berry and I asked him for his autograph.

Considering he'd used our equipment every night I figured it was the least he could do, but I was pissed off by his response. He looked me in the eye and said, 'I only sign one a day and I've already done it.'

Perhaps there's some truth in the old adage that you should never meet your heroes.

The continuing story of Charlie Wykes was a wonderful one. He didn't have a clue about being a roadie, but he could lift things and he was a hard worker. He was gradually learning how to fix things, how to put drums up and all of the good stuff. We were in the early days of U.S.A. and the concert chairman said, 'I've heard about you buggers, I heard you're too loud. If you're too loud, I'll pay ye off and you'll never work round these areas again.'

We needed the money. And Vic Malcolm said, 'Charlie, when you're out the front tonight, if anything goes wrong, anything that's too loud – in fact if anything at all goes wrong, just wave your hands and we will stop.'

So there we were on about the third song, and Charlie started waving his hands, flapping furiously. Vic went, 'STOP, STOP! Charlie, what's wrong?'

'They've run out of Brown Ale!' said Charlie.

***

Our transport problems were eventually solved by Ellis, who sent us a gorgeous, brand-new Mercedes van, which seemed very generous of him, until we realized that for the privilege of using it, we would have to appear in a Mercedes advertising campaign.*

We weren't complaining, though. The van was not only a huge improvement over the Transit, but also a sign that we were on the up-and-up as a band.

Then when our next single entered the charts at No. 27 – 'All Because of You' was the title, another foot-stomper, with a sped-up vocal intro, more band shouts and a middle section inspired by The Beatles' 'Twist and Shout' – Red Bus outdid themselves and also sent us a brand-new Ford Granada. The idea being that the roadies would drive our gear around in the van, while we'd arrive in style in this very posh four-door saloon.

I felt like a kid again when we got the keys to that car. I mean, a Granada was almost as luxurious as a Jaguar in those days – a proper executive limo. But then, of course, the fights started over who got to take it home when we weren't touring. 'Well, I want it this weekend', 'Fuck you, you had it last weekend.' That kind of thing. Everybody wanted a Ford Granada parked outside their house. Being a married man, I couldn't use it to pick up any girls, but I could at least take my wife out in some style.

The only one who didn't care about the Granada was Vic. As the main songwriter, he'd got his own deal for the publishing side of things – and he must have got a pretty decent advance because he went out and bought himself a

---

* 'The New Musical Express' was the tag-line of the magazine and billboard campaign, with a picture of us standing next to the van with our gear.

brand-new Reliant Scimitar – one of the coolest cars ever, even if it was made by the same company that gave Britain the three-wheeled Reliant Regal van.

Meanwhile, Vic had also started going out with a girl who had her own flat in Chiswick, a very nice part of west London. So, whenever we were in the capital, we'd all have to stay at this nasty little council flat in Hackney that Red Bus had rented for us, literally just a room with four mattresses on the floor, while Vic was enjoying the good life on the other side of town. After a long day in the studio, Vic would get a nice home-cooked meal from his girlfriend, while we'd be hunting around Soho for a plate of cheap spaghetti at an Italian café.

But as much as we all thought Vic was a lucky bugger, no one really begrudged him his lifestyle.

Or at least not until later on, when everything started to fall apart.

After our *Top of the Pops* debut, Geordie appeared on the programme something like fourteen more times, if you can believe it.

But it was our second appearance, to promote 'All Because of You', that was the most memorable for me – mainly because amongst the other guests was one of my all-time rock'n'roll heroes, Roger Daltrey. He was in the charts that week with his first solo single, 'Giving It All Away'.

We couldn't believe our luck to be playing on the same show as a real-deal rock God.

Once again, we had to fake the re-recording of our single before we headed to White City for the taping. Then, as we walked into the Television Centre, I spotted a horrible yellow Jaguar E-Type with a oo-something vanity plate parked outside, and it made me shudder, because there was only one man who would ruin such a beautiful car in that way – the dreadful Jimmy Savile. He would be the host of that week's episode.

Other than watching Savile walk past us down a corridor by himself with his terrible blond hair and full-length fur coat and jangling medallion necklaces, I'm happy to say that I didn't have to speak to him. But just seeing him there alone, with no one going near him, was enough to tell you that he was one strange cat. Even back then – decades before it was revealed just how sick the guy was – I never understood his appeal. I mean, whether he was on the radio or presenting *Top of the Pops* or doing anything else, he didn't talk, he just made noises with his mouth. 'Now then, now then, now then guys and gals, *uhuhuhuhuh*, goodness gracious, how's about that then.' It was gibberish. But for some reason, the BBC kept giving him more gigs and more money – and the British public kept lapping it up.

After the taping, off we went to the green room again for a couple of beers, fully expecting to get thrown out after an hour for not being famous enough. But it didn't happen – probably because Roger unexpectedly introduced himself to us at the bar. 'Hello lads, how are you doin'?' I was intimidated at first – I mean, the guy was an absolute icon, and he was wearing the coolest flared dungarees with just his suntan underneath and a golden crucifix around his neck – but he turned out to be a regular lad, and he couldn't have been friendlier. In fact, he went out of his way to tell me that I had 'great pipes' – which, coming from the guy who'd sung 'Won't Get Fooled Again', was the greatest compliment I'd ever been given. I don't remember much of the rest of our conversation, other than him asking where I was staying while I was in London, and me telling him about the filthy council flat with mattresses on the floor that we all had to share in

Hackney. Then before we went our separate ways at the end of the night, he took me aside and said, 'Do you wanna come over for lunch on Sunday – have a chat?'

I thought, does Rose Kennedy have a black dress? Of course I do!

Next thing I knew, he'd written down the address of his country house, and the name of the nearest village, and all I could think was, *this is it*, this is the stuff you read about in the papers – stars getting together for drinks, being daft, doing whatever they want to. The rock'n'roll lifestyle that I'd heard so much about.

Someone else had won the fight for the Granada that weekend, of course. So, I had to drive there in the Mercedes van, still packed full of our gear. It was a long way – almost at the southern coast, in fact – and the scenery was just stunning down there. I remember the lanes getting narrower and narrower, and the van seeming to get wider and wider, until eventually, there it was . . . a gate followed by a long gravel driveway leading up to this absolutely stunning seventeenth-century manor house.

When I rang the bell at the gate, I wondered if Roger (it felt strange even thinking of him as *Roger*) would remember who I was – never mind having invited me over for lunch.

'Hello?' said a woman's voice through the intercom. 'Who is it?'

'Hi . . . I'm Brian, Brian Johnson. From the band Geordie . . .'

'Oh . . . Roger's not here right now, but if you drive up and park in front of the house, he'll be back soon.'

So, I drove in and waited in the van. Then suddenly I heard the thud of approaching hooves, and when I looked up, I was treated to the most sensational sight – a beautiful white horse galloping towards me, no saddle, ridden by a bare-chested and barefoot man in powder blue jeans, with long, golden curly hair. He seemed to be holding onto the horse *just by its mane.*

If this isn't rock star, I thought to myself, I don't know what is.

'Alright mate,' said Roger, as he brought the horse to a halt right in front of me, 'you been here long?'

He ended up taking me to a barn, which he'd had converted into a state-of-the-art recording studio.

'Townshend's outdone himself this time,' he said, 'I just got this back. See what you think.' It was a studio tape of The Who's new album: *Quadrophenia.*

This was a moment.

We ended up listening to a few of the tracks and, of course, they were brilliant, soon to become classics. Then Roger asked if I was hungry. I admitted that I was pretty starving after the long drive, and off we went back to the main house.

The manor and the lunch were everything that I'd imagined they would be and more. The dining room was all huge fireplaces, thick floorboards, high ceilings and views of rolling countryside. It was grand and stately and homely all at the same time. The dining table was the size of a football field. And we ate the most delicious meal of roast beef, Yorkshire puddings, English vegetables, the works. I felt like I was dreaming. And Roger's wife Heather – the lady who'd spoken to me through the intercom at the gate – was lovely.

It was just as I was leaving that Roger finally explained why he'd invited me in the first place.

'You told me that you were living in a filthy flat in

Hackney,' he said. 'Well, me and the missus went through all of that. So, I wanted to bring you here and show you what you can do if you stick at it, because there's really no easy way – and if our paths never cross again, I just want to say that I really hope everything works out for you.'

What struck me most was that you could tell he really meant it. From one singer to another – even though he was this huge rock star, and I was just a guy in a struggling band from Newcastle – he genuinely wanted me to succeed. 'The secret is,' he added, 'don't give up. *Never* give up.'

The following week, thanks to our appearance on *Top of the Pops*, 'All Because of You' rose to No. 6 in the charts. It was our first Top 10 single. It would also be our last.

Later on, when the lean years hit and my days of fame faded like a politician's promise, there were times when Roger's words were a distant memory. But I clung on to them all the same, never giving up hope, even after my thirties crept up on me and kidnapped my twenties, even after I had to give up being a musician and get a 'real job' again.

Roger had been right all along, of course – like everything else in life, there really *isn't* an easy way.

Meanwhile, I'm happy to report that our paths did cross again.

In fact, we still talk to this day.

I might have been only twenty-six years old, but I was very married, and after the arrival of Kala* – which I rushed home for during the tour, all the way from Somerset – I was the father of two little girls who I absolutely loved. So, the best I could do was cheer from the sidelines as my very single

* Pronounced Kah-la – it's Indian in origin.

and free bandmates, the jammy bastards, went out and had themselves a good time.

But my marriage had never been a happy one, and when you added long periods away from home to the mix, things started to fall apart. I'm sure that it wasn't just me who often ended up wondering what life would have been like if different choices had been made.

Which brings me to one night not long after our second *Top of the Pops* appearance.

We were playing a show out in the countryside – the posh countryside, down south – and a girl came up to me afterwards and, in this fabulous Julie Christie accent, she said, 'Gosh, I thought that was just so awfully good.' I was instantly smitten. I mean, she was just gorgeous, early twenties, confident, so stylish, with short black bobbed hair. I've forgotten her name, which is terrible, but probably just as well. Anyway, we got talking and after a few drinks, she was going, 'Brian, do come and visit at the weekend, I live in Bagshot in Surrey. I would love so much for you to meet Mummy and Daddy.'

Now, I had no idea where Bagshot was – I certainly didn't know it was right next to the Royal Military Academy Sandhurst. The only clothes I had were my stack-heeled boots, my hillbilly dungarees and a yellow jumper. And as usual, someone else had nabbed the Granada, so I was driving the Mercedes van.

An hour or so later, I was pulling into the gravel driveway of this lovely big house. Then the girl introduces me to her mum, who's probably only about forty and very attractive, then I meet her dad and . . . holy shit, he's a high-ranking army officer. And I'm thinking, Brian, what the fuck are you doing here? I mean, my hair was a mess, I was sweaty, my clothes were dirty from last night's show – The Pig would have taken me around the back of the house for a good hiding. But her dad couldn't have been nicer. And he had the poshest Fiat that you could buy, a four-door 132, a choice I respected so much because the obvious car for a guy like that was a Rover. But no, he'd gone for this beautiful Italian saloon instead.

'Are you staying for dinner?' asked the girl's mum.

'Well, if that's alright,' I said, 'I don't need to get back to London for a little while.'

'Oh, never you mind about getting back,' she said. 'I'll tell you what, go to the pub with John and have a couple of pints, and by the time you're finished, we'll have dinner ready.'

So off I went with her father – I couldn't bring myself to call him John – and sure enough, when we got back, there was a beautiful table set, the smell of a casserole wafting through the house, and all these bottles of expensive French red open.

All through dinner, we're getting through the wine and I'm getting a little tiddly and this lass is just making eyes at me. Then her mum says, 'Oh, there's no need to go back to London, Brian, you can sleep here. We've got a spare bed.' And the General chips in, 'Yes, no need to travel on a Saturday, bloody waste of time.'

Later on that night, of course, I got a knock on the door.

I forgot to mention that I was married, of course.

But she'd already guessed.

'If you don't love your wife, why don't you leave her?'

'Because she'd take everything,' I sighed.

'Oh, don't be silly,' she replied, with her lovely smile. 'You don't *have* anything.'

She wasn't wrong.

13
Highway to . . . Nowhere

⚡

A month after the triumph of 'All Because of You' entering the Top 10, we found ourselves in Torquay, on the coast of Devon. It was Easter Monday, 23 April 1973. The date sticks in my mind because it was one of those days when the universe seemed to be trying to tell me something.

Now, Torquay is only about fifty miles across the English Channel from France, and we'd been told that it had a near-tropical climate with palm trees lining the streets. And being naive Geordies, we believed it, booking ourselves into a B&B right on the seafront, and making sure to pack our swimming trunks and suntan lotion.

It was the coldest night in Torquay's history. The wind blowing in from the Channel was just as bad as the North Sea gales back home, and it wasn't raining, it was *sleeting*. Earlier that morning, there'd even been a layer of frost on the ground.

Our accommodation was one room between four grown men with each of us on one of those little divan beds that you fall out of if you roll over in the night. The paint was peeling off the walls. The sheets were made from the kind of nylon that gives you electric shocks whenever you move. And, of course, there was no heat, unless you fed 5p pieces into the meter in the room – which we stopped doing when we realized 5p got you about five minutes of warmth. The heat just went straight out of the cracks around the window frames.

At least we *had* a place to sleep. In those days, the owners of B&Bs were notorious for giving away your room before you showed up, especially if you got in late.

Not that our landlady was in any way welcoming.

'I lock the door at midnight on the dot, so if you're not back by then, hard luck.' As for breakfast, she added, there'd be a toaster and some bread made available at the crack of dawn for about twenty minutes.

'And if we miss it?' I asked.

'You'll do without.'

The show that night was at Torquay Town Hall. Everyone from The Rolling Stones to The Who had played there, and David Bowie was booked to do a show a few months after us.

The first thing we noticed when we pulled up was the bus parked outside. Not a normal bus, but a gigantic American model from the early 1950s, with stainless-steel side panels and a bullet-shaped back end. It was a Flxible Clipper, which I later found out had been built for an Australian tour operator, which explained why it was right-hand drive. I couldn't believe that anyone had managed to get a vehicle of that size and shape into the country.

'Whose is *that*?'

'Must be the support band's,' shrugged Vic. Support bands were usually even more broke than we were. So how could they afford transport like that?

When we walked in, the support band in question were still on stage, with about fifteen minutes left to go – so we got some beers in, sat down at the bar, and had a listen.

The band were from Australia and had just changed their name from Fraternity to Fang after messing up their U.K. debut the previous year. I couldn't stop looking at the lead singer, because he was one of the wildest-looking cats that

I'd ever seen. Coconut-bob hair. One tooth missing. Abe Lincoln beard. He looked like an elf. But, fuck me, the guy could sing. What he was singing wasn't rock'n'roll, though. It was more like . . . prog-folk. Along the lines of Jethro Tull's *Living in the Past*. Only proggier. And folkier. At one point, he even whipped out a wooden recorder and started to play it in a way that would have brought tears to the eyes of Mrs. Patterson, my old teacher. Then at the end, he swapped the recorder for this thing that looked like a cross between a bong and a rocket launcher. It was a bassoon, apparently.

As Fang finished up, we drained our beers and headed backstage.

'Who's that singer?' I asked a guy wearing a now-out-of-date Fraternity T-shirt.

Because there was no doubt about it, Bon Scott was clearly no ordinary singer.

I'd love to tell you that I made a note to look up all of Bon's previous work, but Fang weren't really my cup of tea – and by the end of the night, we were exhausted and frazzled from the show and from all the driving earlier on in the day. So, we headed back to the B&B, teeth chattering in the cold, and the decision was made to break open the coin box on the meter, so we could keep putting in the same 5p, over and over again.

It worked like a charm. But just as we were finally starting to warm up . . .

Tap-tap-tap.

'What's that noise?' asked Tom.

Tap-tap-tap.

'Shit!' hissed Vic. 'The landlady must have heard us breaking the coin box! Quick, put it back on!'

A mad scramble followed as we tried to unbreak the

electric meter, until we realized that the knocking wasn't coming from the door. It was coming from the window.

Then we heard the whispers. 'Pssst. Hey? Hey lads? Open the window! It's us . . . Fang!'

I was drunk and I can't remember much but I am told that when we pulled back the curtains, there was Bon and a couple of the boys from Fang, shivering on the street outside. Their tour bus had broken down, which meant no heater – and because the bus's side panels were made of stainless steel, it had become like a fridge inside. A mechanic was already working on it, they said – although where on earth they'd found a guy in Torquay at 11.30 p.m. on an Easter Monday who knew his way around a big-block American diesel, I had no idea. Whatever the case, Fang desperately needed somewhere to get out of the cold, especially since it had started to sleet again. So, we forced open the window sash and heaved the boys from Fang inside, while trying not to wake the landlady. I'm not sure if this really happened, but I was told it did. But being so drunk, I have an excuse.

Eventually, Fang's roadie knocked on the window to say that he'd finally got the bus started again.

The next night we played at Plymouth Guildhall, with Fang once again in support.

I remember nothing of the show apart from the fact that about two-thirds of the way through, I suddenly got an absolutely terrible pain in my gut and collapsed on the stage and started to roll around, moaning and howling. The crowd thought it was all part of the act and were lapping it up and going crazy, so I forced myself back on my feet and carried on with the song that I was doing, but that was it – we finished twenty minutes early, I was off to A&E.

I'd come down with a bout of appendicitis. Not bad enough to require emergency surgery, thankfully – but I did need to go on a long course of antibiotics.

The tour went on regardless, night after night, six or seven days a week. We were driving hundreds of miles a day, sometimes in the Granada, sometimes in the van. But we were so young and so excited – and our hopes were still so high – it was a magical time.

I never saw Bon again, I'm very sorry to say. But it's so strange to me that our fates entwined on that one night on the Torquay seafront in the freezing cold.

I wish that I could have got to know him better.

On the road, it was becoming increasingly obvious that Geordie were two different bands. The first band was just kinda poppy and played songs like 'Don't Do That' and 'All Because of You' – with the teenybopper magazines running profiles of us and organizing competitions like, 'Win a day with Geordie at a fun fair!' The other band, meanwhile, was represented by tracks like 'Black Cat Woman' and 'Keep on Rockin'', and had more in common with Led Zeppelin or Black Sabbath than anything glam. But the press only ever seemed to notice the first band and kept comparing us with Slade – which started to get pretty frustrating after a while – and our management was firmly of the opinion that we belonged in the pop world.

I wasn't so sure. And one of the moments that persuaded me was in, of all places, Faslane submarine base.

Geordie were playing at the base club. We were headlining and a Scottish band called Nazareth were the support. I had never heard of them; not many people outside of Glasgow had. Before the show, I started chatting with their singer Dan McCafferty and we got on immediately. We were from the same background of council houses and industry, and both had been apprentices.

The audience was made up of uniformed sailors and some in their civvies. They lined the walls and bar that surrounded the dance floor, and then in came the girls. It was the perfect Friday night for a fight, especially because submariners didn't like sailors and vice versa. The air was electric with trouble, you could actually touch it.

Dan said, 'Well, we'd better get on before they get a wee edgy.' I thought I'd stay and watch and Nazareth came on and started. I was mesmerized. It was a thunderbolt. They were loud and rocking and so very tight and I thought, I wanna be in a band like that. All the tenseness went out of the room, everyone was locked into this brilliant band. The next thing I thought was, how the hell are we going to follow that? They finished to howls of 'MORE, MORE'.

And then it was our turn. Although we were a tight rocky little band, our singles had been a tad poppy. We gave it our best shot, the boys were playing up a storm, but we were following a hurricane and tornado all in one.

Halfway through the set, I saw the first bottle fly at the sailors, and then a chair at the submariners, and then the world went mad. There was blood. There were people running on stage for safety. These were not Jolly Jack Tars.

We somehow kept going, it was a mad house. Military police were called and it slowly emptied. Dan came over and gave me a whisky and said, 'Oh dinnae worry, it was much worse last week . . .'

We worked our arses off during the rest of 1973 to try and build on the success of 'All Because of You' and get to the next level. But our album, *Hope You Like It*, wasn't selling enough to turn us into a proper headline act, meaning we had to keep putting out more singles to keep the momentum going. We released three more singles that year – 'Can You Do It', 'Electric Lady' and 'Black Cat Woman' – with only 'Can You Do It' getting into the Top 20. The others didn't even chart.

As much as this wasn't exactly an encouraging sign, we just thought we needed a new album.

So back we went to Pye Studios in Marble Arch and Lansdowne Studios in Holland Park, with the wildly eccentric Roberto Danova once again producing, and we made *Don't Be Fooled by the Name*. For the cover photo, we dressed up like Al Capone-style gangsters, complete with black hats and black suits, me with a cigar in my mouth. The idea being that we'd grown up a bit after the more light-hearted *Hope You Like It*.

One of the best parts of making the album for me was getting to know André Jacquemin, a composer, producer and arranger who'd just moved his studio from his dad's greenhouse into Red Bus's building on Wardour Street. He was the guy who Monty Python used to produce all their albums – he'd later write the James Bond-esque theme tune for *Life of Brian* – and being a massive Python fan myself, I couldn't hear enough of his stories. Mind you, André also nearly got us both killed because he had a Bond Bug,* which was a three-wheeled 'microcar' shaped like a wedge, with screens instead of doors. It looked like a slice of orange with a sense of humour – it only came in that colour – but André was so proud of it he insisted on taking me for a ride, and we very nearly ended up under the wheels of a London bus.

Another memorable moment for me from those studio

* People still love them today – a pristine 1973 example sold for £29,582 at auction in 2021.

sessions was when we recorded our cover of 'The House of the Rising Sun' – which I'd first performed all those years ago at Sunniside Working Men's Club. After running through it a few times, I felt like I'd nailed the vocals, but Roberto kept saying, 'It's just-a missing . . . *something.*' Then inspiration struck and he started rushing around the studio, setting up microphones all over the place, and making all these humming noises into them. When he was done, the track began with what sounded like a drone, which fitted the dramatic, ominous tone of the song perfectly.

Not that anyone ever heard it, of course . . . because no one bought the album.

A tour of Australia and Japan was seen as the answer to our problems, so in early 1974, we packed our bags and off we went. We had to sit all the way in the back of the plane, obviously, but we stocked up on duty-free tabs and whisky and spent most of the flight getting through it all. (Even when they banned smoking on flights in the 1980s, routes to Australia were exempt because *no one* could go without a tab for that long.)

It felt like it took three days to get there (actually, it probably did). We flew to Bahrain first, then to Singapore, then on to Sydney. But we didn't care because we were so excited, especially when the Australian promoter, who was a bit of a lad, told us that we'd be staying on Bondi Beach. We couldn't believe that we'd be right there on the shore of the South Pacific, looking out over the beach and all the Aussie girls in their tiny bikinis. And we were right not to believe it because it was absolute bullshit. We had a room with two bunk beds, no view and no air conditioning, a good mile from the ocean.

Then all the other usual scams began. We had to rent the P.A. system from the same guy who was doing our booking – his wildly over-inflated fee deducted from the ticket sales before we saw a penny – and the guy in charge of transport supplied us with an old Post Office van, not a real truck. But we couldn't pick up the phone to Ellis and ask him to sort it out. Once you were Down Under, you were fucking Down Under, mate!

Our first show was a festival-type deal at E. S. Marks Athletic Field – a big open-air space with a covered grandstand – and we were the headliners. When we went on, it felt like Woodstock – big stage, big sound system, huge crowd of several thousand Aussies, everyone cheering and whooping. It was fantastic, a huge morale booster.

But two days later, we were playing a working men's club out in the sticks, in the middle of the afternoon, when it was about 120 degrees in the shade. The place was an absolute dump. All tin huts and rusted-out cars. The crowd was small, sweaty and drunk – and didn't much care for Poms. Later, as we were getting out of our stage gear in the dressing room, a huge snake appeared, and the four of us bolted out of there in our underpants, screaming. I mean, we were Geordies – the only snakes we'd ever seen were in Tarzan movies. When we told the venue manager, he muttered 'Fucking Poms', strolled into the dressing room, came out holding the snake, and went, 'It's not even poisonous, you wankers.' At which point we began to suspect that someone had deliberately put it there.

By the time we got back to Sydney, we were starting to wonder if the tour had ever been a good idea. In the meantime, though, we discovered these amazing parks where you could bring your own steak and beer and make your own barbeque, and we went to the pictures to see *The Exorcist*, which scared the living shit out of us.

The climax of the trip was two nights at Chequers, the famous Sydney nightclub – and on one of those nights, if I'd

THE LIVES OF BRIAN

known where to look, I could have seen Malcolm Young standing at the back. He'd gone there to pick up a cheque that he was owed by the venue management, but decided to stay for the show, having heard about my James Brown antics from Bon. I don't know if it's true but I heard Angus was there a week later when we played the Hornsby Police Boys Club, out in the Sydney suburbs (not to see us, he was just there). There was no writhing around on the floor and moaning for me on either of those nights, of course – although, as usual, Tom Hill spent a lot of both gigs on my shoulders.

Then it was time to fly to Tokyo, where we were met by the legendary promoter Mr. Udo, who'd organized Led Zeppelin's tour of Japan a couple of years earlier.

We couldn't believe Japan. It was just stunning. No dirt on the streets. Construction workers who bowed. Everyone wearing white gloves. Taxis with doors that opened automatically. We even got a *room each* at the hotel, an unheard-of luxury.

Mr. Udo took us to dinner at a teppanyaki place, where the Kobe beef was as tender as marshmallow. It was hands-down one of the best meals of our lives. We were also introduced to sake, which we started to guzzle down in mugs. This was good stuff, and if you drank enough of it, you started to sing Japanese folk songs, in Japanese.

We did about four shows in Japan, if I remember correctly, travelling between them via bullet train – something that I'd heard of, but almost didn't believe existed. It was an extraordinary experience, sitting in the restaurant car of a train going at over 100 mph, no rattles or shaking. The Japanese really were light-years ahead of the rest of the world.

The gigs were strange affairs, though. You'd play a song and get a little ripple of polite applause at the end, then silence. You couldn't help but wonder if they even liked the music.

Then at one show, a kid got so excited he stood up and clapped.

He was promptly grabbed by security and thrown out.

We ended the year supporting Deep Purple on their tour of Germany. This was going to be pretty exciting; they were absolutely huge. But the contrast between the success we'd enjoyed and Ritchie Blackmore's juggernaut – the latest Deep Purple album *Burn* had become a Top 10 hit on both sides of the Atlantic in spite of a radical line-up change that saw David Coverdale take over from Ian Gillan on vocals – was stark.

I mean, the fans at those shows had come to see only one band. So even though we were doing well and the band was tight, no one was really paying attention.

Another of the support acts on that tour was The Sensational Alex Harvey Band, fronted by the Glaswegian madman of the same name. His live version of 'Delilah' – heavier and darker than the original, to put it mildly – was something to behold, and would become a Top 10 hit for him the following year. At the time, though, Alex was still a cult act and, like us, very much in the shadow of Deep Purple.

'You know, Brian,' he said to me before one show, in his broad Glaswegian accent, 'the secret to success in this business is that you've got tae get a *reaction*. That's how you make an impact! So, I think I'll switch up the show a wee bit tonight . . .'

I didn't think much more of it until 8 p.m., when it was time for Alex to make his usual entrance against a moodily lit brick wall, holding a can of spray paint. He'd then graffiti the word 'Vambo' on the wall, the lights would come up, and the band would launch into the blistering wah-wah guitar intro of a song called 'Vambo Marble Eye'. (Vambo being some kind of super-hero figure from Alex's imagination.) On this particular night, though, he didn't do any of that. Instead, he goose-stepped on stage, wearing a Nazi military peaked cap with a little stick-on button moustache. Remember this was *Germany*, with World War II still a recent memory. The howls of shock and boos of disbelief were deafening. Glasses and chairs flew at him, but he just smiled and waved back – before making a very swift exit.

I was at the side of the stage when he came off. 'Now, *that's* a reaction!' he grinned as he rushed by. And we were next. Thanks, Alex . . .

The guy just had no fear whatsoever. He was also one of the most gifted lyricists I ever met – his songs like 'The Faith Healer', 'Hammer Song', 'Sergeant Fury' and 'Boston Tea Party' are absolute classics. Do yourself a favour and listen to all of his albums.

My last encounter with Alex was in our shared dressing room, at a point in the tour where I was starting to get friendly with one of his girlfriends – a dark-haired German lass who dressed entirely in shiny black leather, from her skirt to her knee-high boots. She was hot, to say the least – especially since her accent kept giving me flashbacks to my night in the nettles around the back of Walker Boys' Club.

On the night in question, this girl had decided to hang out in the dressing room during Alex's show, and when she realized that we were alone, she gestured to me in a way that didn't require any translation. Next thing I knew, her skirt was up, my trousers were down . . . then right on cue, in walked Alex, and we were caught *in flagrante*.

'JOHNSON' he boomed, pointing his cane at me. 'THAT'S MY CABARET YOU'RE FUCKING. I WANT A REPORT ON MY DESK IN THE MORNING IN TRIPLICATE!'

No fall out, no repercussions. Just a sly wink.

To this day, I have never met another man like him. God rest you, my son.

Geordie desperately needed to try something new, given that *Don't Be Fooled by the Name* had failed to produce a single hit. But what ended up happening made no sense to me at all.

All of a sudden, Vic just wasn't there any more. To this day, I've no idea what happened – no one told me anything. One minute, Vic had been our main songwriter and guitarist. The next, he was out of the band. Which seemed very unfair given that he'd been the one who'd put the band together in the first place.

The lead guitarist ended up being a guy named Micky Bennison – an old friend of Tom's. He was a nice lad and a good guitarist who loved American cars and had an import business nicknamed Third Leg Motors. But by the time we'd put some new songs together and gone back on the road . . . nobody cared. And when we played the old Geordie songs, they just sounded so dismal and undistinguished without Vic's guitar sounds. Worst of all, now that I was stuck in the back of a van with a guy I barely knew, it just wasn't fun anymore. All of the camaraderie had gone.

It was clear that Tom and the other Brian had also lost their enthusiasm. When we got back from Germany, they opened a shop in Newcastle – it was called Geordie the Boutique, just across from the Theatre Royal – and it took up most of their time. Tom was a bit of a fashionista and he'd go shopping down in London and bring up all the latest clobber – the stuff you couldn't find up north – then the two of them would resell it. They seemed much more excited about that than Geordie.

Meanwhile, I was just sitting around waiting for something

to happen. My £45-a-week salary was put on hold for weeks at a time because we were no longer playing regularly – not because we didn't want to, but because we couldn't get any gigs. Reality was starting to bite and it was apparent we were past our sell-by date.

Then one night, a guy from EMI Records came up to Newcastle and took me out for an Indian meal. He asked me what I was doing with myself these days. 'Nothing much, to be honest,' I said. Then he asked me if I'd ever consider working for a record company. 'Oh, I'd *love* to work for a record company,' I told him, not really taking the question seriously, 'they always seem to have more money than me . . .'

'You could be a rep,' he replied, looking me dead in the eye – at which point I realized that this wasn't a hypothetical conversation. He was actually sounding me out for a job.

'You really think . . . I could do that?' I asked.

'Of course,' he said. 'You're a funny guy, you get on well with people, you've been on *Top of the Pops*. That's exactly what we need. You'd be a huge asset for the company.'

'Oh, mate,' I said, trying not to get emotional, 'that would be a dream come—'

'We could also get you a company car.'

'Okay, where do I sign?' I said. I wasn't joking.

Unfortunately for me, though, the EMI guy went out for dinner the next night with the radio presenter James Whale, then a friend of mine and the host of *Night Owls* on Metro Radio. And thinking he had my best interests at heart, James talked the guy out of making the offer official. 'Oh no, no, no, Brian's no good for that, he's a *singer*!' he told him. 'You can't ruin his career by making him a record rep!'

I could have killed him. I mean, I needed the money so badly. 'You fucking moron, *why* did you say that?!' James was unapologetic. He told me that he'd just spoken his mind – that he truly believed that I was destined for bigger things. I didn't know whether to say thank you or fuck you.

The situation at home was dire. But I couldn't face the thought of going cap in hand back to Parsons and asking for my old job. The smug 'I told you so' lectures that I'd get from the likes of Harry Blair would be unbearable. Besides, my old job probably didn't exist anyway. As for going on the dole – I was too proud to take money from the government.

Carol was at her wits' end. We both were. And, of course, that kind of stress isn't exactly conducive to marital bliss. We were constantly at each other's throats.

Then one day the phone rang.

'How's my favourite rock star?' asked the instantly familiar voice on the other end of the line.

'I'm broke, Ellis, because you're not paying me,' I replied, through gritted teeth.

'Really? Gosh, well, I'll have to talk to accounts about that, that doesn't seem right. Anyway, er, how would you like to come down to London and start work on the new album?'

'*What* new album?'

'The new Geordie album.'

'Ellis . . . there's no Geordie without Vic. It's not the same. Anyway, I'm done with this business. It's just one scam after the other and I can't take it any more. I need a *real* job.'

'Hmm,' said Ellis, thinking for a moment. 'What if we got you a new house? Would *that* help?'

Oh, for God's sake, I thought. Here we go again . . .

14

Stowaway

⚡

The house was in Preston Grange, a posh suburb near Tyne-mouth Golf Club. I could never have afforded anything like it on my own. It was brand new with big modern windows, central heating, a garage, a driveway and back garden – the perfect home for a young middle-class family. It seemed too good to be true, honestly, given how few records Geordie had been selling since our one and only Top 10 hit.

Then again, I told myself, Ellis was getting a new album in return. And it certainly wasn't unheard of in those days for a band like ours to make a mid-career comeback – even if Vic, the guy who'd been the driving force behind it all, was now gone.

It was going to be a tricky balancing act, though. On one hand, we needed to move on from the old Geordie and end the comparisons with Slade. But on the other hand, we also didn't want to lose our old fans . . . or what few of them we had left.

Red Bus was at least taking the project seriously, which you could tell by the fact that they'd hired Philip 'Pip' Williams as the producer – he'd previously worked with The Kinks and The Moody Blues and would go on to produce Status Quo's *Rockin' All Over the World*. So, we were in good hands. But, of course, Red Bus, always trying to save money, had given us only a few days of studio time. And because work on the songs had started before Vic was fired, the material was all over the place.

The lead single was 'She's a Teaser' – a tight, hard-rocking number, but with a lot of brass added in the studio, which made it sound like a bit of a sell-out. (That song had been finished *long* before the main album sessions began.)

By the time I got to London to record the vocals, all the backing tracks had already been done. That in itself should have been a warning sign. I mean, there was just no band spirit at all. Then when Pip played the tapes back for me, I couldn't hide the look of disappointment on my face.

'I know what you're thinking,' said Pip. 'They're not quite there yet. That's why *you're* here . . .'

The next few days were the closest that I'd ever worked with a producer before – and it gave me a lot of respect for what it takes to do that job. I mean, to be a good producer, you've got to be a United Nations-worthy diplomat, a musical genius, and a technical wizard all in one. Pip was all of those things and more. He also looked the part, wearing this fabulous buckskin jacket with all the tassels on the arms, like something an American frontiersman would have worn. It was the coolest, most rock'n'roll piece of clothing that I'd ever set eyes on.

So, there I was with the words, and a rough idea of the melody, and I just had to make it work. And, of course, the first few times I went through it, I was just trying to get to the end without messing it up – that's always the way, unless you wrote the song yourselves – then after that I started to loosen up, improvise a bit, have some fun.

The beautiful thing about Pip was that he could read my mood and adapt accordingly. He'd be like, 'Let's have a break,

Brian, we've worked long enough. Do you think you could manage another hour after dinner? I don't like singers to sing after dinner.'

Of course, I was still a young man then, so I was thinking, I can sing after *anything*.

The worst parts of it all were the mealtimes because I couldn't afford to eat out. Pip would name a restaurant that he wanted to go to, then he'd look at my face and go, 'Oh . . . is it expensive there?' I ended up bringing sandwiches to avoid the issue. I mean, eating out at restaurants wasn't something that I was used to anyway. Even at the height of Geordie's success – when we were on *Top of the Pops* every other week – a meal out for us was stopping at a Little Chef roadside café on the A1 or the inevitable Indian restaurant.

Mind you, not even the finest of Michelin-starred cuisine could compete with a Little Chef 'Olympic breakfast' when you were starving at 6 a.m. after driving all night.

We recorded about a dozen tracks in three days, after which Pip invited me out for a drink to celebrate.

'I'd love to, Pip,' I told him, 'but my train home leaves at 7 p.m. – so I'd better get going.'

'Well, you're cutting it close,' he said, checking his watch. 'C'mon, let's get you a black cab.'

'I'll take the Tube, Pip, it's alright.'

'You'll never get there on time on the Tube, Brian. They're on strike, anyway. You need a cab.'

That was when I had to admit that I had only enough money for the Underground fare and a beer and sandwich on the way home. Pip told me not to say another word. Then he fished into his pocket and pulled out a £20 note, the equivalent of about £150 today. I told him that I couldn't possibly take that amount of money. But he shoved it into my jeans pocket. 'Brian, please,' he said, 'I want you to take it.'

A couple of minutes later, we were standing outside, waiting for a cab. Pip pointed to my faded denim jacket, which must have dated back to the days of The Gobi Desert Kanoe Klub. It was old and falling apart. 'How long have you had that?' he asked.

'I'm not sure,' I shrugged. 'Why?'

'Try this on,' he said, taking off his own jacket – the fabulous buckskin one. 'You'll look good in it.'

'Pip, I can't take the jacket off your own back,' I protested, 'I've only known you for three days! And look at that thing – where did you get it? It must have cost an arm and a leg!'

'Three days in a studio is a long time, Brian. We're friends now. And the jacket suits you better.'

'Pip, I can't, I just can't, I'm fine – stop giving me things!'

Then, a cab pulled up and Pip dropped the jacket on the floor in front of me and walked away. 'I'll be seeing you, Brian,' he called out over his shoulder. 'Safe travels home. And take the jacket! You're a rock star – so you should dress like one.'

That was a special moment for me. I felt like I was stealing it when I picked it up and put it on. And, of course, it made everything else that I was wearing look filthy and worn-out – especially my shoes.

'King's Cross station,' I told the driver through the window. He nodded okay and I climbed into the back . . . while hoping to God that my brother Maurice would be on the train.

If you're wondering why Maurice hasn't featured more in this book, it's because he was away most of the time.

At the age of fifteen, when I was just starting full-time at Parsons, he decided that he wanted to be a chef, and went to work at The County Hotel, opposite Newcastle's Central Station. They made him work as a bellboy first. Then he moved up to become a commis waiter, or an apprentice waiter, and from there he became a commis chef. He'd even practise at home. 'Boiled potatoes, Ma'am?' he'd say to my ma, as he doled out Sunday lunch. 'And would Ma'am care for some carrots?'

Then one night, we found him packing his bags. He told us that he was going to Jersey, in the Channel Islands, to work at a much bigger hotel in the main town there, St. Helier. It was the first that any of us had ever heard of it, because Maurice didn't speak much. There were no fond farewells. He just got on the train and went.

Next thing we knew, he'd come back and bought himself a Mod-style Lambretta scooter – silver, twin chrome tail pipes, and the spare wheel on the back. It was fabulous. Although the first time I borrowed it – to go to the pictures – someone nicked the spare wheel. Which I still feel bad about to this day.

Then off Maurice went again, returning this time with a Triumph Spitfire sports car.

I remember coming home and seeing it parked outside our house and going, 'Whose is *that*?' Nobody had anything like it on our estate. Then Maurice appeared, but I hardly recognized him because he'd grown another foot and had a moustache.

Before he took me for a ride in the car – he had the leather gloves, the herringbone cloth cap, the whole old-school driving get-up – he made me take off all my dirty work clothes and wash my hands. Twice. I didn't blame him. What a glorious machine that Spitfire was. It had all the dials, gauges and buttons, even indicator stalks, and when you changed gears, the engine made all these satanic woofling noises.

I was in awe of Maurice. I'd always been a good student at school – until the end, anyway – and I worked at one of the world's best engineering companies, while earning money from gigs on the side. But I was flat broke. Meanwhile, Maurice – who'd failed every test ever put in front of him – was driving around in *this*.

But that's the thing with Maurice. He plays dumb, but he's smarter than anyone. And he's the most lovable guy you could ever meet. For as long as I can remember, people have been coming up to me, saying, 'How's Maurice? I love Maurice.' He's just one of those guys.

Anyway . . . after coming back from Jersey for good, Maurice got himself a job as chief steward on the London to Newcastle train service, in the first-class section. And if you found yourself on the same train as him – even in the cheapest seat you could buy – he would always look after you. Everybody looked after everybody's family in those days. It was an unspoken rule. But Maurice, being a lovely lad, extended the courtesy to friends too. My great pal Brendan Healy, who often had to go to London for auditions – there'll be more on Brendan and his many talents later on – used to call him 'The Good Samaritan of King's Cross'.

I heard Maurice's voice before I saw him.

'Brian???'

Instant relief. Then I looked around and saw him hanging out of the first-class carriage.

'Are you going to a Cowboys-and-Indians fancy dress party?' he asked, staring at my jacket.

'Fuck off, Maurice,' I smiled.

'Come on then, get yourself in here.'

It was a well-oiled routine with Maurice. You'd walk purposefully past the restaurant car, ticket in hand – as if heading to your seat in economy class – then a service door would open next to you, and you'd duck inside. Then you'd sit against the wall in the kitchen, out of sight, smoking a cigarette, until the train started to move. A nod and a wink would be exchanged, then you'd be ushered to a window seat in the dining carriage, with a white tablecloth in front of you, and proceed to enjoy a silver-service steak dinner with as many beers as you could drink.

'Boiled potatoes, sir?' Maurice would ask with a flourish, to ensure that none of the paying passengers suspected what was going on. 'And would sir care for some carrots?'

The best part of the journey, of course, was when the train crossed the River Tyne to Central Station – those last few seconds giving you the most spectacular view of the Tyne Bridge, all lit up from underneath. That was the beautiful thing about the King's Cross to Newcastle train service – it made coming home feel so good.

The album vanished without a trace. There were no survivors. Not even a life belt was found. But unlike the case of the *Mary Celeste*, this was no mystery – the album was just crap.

The marketing of it had *also* been pretty dire, mind you.

Red Bus's solution to the problem of Geordie needing to move on without alienating our old fans was to make it a 'faceless' album with a cover featuring a naked woman shooting out of the earth, holding up a shining light. The title was *Save the World*, 'featuring Brian Johnson'. But, of course, the album didn't save anything. Not the world. Certainly not Geordie.

I remember Maurice driving over to the house in Preston Grange one morning, asking, 'So what's happening with the record? I've heard nowt on the radio . . .'

I told him that it hadn't been officially released yet – which it hadn't – but, of course, an album would usually be hyped through the roof long before it came out. But neither of the two singles we'd released – 'She's a Teaser' and 'Goodbye Love' – had come even close to bothering the charts.

'Can I at least *hear* it?' asked Maurice.

'I don't have a copy,' I shrugged – and it was true. I mean, it was hard to care when no one else did . . .

People often ask me how and when Geordie eventually broke up. But the truth is, we never really did. There was no big argument or walk-out. We didn't lose anyone to drink or drugs. We were never even dumped by our record company.

It all just kind of . . . fizzled out.

15

Bailiff Blues

⚡

If there was a moment when my first career as a professional singer came to an end, it was when I was at home one day in Preston Grange and heard a rap of knuckles on the front door.

'Mr. Johnson, I presume?' asked the man in a bowler hat who I found standing on the mat. Before I could answer, a couple of big, nasty-looking lads appeared behind him – a brick wall of Geordie muscle – and my heart almost stopped.

'My name is Mr. Such and Such and I'll be your bailiff today,' bowler hat man said, as I just stood there, my jaw hanging open. 'Now, if you don't mind, these two nice young gentlemen are going to come into your house and secure your furniture as collateral – including your television, if you have one. Oh, and your fridge. And by secure, I mean remove. You'll get them back as soon as you settle your debts.'

By now it was the winter of 1978 – one of the coldest, bleakest, most depressing winters in the history of Great Britain. Nonstop strikes had seen rubbish piling up on the streets – even the dead going unburied. Meanwhile, the IRA were setting off bombs all over the place.

'The Winter of Discontent', the newspapers were calling it, which seemed about right . . . if only to describe my personal circumstances. I hadn't had a gig in months, leaving me and Carol so broke we were back to choosing between heating the house or putting food on the table. And, of course, the arguments at home were more ferocious than ever, with poor little Joanne and Kala – now about ten and five years old – caught in the middle of it all.

It had always seemed too good to be true that Red Bus were willing to pay the mortgage on the house in Preston Grange – and now that I was looking at this bailiff in front of me, I realized that I should have listened to my gut.

'What's all this about then?' I finally managed to stammer, fearing the answer.

'We've got a court order here, on behalf of Leeds Permanent Building Society, to seize collateral against your missed mortgage payments in the amount of £500,' explained the bailiff, holding up a piece of paper with a signature and wax seal on it.

'But I haven't *made* any payments,' I told him.

'Well, I admire your honesty,' came the reply. 'Most people claim the cheques are in the post.'

'No, I mean . . . my *record company* makes the payments.'

Or so I thought.

With the bailiff in the house, I managed to get Ellis Elias on the phone – 'Hello Brian, how fab to hear from you, gosh, I'm terribly sorry about all this, there must have been a mix-up, let me talk to this bailiff fellow . . .'

Thanks to Ellis's bullshit, I got a forty-eight-hour reprieve.

But there hadn't been a mix-up. Red Bus had simply stopped paying the mortgage because I wasn't making any money. And the mortgage was in my name – as was the house – so I was on the hook for everything. I should have known, but I've always been naive like that.

Next thing I knew, I was at Newcastle Crown Court.

I got lucky in two ways. First, the judge was sympathetic to a guy who was about to lose his house and couldn't afford a lawyer. And second, Leeds Permanent sent this awful, slimy little puffed-up creep of a mortgage arrears guy to represent them.

When the judge realized I wasn't making up the story about my contract with Red Bus, he gave the Leeds guy a proper bollocking. 'If Mr. Johnson owned and lived in the house, why did you keep sending letters to a record company on Wardour Street in London?' he scolded. 'You knew four months ago that this company had stopped paying! So why didn't you go and see Mr. Johnson then? Why wait all this time and then ambush him, threatening to take away all his possessions and put him and his wife and children out on the street? I think you did it because you just wanted the house back. You didn't *want* to give him a chance!'

Then the judge turned to me and said, 'Mr. Johnson, what can you afford to pay a month?'

The correct answer was 'Absolutely jack shit, Your Honour.' But for some reason I blurted out seventy quid.

'So, you're going to need to get a job, yes?' he said. 'A *real* job. Not as, ahem . . . a *musician*.'

Yes, Your Honour. Whatever you say, Your Honour.

He banged his gavel. 'Leeds Permanent is hereby instructed to add the amount owed to the principal balance and draw up a new mortgage agreement with payments of £70 per month. And Mr. Johnson, you need to find employment, quickly – and don't ever miss another payment again.'

The satisfaction of defending myself and winning – and keeping the house – lasted for all of a couple of hours.

That was when Carol said that she was 'going out with the girls' to celebrate, which somehow escalated into another argument, and it was just so obvious in that moment that we had no marriage left to save. That was when I finally realized that we had to call it quits. It just wasn't fair on the kids. So, I packed my bags, got into my car – now a very used and rusty VW Beetle with a six-volt battery that could barely pull your cap off, never mind power both headlamps at the same time – and started to drive. Slowly.

There was only one place I could go, of course – No. 1 Beech Drive.

That night, I moved back into the same room that I'd once shared with Maurice and Victor, my dog-eared copy of *The Morley Method of Scientific Height Development* still under the bed. And when I got up the next morning and looked out over the slag heaps, railway lines and the Vickers tank factory on the banks of the Tyne, I couldn't help but wonder how I'd gone from appearing on *Top of the Pops* with Roger Daltrey to this. At the age of thirty-one, I'd lost everything. My marriage, my career, my house . . . although at least the kids got to stay in Preston Grange with their mother.*

I can still remember the awful feeling of failure like it was yesterday. It was a horrible, confusing, draining time. I couldn't sleep. I could barely eat. I didn't even want to see my friends because I didn't want to feel their pity – or worse, accept their charity.

Meanwhile, it was hard to watch other bands, given how badly I wished I was out there doing the same thing. But, of course, I couldn't resist. And the funny thing is, the one band

---

* I would get back together and break up again with my wife *many* times over the months and years that followed, and later on, we tried hard to give it another shot for the sake of the kids – but in spite of our good intentions, that proved to be very naive.

that I remember seeing during that period was AC/DC. Not live, but on *Rock Goes to College*, a series on BBC Two that showcased 'up and coming' acts by broadcasting live gigs from various Students' Unions around the country. There was a huge buzz about AC/DC, who'd been playing at Essex University. People kept telling me, 'You've *got* to see these guys.'

What a show it was. They were so different to everything else out there, I couldn't quite believe it. Angus was just manic. He must have only been about twenty-two at the time. He had the schoolboy outfit on, of course, and he did his striptease routine to 'Bad Boy Boogie'. As for the singer – he was a natural-born frontman with tight black trousers, tattoos up his arms, and what looked like a rum and Coke in his hand. It didn't occur to me for one second that he was the same guy that I'd met in Torquay. In fact, I wouldn't have believed you if you'd told me. There was just no resemblance whatsoever. This was a *rock'n'roll* singer, not a folk guy.

I loved every second of it. But, of course, it was also a reminder that I'd had my shot and blown it. I mean, at my age in the rock'n'roll business, unless you were already a star, it was all over. Like the judge had told me, it was time to find a real job.

Even if I could have faced going back to Parsons, it was too late now. The place was a shell of what it used to be. I was going to have to aim lower. So, I picked up a copy of the *Evening Chronicle* – the same paper that had once declared me a 'Star of the Future' – and started to thumb my way through the job classifieds.

'Windscreen fitter needed,' said the first ad I saw, with a telephone number next to it. I can't even remember what the other jobs were on the page. I just saw the words 'windscreen fitter' and thought . . . well, how hard can *that* be? I mean, I used to prepare drawings of steam turbines for power stations, where if you got a measurement wrong within a thousandth of an inch, you could cause disaster. Sticking a piece of glass to a car wasn't going to use up many brain cells.

When I called the number, a guy named Peter answered. It wasn't the usual 'Hallow?' that you'd get from your usual Geordie working man, though. Oh no. Peter was in a different class. Or at least he thought he was. 'Good afternoon,' he went, in this very pompous voice, like he was a Concorde captain about to take off for New York. 'This is Peter, North East Manager of Windshields, Ltd. How may I help you?'

I wanted to beat my head against the wall and scream.

But I needed this job – *badly* – so I swallowed my pride and stayed on the line.

Peter informed me that I'd have to attend a 'preliminary interview' at Windshields, Ltd's 'roadside service forward operating headquarters', which, at the end of the call, turned out to mean the passenger seat of his Ford Escort Estate, which he would park in front of Birtley Services on the A1, about fifteen miles south of Newcastle.

I was actually relieved that Peter was based so far out of town because that meant there was less chance he'd recognize me. I mean, Geordie had been solid B-list celebrities in Newcastle for a while. Metro Radio were always playing our singles – especially 'Geordie's Lost His Liggie' – and Tyne Tees Television often featured us on a show called *The Geordie Scene*. And, of course, I wasn't exactly hard to miss with my mass of curly hair.

But now that I was going back to civilian life with my tail between my legs, I wanted to be invisible.

***

The interview was early on a Friday.

My biggest worry was that the Beetle wouldn't make it. The key had long ago snapped off in the ignition, so you had to do this trick with the handle of a teaspoon to turn on the ignition.

It was raining that morning, of course. More than raining, in fact. It was like Thor the Thunder God was taking a piss after a night out and it was all landing on me. And, of course, the Beetle's floor had a hole in it, and each wiper went at a different speed, and every so often smoke would billow out of the front of the car, which was strange, because the engine was in the back.

As promised, Peter had parked his Escort next to the entrance. So, I pulled up behind it. Then I jumped out of the Beetle, wincing as the rain lashed down on top of me, and I tapped on his passenger window, expecting him to reach over and let me in.

But nothing in my life was ever that easy.

Peter glanced up at me briefly, put up his index finger, and mouthed, 'One moment.'

I looked back at him through the window in just utter disbelief. I mean, every second that passed, another ten gallons of rainwater were soaking through my clothes and filling up my shoes. I was like, what the fuck do you have to do that's so important you can't let me in your car? He didn't even have a phone or a laptop to pretend to type on. This was 1978! He just had a little notepad and a pencil.

I tapped on the window again, trying not to make it sound as pissed off as I was feeling.

This time, he didn't even bother to look up.

By the time he opened the door, I looked like an unsqueezed chamois leather.

'Okay then, Brian,' he goes, as water's dripping off the end of my nose and I'm wondering if I'm going to end up with hypothermia. 'One of my *many* responsibilities here at Wind-shields, Ltd, is to ensure that all prospective fitters have the skills and dedication for such a demanding line of work. So, tell me – what qualifications do you have?'

'I used to be a draughtsman,' I told him. 'So, I've got my City & Guilds and my Tech Three certificate.'

Surely, I thought, he's got to be impressed by this. I mean, these were serious qualifications that took a five-year appren-ticeship and many exams to get.

'Oh,' he said, looking back at me blankly. 'You sound a bit overqualified to me.'

Please, just get me out of here, I thought.

Peter rang me that night to tell me he'd given the job to someone with experience. 'Okay, fair do's,' I told him, and hung up. Then he called back a few minutes later to tell me that, actually, the more experienced person had turned down the job because there wasn't enough money in it, so, er . . . would I still be interested in taking the position?

A couple of days later, I was up at Windshields, Ltd's main warehouse in Darlington for a week of what Peter called 'training'.

Or, to use the technical term, 'learning how to replace a windscreen'.

They kept glass for every make and type of vehicle you could imagine at that warehouse, along with a fleet of beauti-ful white Ford Transit vans with orange lights on the top. When I first saw those vans, I have to admit I started to feel a bit better about the whole situation. I couldn't *wait* to get behind the wheel of one of them.

The guy I had to follow around for the week was a man of

very few words called Norman. He was probably only in his thirties, but he wore spectacles of the jam jar-bottom variety and dressed like he was in his sixties. He didn't seem too pleased to have me as company.

The first call we got over his walkie-talkie radio was for a Peugeot with a broken windscreen at a garage near Boldon Colliery. So off we went in the van – in silence – until Norman grunted something about needing to stop at his house to pick up his lunch from his wife.

So, we drove to his house, in silence.

Then we pulled up next to it, in silence.

Then we sat there for a moment, still in silence, looking in through the window at his wife doing the dishes. Finally, he let out a sigh and said, 'Christ, she's got a face on her like a bull-dog sucking piss off a nettle. Stay here. *And keep your head down.*'

This is gonna be the longest week of my life, I thought.

Over the days that followed, I discovered that replacing windscreens didn't exactly require the skills, dedication and qualifications that Peter had suggested it would.

The first time Norman let me help – instead of just having to stand there, watching – he made me down tools halfway through the job so he could 'go for a slash', which I knew from experience meant a cup of tea, three tabs, a bowel movement, and a long look at Page 3.

But I got bored while he was gone and just finished it.

I couldn't help myself. I was just so impatient to get going – to start making a living again.

Norman looked at me like I was Judas when he got back. 'What did you do *that* for? If you work at that speed, they'll just give us more jobs!'

I'm pretty sure that he stopped speaking to me after that.

Although to be fair, it was hard to tell the difference.

16

A Sign from Above

Once my training was over, I got my very own Transit van with an orange light on top, and I was told that I would be on-call every other two nights. I also got my own walkie-talkie and, even better, my very own call signal – 'Whisky Oscar, One-One-One'. Not the coolest of call signals, I'll grant you that – and good luck saying it after a few beers – but I couldn't have cared less, because I absolutely *loved* my new job.

It wasn't just that I was finally free of Red Bus and all the bullshit of the music industry. And it wasn't just relief that I was finally making a steady living. When I was out in my little van . . . I felt like I was performing an important service.

In those days, you've got to remember, if your windscreen broke when you were driving down the A1, you couldn't just pick up your phone and call for help. You had to get out of the car and *walk* to the nearest emergency telephone. And if you were a long way between phones, or if it was dark and pissing it down – and as I may have already mentioned, it was often pissing it down – it could be a frightening, exhausting experience. You could end up freezing to death in winter if you weren't careful. And this being 1970s Britain, often the first phone you tried didn't even work. Which meant you had to walk to the *next* one. Then all the way back to your car.

Needless to say, by the time my van pulled up, most

people were over the moon to see me – and I got a great sense of pleasure watching a family of four in their little Austin Maxi toddle off after I'd got them back on the road again. I even started to think about going into business on my own – that's how much I'd accepted the fact that this was going to be my life from now on. It wasn't that I'd given up on singing – I'd just convinced myself to treat it as a hobby now. Even if, deep down, a part of me still burned to prove that I could do more and hold my own with the best of them.

Like any job, of course, there were days when fitting windscreens could be a grind.

It was hard physical work, for a start – and you'd find yourself coming home with bits of glass and glue in your hair and your hands sticky and black from handling the windscreen rubber. And sometimes the customers could be difficult – or just weird.

One time, I got called out at about 11.30 p.m. to a huge articulated lorry with its front window out. This was at Scotch Corner, about fifty miles south of Newcastle. And, of course, it was lashing it down at the time, and there was a ferocious gale blowing.

Now, the glass for a lorry is huge and extremely heavy and the only way I could reach the opening was by standing on the roof of the van. I was terrified the wind would catch me – or the glass – so I said to the driver, 'Is there any way that you can hold one end while I get it into place?' He looked back at me, unscrewed the cap of his flask, poured himself a nice hot cup of tea, and went, 'Not my job'.

That was a fun night.

Then there was the time I got called out to a Ford Cortina in the middle of nowhere, only to find the driver sitting in the boot, drinking from a pile of miniature whisky bottles, absolutely off his head. On closer inspection, both the front *and* the back windscreens were out.

I got the fright of my life when I saw that mess.

Whatever he'd hit had gone in one end at such speed that it had come out the other. I'd never seen that before. And he had all the booze in the boot because he was a whisky sales-man from Edinburgh who was dropping off samples at all the hotels along the A1.

He was unintelligible.

'B . . . Br . . .' he couldn't get the words out. 'Fucking, Bri . . .' I thought he said bird. It must have been a big bugger.

'No, *brick* . . .' he finally managed. Ah, that explained why it had gone straight through. No wonder the guy was para-lytic. The brick had been trapped between the two rear tyres of a truck he was behind, worked itself loose, then been shot right through his car, missing his head by inches.

Then I looked back at him, wondering how on earth he'd ever get himself in a fit enough state to drive the hundred-odd miles back home. But those were different times. People did shit every day of their lives that you'd get locked up for today. But I'd done my best for him. And he did give me six bottles of whisky as a tip.

By the time Margaret Thatcher became Britain's new prime minister in May 1979, I honestly don't think you could have found a faster, harder-working windscreen fitter in the entire country than yours truly. I had that job down to a fine art. And I was making money. In fact, if it hadn't been for what happened next, I might never have given it up . . .

It was about three or four o'clock in the afternoon – the beginnings of what passed for rush hour in those days – when my walkie-talkie crackled to life. 'Brian?' said the dispatcher.

'Please, fast as you can, son, we've got a black Ford Cortina Mark IV just north of Scotch Corner. They're in an awful hurry.'

Now, a brand-new Cortina Mark IV was a very nice ride in those days, and in black it would look the absolute business. So, when I jumped into the van and sped off towards the A1, I already knew that this was going to be a higher class of customer.

I wasn't wrong.

From the moment I set eyes on the car, I could tell there'd be something different about this job. There were two guys in the back, one of them wearing a panama hat with dark glasses. Another two guys were outside, leaning on the bonnet, smoking, both dressed in black. They just had this sense of . . . *freedom* about them. Like they didn't belong in the normal, nine-to-five world. It was something that I hadn't been around for a long time. Something that I missed . . .

A lot.

'What's your name?' asked one of the smokers in this very smooth, commanding voice.

'Brian,' I said.

'Okay Brian,' he said. 'Here's the situation. We've got a V.I.P. in the back and he's due on stage at Hammersmith Odeon at 9 p.m. tonight. It's 4.15 p.m. now – and it's a five-hour drive to London . . . maybe a bit less if we put our foot down.' He pointed to the Cortina's smashed windscreen. 'How quickly can you pop a new one of these in? There are 3,500 people relying on us to get to that venue on time.'

Holy shit, I thought.

'Give me fifteen minutes,' I said.

'C'mon, son. Realistically . . . how long?'

'Fifteen minutes.'

I worked so fast, it was like I was in a trance. I got the old windscreen out in two minutes, no problem. Then I dove into the cabin with the portable vacuum, resisting the urge to try and catch a glimpse of the V.I.P. in the back. Then I ran back to the van. Found the replacement glass. On went the new rubber. Then I wrapped the cord into the channel, carried the glass over to the car, placed it over the opening – *bash-yank, bash-yank, bash-yank* – until finally, it locked into place over the lip.

'Done,' I said, sweat pouring down my face.

'That wasn't fifteen minutes,' the guy said. 'It was more like twelve. What's the damage?'

'Twenty-five pounds.'

He pulled out his wallet, took out two crisp twenties, and pushed them into my hand.

'Keep the change,' he said.

Holy shit.

Then he jumped into the driver's seat, fired up the engine and began to pull away . . . just as I realized that I'd forgotten to ask the V.I.P.'s name.

But I found out anyway, because the car jerked to a halt as the rear window drew up alongside me. Down rolled the glass. Then out came a pale, hairy arm, holding up a T-shirt.

'Here you go,' a voice said, in a Cockney accent that sent a shiver down my spine.

The voice was unmistakable. At that time, it was being played all over the radio, at all hours of the day, all over the world. I couldn't believe it. I was being given a T-shirt, personally, by none other than Ian Dury . . . whose latest single, 'Hit Me with Your Rhythm Stick', was currently at No. 1 in the U.K. charts.

I took the T-shirt – dumbstruck – while staring at my reflection in Dury's glasses.

The window rolled back up . . .

Then with a squeal of tyres, the Cortina roared away in the direction of Hammersmith Odeon.

I wish that was me, I thought.

I looked down at the T-shirt – which was black with 'IAN DURY AND THE BLOCKHEADS' written on it in white – while trying to catch my breath. Every nerve-ending in my body felt like it was on fire. It wasn't just that I'd met a rock'n'roll star. Suddenly, I just *knew* that I could do it again – even in my thirties, even after trying and failing to make it once.

The truth was, of course, it wasn't even really a choice.

That energy, that sense of freedom – I belonged around it.

It wasn't just a part of me.

It *was* me.

I had to find a way to get back in the game.

PART THREE

17

Lobley Hill

⚡

With a sound like a large animal being castrated, the steel shutter rolled up, and there it was – my old P.A. system.

It had taken some detective work to find it. After calling all of Geordie's old roadies and drivers and getting nowhere, it was Ellis who finally pointed me in the direction of the warehouse just outside London where it was being stored. He told me that I could come down and get it any time – it was mine, after all – but he couldn't promise that it still worked. It had been almost two years since Geordie's last show.

The speakers were covered in cobwebs and dented and scratched from years on the road – but all the bits and pieces were there and intact. The system had been added onto and improved over the years, now boasting 300 Watts of power, a mixing desk, and a pair of enormous JBL trumpet side speakers, enough to fill even the biggest of gigs. I mean, okay, it was now badly out of date, and it had taken a beating on its travels, but as long as I could get the thing powered up again, I didn't care.

Hauling the amp and speaker cabinets out of the warehouse and into the back of the Transit was the next order of business – and hard work, given the weight and bulk of the equipment. To help, I'd brought along an aspiring roadie, a soft-spoken blond-haired kid named Derek Underhill, still in his teens, who loved being around bands.

Soon enough, the van was loaded up – and off we went, back up the A1 to Newcastle.

Now, at this point, you might be wondering *why* I needed my old P.A. back.

Well, I'd started a new band, of course . . .

Semi-professional, this time, so I could keep my day-job as a mobile windshield fitter.

And the name?

Geordie II. Very original.

Other than yours truly, Geordie II had no carry-overs from the old band.

The rest of the line-up was Derek Rootham on guitar, Dave Robson on bass, and a lovable lunatic named Davy Whittaker on drums. They'd all previously played in a New-castle band called Fogg with a singer from London, Chris McPherson. Fogg had released one album in 1974, entitled *This Is It*. We'd done gigs together in the clubs and the pubs.

The singer of Fogg, Chris, was quite a character, with a Cockney accent that stood out like a donkey's dick in the North East, and a love of dramatic stage effects. And by dra-matic stage effects, I mean *fog* – which made sense, I suppose, given the name of his band.

In fact, the one time I went to see Chris's new band was when they were trying out a new opening with a fog machine. The idea was that all the lights would go out before they went on, the theme from *2001: A Space Odyssey* would begin to play, a blanket of fog would creep out over the floor, then the band members would enter from the back of the room, and make their way dramatically through the tables and chairs to the stage. All of which sounded very cool in theory. But what the lads hadn't realized was that they'd rented a fog machine that was far too powerful for the venue, and that the ceilings were unusually low, which meant that once the fog had covered the floor and started to rise – not a problem in City Hall or the Theatre Royal – it had nowhere to go.

So, out went the lights. On came 'Space Odyssey'. Then – *phhhhsssssst* – all this fog started to appear, first covering the floor, then rising, then hitting the ceiling, then coming back down again, until within a minute or two, it felt like being trapped inside a house fire. I mean, you couldn't see your own hand in front of your face – it was fucking scary. And, of course, the band couldn't see where they were going, so they ended up just stranded at the back. By the time 'Space Odyssey' came to an end, the band hadn't moved an inch, people were coughing and wiping their eyes and running for the exit, and the concert chairman had to switch the lights back on and open all the windows, just so the band could find the stage. It was the funniest thing I'd ever seen.

All Geordie II had needed was a P.A. system, which, thanks to finding my old gear, hadn't cost us a thing.

Geordie II's first show was on a Friday night at Shiremoor Working Men's Club, not far from Preston Grange.

It was a typical club set-up, with rows of long tables and vinyl-covered chairs in front of a little stage with a glittery backdrop, with a men-only bar, a lounge for couples and the concert room for live music. We'd had some rehearsals and we were instantly tight. The band gelled immediately. It was fantastic and we were really looking forward to rocking, then the P.A. packed up about three songs in.

But we had a great roadie named Frankie who, with Derek as an assistant, managed to get it working again.

I'm not going to pretend that it wasn't difficult going back to such small-time venues. With the original Geordie, I'd been spoiled by playing big venues and universities. After a few more gigs, though, I started to get the hang of things.

You'd go on, and for the first four or five songs, you'd get absolutely nothing in return – nobody wanted to be the first one to clap. If there was any reaction at all, it would be somebody shouting 'Turn it down!' But, as long as there was no booing, you were doing okay. Then at the end of the first half, you'd get a smattering of applause before the concert chairman rushed over and told you to shut up and get out, because the bingo was about to start.

Now, the bingo was a life-or-death business in those days, and a working-class institution. You'd have been strung up from the rafters if you'd have so much as farted between the calls of 'two fat ladies, 88!', 'top of the shop, 100!' and 'key to the door, 21!' It was so serious, some of the clubs were even networked together using early telephone technology, so the jackpots would be bigger – with the caller's voice piped into every room through speakers in the ceiling. Some jackpots would run for weeks on end, with the prize money growing all the time. One week, I remember the jackpot reaching the absolutely *mind-boggling* sum of £800. There was absolute silence as the players chewed on their pencils and looked at each other furtively, before some old lady at the back leapt to her feet and screamed 'Bingo!'

Then suddenly the bingo cards would be put away, and it would be time for us to go back on.

By that time, people had relaxed enough – and drunk enough – to loosen up and have some fun. They'd piss themselves laughing when you told a joke. They'd cheer when they recognized a song. And, of course, you could *never* play an original song to a crowd like that, because the last thing that anyone wanted to do on a Friday or Saturday night was concentrate. But we found ways around that by taking songs that everyone knew, like 'Don't Let Me Be Misunderstood' and 'We Gotta Get Out of This Place' and rocking them up beyond belief. We also introduced them to songs they didn't hear on the radio from the likes of Boz Scaggs, Bob Seger, Bruce Springsteen, Whitesnake, Deep Purple and AC/DC.

But one song we would never do was 'We Are Sailing' by Rod Stewart – they literally had signs up backstage that read 'No Sailing!' – because people would end up standing on the tables, their arms outstretched, singing along. I mean, I'm sure it had been a good laugh the first time it happened, but it had got to the point that once the song had started, you couldn't get it to stop.*

Anyway . . . as time went by, even though we were a barely semi-professional outfit, playing these very small and un-glamorous venues, a strange realization came to me.

I was having the time of my life.

One night, I got a telephone call at home from Chris McPherson. My heart skipped a beat when I first heard his Cockney accent because I thought that he might want his old band-mates back.

But no. He had other news.

'Alright, Brian,' he said, sounding very chirpy. 'I'm off to Switzerland tomorrow.'

'Wow, you lucky sod,' I said. 'What for?'

'Rainbow,' he replied. 'Ronnie James Dio just left, so they need a new singer. The audition's in Geneva. And y'know . . .

---

* This became even more of an issue during the Falklands War, because the song was the unofficial anthem of the British naval forces.

I'm feeling good about this. I'll be back amongst my own, know what I mean? They saw me singing in Fogg and they asked for me.'

'How d'ya get *that*, you jammy sod!' I mean, the guy was a good singer . . . but this was as big as it got. 'They just called you out of the blue?' I asked, still reeling.

'Well, not as such, no. They put an advert in the *NME* – and I replied to it. But I'm exactly what they're looking for. To be honest, I think they had me in mind all along.'

'Well, that's great news,' I said, 'Knock 'em dead, mate?'

A few days later, I saw Chris in the Central Arcade, back from his travels. 'I don't think I got it,' he shrugged. 'Fuck 'em, waste of time. But I did mention your name on my way out . . .'

'What? *Really*?'

'You'll owe me a lifetime of beers if you get it, mate.'

I was floored. As much as Chris was a bit full of himself, he was a good lad with a big heart.

He said, 'I left them your number.'

I was sceptical, of course – my years in Geordie had left me a lot more jaded than before. But I couldn't help but feel a *little* bit excited, not only to be on the radar of a big-time band, but also because of the prospect of a free trip abroad.

When the call finally came (and it *did* come), it wasn't Blackmore on the line. It was a Scottish guy who wouldn't even give me his name. All he'd say was that he 'worked with the band'. It was getting too expensive to fly singers to Switzerland, so they were now doing auditions differently. I was disappointed and didn't understand.

'Okay, so how do you want to do this?' I asked. 'Should I make a demo and send it over?'

'Nah,' said the guy. 'Just sing down the phone. Whenever you're ready. I'm all ears.'

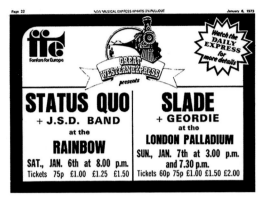

The Slade show was a real step up for us.
Two shows, both sold out, in a day.

This is what we had dreamed of.

Geordie on TOTP.

Roger Daltrey at home on a horse.

Geordie giving it some.

Greyhound pub.

Phil Lynott.

Tits, knickers, gangsters and a Christmas present.

'It's a beautiful mover!' That'll be £350, please.

FOR IMMEDIATE RELEASE
FROM: BOB KAUS
APRIL 15, 1980

AC/DC NAMES BRIAN JOHNSON AS NEW LEAD SINGER

Atlantic recording group AC/DC has announced that Brian Johnson has joined the group as their new lead singer. The news comes after the considerable speculation which followed the tragic and untimely death in February of original AC/DC lead singer/lyricist Bon Scott.

27 year-old Brian, who was born just outside Newcastle (England), was previously with the British group Geordie. They enjoyed two Top 20 hits in the U.K. in 1973, "All Because of You" and "Can You Do It." Most recently, Brian had been singing with a re-formed line-up of Geordie, when he was invited to audition for AC/DC last month. Brian was recommended to the group by their producer, Robert John Lange.

Brian has now joined the other members of AC/DC – Angus Young, Malcolm Young, Phil Rudd & Cliff Williams – in rehearsals for the group's next Atlantic album. Current plans call for the band to enter the studio in early May to commence the recording of the new LP.

AC/DC's last album, "HIGHWAY TO HELL," was recently certified platinum by the RIAA. The group most recently toured the U.S. in the Fall of 1979, with a cross-country headlining itinerary.

Writing lyrics.

Lets put some Back in Black rumours to bed shall we the conspiracy theorists are legion the truth is it was me at the end of the pen, writing on a legal pad, with nothing more than a title given by Malcolm and Angus Thats what happened, thats the truth, now live with it.

Me, Angus and Mal at breakfast in the Bahamas.

Compass Point.

Riffs: Young and Young.
Lyrics: Johnson.

Our first Australian platinum album.
What a cracking day.

One of my first magazine covers. Big stuff to be there
on my own. I thought, 'Cor, I've made it!'

Performing on stage in 1980.

On the road with AC/DC, 1980.

RIP legend Malcolm Young.

My poor dad never got used to press photographers (taken at his working man's club).

Just lovin' every minute.

Suddenly I remembered why I'd come to hate the music industry.

'Are you taking the piss?' I asked, starting to get angry. 'I'm not singing down the phone!'

'Well then, you can't audition.'

'Who the hell are you, anyway?' I asked.

'Look, are you going to sing down the phone or not?'

At that point I snapped. I grabbed the receiver in both hands, took a deep breath, then made the kind of noise down the line that a hyena might make if you shoved a porcupine up its arse. 'FUCKING SUCK ON THAT,' I added, before slamming down the phone.

Funnily enough, I didn't get the job.

The working men's clubs where Geordie II played might not have been very sexy, but they dominated *all* live entertainment in the late 1970s – especially in the North East – and after initially focusing on talent competitions and the like, they'd now fully embraced live music.

Overseen by the Working Men's Club and Institute Union in London, which had branch offices all around the country, there were thousands of clubs across the country, with about four million members in total – and long waiting lists of people who wanted to join. (There was even a working men's club on King's Road in London, if I remember correctly.) Flush with members' subs and other fees – not to mention their bar takings and whatever they made on bingo games – the clubs had more cash than they knew what to do with. And because they were run as co-operatives, the profits were used to benefit the members instead of being paid out to investors.

The names they could afford to book as a result were the

very best acts of the time. Shirley Bassey played at Batley Variety Club. As did Tom Jones and Tina Turner. Even Louis Armstrong. And most unbelievable of all, Roy Orbison recorded an entire live album there. I mean, this was *West Yorkshire* . . . at a club built on top of an old sewage works!

What made it all the more remarkable was the fact that the clubs were run by some of the most awful, officious, small-minded committee men that you could ever imagine. You could spot them immediately by their navy-blue double-breasted suits, club ties and lapel pins – and they always had a new Skoda or Lada parked outside. There was one infamous guy – I forget which club he ran – who'd been accused of embezzling money, so he got up on stage one night and declared, 'It's come to my attention that there are people in this room who have made serious allegations against me, so before we go any further, I want all of the allegators to stand up.'

Those were the kinds of great minds that you were dealing with.

There were a few occasions, of course, when we ended up on the wrong end of a concert chairman's power trip. There was one guy, in particular, who was constantly telling us that if we didn't turn down our amps, he'd send us to a disciplinary tribunal – a very real threat that could have seen us 'banned from the area' because that was the power they had, and they could put you out of business for good. Eventually, he bought himself a decibel meter and sat in the front row, holding it up, to make sure that we didn't go over whatever level he'd deemed acceptable. The night he did that, though, we didn't make any noise at all. We just walked off the stage in protest – and, of course, the guy ended up getting mobbed by the audience, furious that he'd ruined their Saturday night.

Anyone who performed at the clubs, meanwhile, also had to put up with the brutal honesty of the members. There was a certain type of working-class man in the clubs who loved nothing more than to insult someone famous to their face. It was a kind of bragging right – 'You know that so-and-so? I told him he was shite.' Legend has it, there was this one guy, an unemployed miner by day, M.C. by night, and he worked at one of the bigger clubs – again, best not named. Frank Sinatra had played at this place, Engelbert Humperdinck, everyone. And he loved sticking the boot in whenever he could. One night, The Four Tops were on tour in Britain and they were doing a gig at City Hall in Newcastle, but their manager was told that if they came down to this big club and did a thirty-minute set, they would get an extra couple of grand, finish, and be able to drive back to City Hall for the real gig. And just as they were about to go on, they got introduced by this ignorant dummy, who got the mic and said, 'Okay everybody, I've got a lovely surprise for you now. I've no idea who they are . . . but here are four darkies from America!'

The Four Tops just turned around and walked out. They were like, 'Fuck you.' And they'd already been paid, so the club had to take the loss. The guy got the sack and was banned from the club forever – or so the story goes. He told the management that it was 'just a bit of banter'. But that was always the excuse people used for just being disrespectful and nasty – and in this particular case, racist beyond belief.

It was bullshit then, and it's bullshit now.

What made Geordie II so successful in the working men's clubs was that we weren't just a typical rock act. The clubs usually *hated* rock acts, because they were too loud and took themselves too seriously, which turned off the older members. But we had a sense of humour. For example, at random points during the set, Davy Whittaker would get up from his drum stool, push me aside, sing the first line of 'Nessun Dorma' – he didn't know any more of it – then go, 'Thank you very much.' At the end of the night, meanwhile, we'd leave the stage to Ivor Biggun's 'I'm a Wanker' and the place would be in stitches. And all of this created so much goodwill for us, it was rare for even the most puffed-up concert chairmen to give us any trouble.

By the end of 1979, we were getting booked three or four times a week, and our fee just kept getting higher and higher. We were playing so much, there were nights when I forgot where we were. Usually we played Friday, Saturday and Sunday nights, but when our fee hit £250 per show and we became impossible to book because we were so in demand, a lot of clubs started asking if we could do weeknights, even Tuesdays, for a bit less money. We were only too happy to oblige.

These were some of the best nights of my life.

We were supposed to finish our set at 10.30 p.m., but that never happened, it was always fifteen minutes later, then we'd pack up all our stuff, and we'd be home just after midnight, then up at the crack of dawn the next day to go to work. Unless we went out for an Indian afterwards, or down to the Selva Grill at the bottom of Dean Street – the only place in Newcastle that would stay open until 1 a.m.

My days playing the clubs also gave me an appreciation for great comedy – and there were times when I toyed with the idea of becoming a comedian myself if Geordie II ever broke up.

I mean, when I saw my friend Brendan Healy do his act, I couldn't believe it. He'd never meant to be a comedian. He'd started out as a keyboard player and trombonist, then became

a fully-certified concert conductor. But he was a clever, hilarious guy, and at some point he realized that he was good
enough to keep a room hanging on his every word. He'd
walk onto a stage and say, 'Ladies and Gentlemen, I'm very
sorry I'm late. My car broke down and I had to come on a
bus. But it's alright . . . I managed to disguise it as an asthma
attack.' After which there'd be a deafening silence while everyone tried to get the joke. Then just as the first person started
to laugh – which would quickly turn into a deafening roar as
everyone else caught on – Brendan would say, 'Alright, here's
another one you won't get . . .'

From then on, he'd have the audience eating out of the
palm of his hand.*

I'm reminded of the night that our P.A. finally died – this
time in a way that was beyond any repair. There was another
band sharing the bill with us that night – fronted by a local
character named Malcolm Wylie who owned two ice cream
vans† – so we had to go and ask them if we could borrow
their system. They let us plug into their gear, of course, but
what I couldn't get over was just how much of a star their
lead guitarist was. I mean, he was this seventeen-year-old kid
from Cullercoats who'd dropped out of school, and he'd
come up to the front of the stage and you could just smell
the quality. Then he'd do a solo that left me wondering how
on earth he'd learned to play like that – until I found out later
that his teacher had been one Dave Black.

Anyway, I never gave any of this another thought until a

* Brendan Healy once told me that he'd gone to see Pavarotti sing live but had
ended up being thrown out – and banned from any future Pavarotti concerts
for life. When I asked him why, he shrugged and said, 'Apparently he doesn't
like it when you join in.'
† That didn't just sell ice cream!

few years later when I was watching television in America and the video for 'Save a Prayer' by Duran Duran came on.

And fuck me . . . *there he was*!

The kid at the club, I realized, had been a very young Andy Taylor.

Things were going so well with Geordie II, I managed to save up enough money to start my own business. Not windscreens this time, but fitting cars with custom vinyl roofs. It was a great job for a musician because garages didn't open until nine or ten o'clock in the morning, sometimes even later. Which let me catch up on some sleep if I hadn't got back from a show until after midnight, which was most nights of the week.

I'd started out with a business partner called Jim, whose brother bought a van for us. But then I came down with the flu for a week, and because I wasn't able to work, Jim fired me. After that, I was on my own. Instead of going to work for someone else, though, I hired someone I could boss around instead – a lad named Ken Walker – and we opened up a shop under the arches on the Quayside in Newcastle.

The best thing about Ken was his posh voice, which sounded just the part when he answered the phone. He was also just a lovely, handy, hard-working guy, always full of fun – and he was brilliant at taking care of the management side of things.

I almost found a new wife, thanks to that vinyl business.

The girl in question – I won't mention her name, because she went on to marry someone else – came to a Geordie II gig one night with a friend, and they were dancing near the front. You could tell that she was class, right off the bat.* She

---

* Because her tattoos were spelled right . . . just kidding.

was gorgeous, beautifully dressed, having a good time, but not getting too drunk. Anyway, we got talking afterwards, and I asked her if she wanted to join me and the rest of the boys for an Indian meal after the show. So, after our gear was packed up, she and her friend got in their car and followed the band's van to the restaurant.

Over dinner, I told her about my business, and she mentioned that she'd just bought herself a brand-new Datsun Cherry – but she'd gone for the model without the vinyl roof, and now she was regretting it. So, of course, I told her that I did all the vinyl roofs for Datsun in Gateshead, and that I charged them about £40 for the service – after which they would rebadge the car as a 'GL' and raise the price by an outrageous £250. I offered to do hers for cost if she brought her car into my shop.

So that Saturday, she dropped off her car and went shopping for an hour, and by the time she came back, I'd fitted an extra-luxury 'American' roof to her car, with some beautiful trim around the edges. I even threw in a pinstripe. But, of course, I didn't charge her any extra. She couldn't believe how good it looked. That was what I loved the most about my vinyl business – people's reaction when they got their cars back. It gave me such a sense of satisfaction. Some of the cars I did were two or three years old and were starting to look a bit sad, and the vinyl just transformed them.

Before she drove away, I asked her if she wanted to come to another show in Birtley. 'I'd love to,' she smiled, adding that she lived nearby in Chester-le-Street.

Over the weeks that followed, I learned that she was the manager of Timex Watches on a trading estate near where she lived, and that she'd lost her husband to cancer when he was just twenty-five – a heartbreaking story. But that had been a few years before, and now she was almost thirty and tired of being on her own. Then one night she invited me to stay the night at her house . . . and after that, we were an item. Or at least as much of an item as we could be, given that I was only separated from Carol and still years away from being ready to go through a divorce. What she wanted most of all was to settle down and have kids, which might have worked if I'd kept the vinyl business while playing shows with Geordie II on the side. But rock'n'roll had something else in store for me.

The better we got, the more calls I got for auditions.

It was a tricky situation. Although I wanted to stay with the two Daves and Derek, I also felt like I couldn't say no when a bigger band invited me to come in and sing. So, when Manfred Mann's Earth Band got in touch to ask if I wanted to try-out to be their new singer – the great Chris Thompson had just left to form his own band – I couldn't think of a good reason why I shouldn't give it a crack, especially since I had to go to London anyway to pick up some more supplies of vinyl.

First, they sent me a tape of 'Blinded by the Light', which they'd had a No. 1 hit with a couple of years earlier. So, of course, I sang along to it a few times, learning the words, all the while thinking to myself, *this really isn't me*.

The audition was at a studio in London, late morning. As Ken and I were driving down to pick up some vinyl roofs anyway, we thought why not do both? The first person I saw when I walked in there was this very overweight, hippy-looking guy with a beard and long hair, and he told me that he'd just come down from Butlin's, the chain of holiday camps. I asked him if he'd been on holiday there – while thinking to myself, *rather you than me, mate* – and he went, 'Oh no, I play there to make a bit of money when we're not touring.'

That was when I realized that the Earth Band was little more than a collection of hired hands who got together under the Manfred Mann name – founded by Manfred himself, a South African keyboardist who'd had a run of big hits in the 1960s. Then in walked Manfred, wearing his John Lennon glasses and little chin beard, hair all ruffled, and he was reading aloud a letter from his mother, who was telling him about things in her personal life that I'd *never* want to hear from my own ma. I just wanted to get out of there as fast as I possibly could.

'Look,' I said, 'I appreciate the invitation and I wanted to be polite and come down here and have a go singing to the tape, but I think you're going to need somebody who's happy just doing covers. Do you have *any* original material?'

Manfred – or Mr. Mann, or whatever it was that I was supposed to call him – looked at me like I was mad. I mean, the guy had made a very successful career from redoing other people's songs. So, he must have thought that I was taking the piss. I'm not even sure that I sang anything that morning, it was so obvious that it wasn't going to work.

Then a couple of days later, when I was back at the shop, doing a vinyl job, the phone rang again.

'Hello, it's Uriah Heep. We were wondering if—'

I interrupted him with three of the most liberating words in the English language.

'No thank you.'

If my first career as a professional singer had ended with the bailiff's knock in 1978, my second one began one night at

Lobley Hill Social Club in early 1980. Or at least that's where people tell me that the incident in question went down and given that most of Geordie II's gigs have all merged into one in my mind, I'll just have to take their word for it.

I'd come straight from the shop – by then I had contracts with several dealerships around town, and business was booming – so I had bits of glue and vinyl in my hair, my hands were filthy, and my white trainers looked close to surrender . . .

There were no dressing rooms with showers and lockers at venues like Lobley Hill, of course, so I had no choice but to go on stage looking like the working man that I was, which often happened when I had no time to change before a show.

As luck would have it, though, our roadie's assistant – Derek, the soft-spoken, blonde-haired kid – had a spare T-shirt in his bag, and he said I could borrow it. When I put it on, it looked like an American football shirt, blackish-blue in colour, with the number '22' on the front in white, and yellow and white stripes where the shoulders met the arms. But it was clean – well, as clean as a roadie's spare T-shirt ever could be – and it did fit me, so I kept it on and went up on stage to do my thing.

The show that night was electric.

Kids were starting to come from all across the North East to see Geordie II, and there'd been a queue halfway up the street to get in. The place was absolutely jammed. I saw the concert chairman at one point running around, sweat running down his forehead, barely able to believe how much business he was doing. My brother Maurice was also in the crowd that night – as was a representative from Red Bus, which no one had expected. News must have reached Wardour Street that Geordie II was now one of the hottest live acts in the North East.

Lobley Hill being a working men's club, there was an inevitable half-time break for the bingo, and when the concert chairman came over with that 'shut up and make yourself scarce' look in his face, I went outside for a tab. Then Maurice came and found me.

The moment he saw me, he froze.

'What's *wrong*?' he asked.

'What are you talking about?' I replied. 'Nothing's wrong. I mean, I'm bit tired, but—'

'Your eyes,' said Maurice, 'they're all red and puffy.'

'Oh . . . yeah,' I said. You see, I'd been sweating heavily during the show, as always, and the sweat had mixed up with all the glue and shards of glass and other shit in my hair and this toxic brew had been running into my eyes, forcing me to wipe it away with the back of my hand. It happened every time I did a show straight after work. My eyes would sting for a day or two, but then they'd be fine again.

'Here,' said Maurice, taking off his cloth driving cap and holding it out for me, 'put this on – it'll stop the sweat running down your face. You can't keep rubbing your eyes like that, Brian, it's not good for you – you'll end up going blind!'

'I'm not wearing *that* on stage!'

'You'd rather damage your eyes than wear a cap?'

'Maurice, if I was delivering newspapers or going grouse shooting, the cap would be brilliant, but I'm a singer in a band.' Then I had a change of heart. I mean, my eyes were stinging pretty badly, and who cared what I wore? 'Oh alright, give it here . . .'

With the cap on, I was now sporting a very odd combination of an American football shirt with the kind of headwear that every working-class man in Newcastle had worn for the last hundred years. I felt a bit ridiculous, to be honest with you, especially because when I wore the cap, my curls of hair bunched up around the sides and at the back. But when I walked back on stage, the audience went fucking nuts.

'Hey, Geordie boy!' people called out, grinning and cheering.

Even better – it really *did* stop the sweat running into my eyes.

At the end of the night – which we closed again with 'Whole Lotta Rosie' because I couldn't get enough of that song after seeing Bon sing it on *Rock Goes to College* – I tried to give the cap back to Maurice. But by then it looked like a wet rag. 'I don't want *that*, it's disgusting! Keep it.' So, I did. Derek didn't want his T-shirt back, either – even after I'd taken it home to be washed. He said it was too baggy for him, which it was, because the guy was whippet-thin.

It was the cap I loved the most, though. When I wore it out and about during the day, it was like an invisibility cloak. But on stage, it just looked so distinctive, especially when I wore it with a T-shirt or a sleeveless denim jacket. I wore the cap so much, in fact, that I had to replace it after a couple of weeks.

I've been buying them and wearing them ever since. I never felt comfortable without them again.

The crazy thing is that AC/DC played the second-last show of their *Highway to Hell Tour* at my old haunt of the Mayfair Ballroom in Newcastle at about the same time as the Lobley Hill show. I don't know if it was the same night, but the AC/DC gig was on 25 January – it had been postponed due to a fire at the Mayfair earlier in the year – so at most these two events would have been just a few weeks apart. And, of course, Geordie II would have certainly been playing *somewhere* that same Friday.

If you'd been in Newcastle on the night in question, in other words, you could have gone to see AC/DC with Bon on vocals at one venue, then taken a bus to a working men's club on the other side of town and seen me in my cloth cap and '22' shirt singing one of the same songs from their set list.

Not that any of those things seemed important at the time. The cap and the shirt had just happened on the night – and I'm not even sure that I knew AC/DC were playing that week.

With Red Bus sniffing around once again, Geordie II's future was the main thing on my mind.

'Listen, you guys were great, we need to get you to London to start making an album. Y'know, boys, I think Geordie II could be the sequel that's even better than the original . . .' Ellis gushed to us after the Lobley Hill show, much to the delight of the two Daves and Derek, who'd never been on the receiving end of a music manager in full bullshit-mode before.

18

Beautiful Mover

⚡

During those early weeks of 1980, the phone in the vinyl shop never stopped ringing. A dealership with six new cars to do. A new club booking. An audition invitation. My ma wanting me to bring the kids over for Sunday lunch. Another club booking. Ellis's office in Soho on the phone. I was knackered.

Then one morning in early March, I picked up the phone to hear a woman with a very thick East German accent on the line. And maybe because I'd seen one too many war films, she sounded like she was about to give me the third degree.

'Is zis Brian Yonson?' she demanded to know.

'Who's asking?' I replied.*

'Zat is not important. Vat is important is zat you must come to Londe-on to sink wiss a gruppen.'

'Sink?'

'Sink. You are Brian Yonson, ze sinker, ja?'

'Oh . . . you mean *singer* . . . yes, that's me. And, er . . . what exactly do you want me to do again?'

'Sink.'

'Yes, I got that part . . .'

'Wit eine rock gruppen.'

'Okay, look, I'm sorry, but I've stopped doing auditions. I'm already in a band and we're about to—'

---

* The first rule of war films is that a question is *always* answered with a question.

261

'I cannot tell you ze name of zis gruppen.'

'Okay, well that's probably just as well, because like I said, I'm not doing any more auditions.'

There was a long pause. 'If you knew ze name,' she said, 'you vould *not* be saying nein.'

I was getting a bit annoyed at this point because I really needed to get back to work . . . but I was also curious. 'Look, if this "rock gruppen" is that big of a deal,' I told her, 'maybe you can give me a *hint*?'

Another long pause. Then a heavy sigh. 'I suppose I can tell you ze initials,' she said.

'Okay then . . .'

'A. Z.'

I racked my brain, but no band came to mind. 'I'm sorry,' I said, 'but that doesn't really ring a—'

'Und D. Z.'

Now it was my turn to go very quiet. Because I was having trouble believing my own ears. I mean, there was surely no way on earth that this woman worked for . . .

'You mean . . . *AC/DC*?!'

'Scheisse! I've said too much!'

Before I go any further, I should probably mention that the period between the show at Lobley Hill and the call from the East German woman had been really frustrating.

That was mainly thanks to Davy Whittaker's boss, who'd dug his heels in and refused to give him any time off during the week so we could go to London and start putting down some tracks. Red Bus had their own studio by now, and that was where they wanted us to record – but there just wasn't enough time between Davy clocking off work on a Friday evening and him clocking back in on a Monday morning to drive the

300 miles down there and 300 miles back again and get any real work done in between. We did manage to get *one* song on tape – 'Rockin' with the Boys' was the title, written by yours truly with Derek and Dave Robson – but Red Bus wouldn't release it until an entire album's worth of material was ready.* Until we had a single in the charts, though, Davy was never going to leave his job – and in the meantime, his boss was never going to give him a day off to help him with his musical career. It was the kind of classic Catch-22 situation.

Eventually, I took matters into my own hands and phoned Davy's boss myself – probably not the greatest idea. Davy worked as a delivery driver for Calor Gas, and he knew all of the company's customers, where they lived, and what kind of gas they needed and when, so of course the last thing his boss wanted was to lose him.

The second the guy answered the phone, I realized that I didn't have a leg to stand on. It wasn't like I was famous or anything. All I could do was appeal to his sense of fairness.

'Hi, my name's Brian,' I said. 'I'm the singer in Davy's band. We've been given the chance to make a record in London. We just need to drive down to London on a Sunday night, stay at a hotel, and Davy will be back by Thursday.'

'No,' came the reply.

'. . . can I ask *why*?' I asked.

'No.'

'Have you even given this any thought, or are you just saying "no" because you can?'

'The answer was no yesterday. The answer's no today. And the answer will be no tomorrow.'

---

* The song never was released, but after I joined AC/DC, it got a lot of airplay in America, and you can find it online today, with an anime-style video.

'Oh, come on, give the lad a chance!' I blurted. 'He's a great drummer and this is a huge opportunity for us. Surely you've got someone who can cover for him? It's just four days, then he'll be back and he can work extra shifts to make up for it.'

'If he goes to London,' he said, 'I'll sack him.'

That was too much for me. 'You know what?' I said. 'You're a fucking arsehole.'

'Excuse me?'

'YOU ... ARE A FUCKING ... ARSEHOLE.'

Slam.

In the end, Davy worked at Calor Gas until he retired, which just made no sense to me at all.

To say that I had mixed feelings about getting a call from AC/DC wouldn't really go far enough. I mean, the second that I heard the band's name, I remembered the tragic event from just a few weeks earlier.

It was Ken who'd first broken the news to me at the vinyl shop.

'Hey Brian, you know that song you sing – "Whole Lotta Rosie"?'

'Yeah?'

'The guy who sings it is dead.'

'No, he's not. I just saw him on *Top of the Pops*. He's as fit as a butcher's dog.'

'Well, it says here that he was found dead inside someone's car – "death by misadventure" they're calling it.'

'What? That can't be right . . . give it here.'

I took the paper from him and read the story myself . . . but I just couldn't understand how it had happened. In those days, I was completely ignorant about the dangers of drinking to excess or taking any kind of drug. Part of it was the fact that no one in my world ever had enough money for drugs and we all had to get up at the crack of dawn most days to go to work, so getting drunk to the point of losing consciousness wasn't exactly an option. Meanwhile, I'd never smoked a joint – and as for harder drugs, I'd never been offered them, never known anyone who'd taken them, they were completely beyond my experience. So, it was shocking to me that a lad like Bon, who was just a year older than me, fighting fit, and in the prime of his life, could die like that.

Most of all, though, it was the tragedy of it that struck me – not only for Bon's family, bandmates and friends, but also for anyone who loved rock music. 'Whole Lotta Rosie' was one of the greatest rock songs of all time, as far as I was concerned, and it was just one of many classics that he'd written and recorded with AC/DC, from *Let There Be Rock* to *Dirty Deeds Done Dirt Cheap*. And, of course, Bon and the boys had outdone themselves the previous summer with their *Highway to Hell* album. Thanks to that gem – and the title song about the hardships of life on the road – they'd finally broken through after six years of non-stop gigging to become a major headline act. Meanwhile, the album had gone all the way to No. 8 in the British charts and to No. 17 in America – where they were becoming an even bigger deal than they were in Europe. The lads had even got onto *Top of the Pops* with their second single, 'Touch Too Much'. I'd watched it myself at home just a couple of weeks earlier. Bon had looked like he was having the time of his life. After all, thanks to *Highway to Hell*, he must have known that AC/DC were on their way to becoming a huge band.

Meanwhile, it *still* hadn't clicked in my head that Bon was the guy from Fang whom I'd shivered with in freezing Torquay, seven years earlier. And it would take a while yet . . .

The East German woman who'd called me wouldn't tell me her name, so I came up with one myself – 'Olga from the Volga'. From what I could gather, Olga worked in the office of a guy called Peter Mensch, a tour accountant turned manager, but whenever I asked her a question, it was met either by stony silence or 'Zis, I cannot say.'

What puzzled me was how my name had ended up on their list of singers to call. It made no sense. By now, it had been seven years since Geordie's run of minor hit singles, and I was only a household name in the sense that everyone in my house knew my name.

What I'd find out later – much later – was that my name had actually been put forward by several different people. There was an AC/DC fan in Cleveland, Ohio, who'd seen Geordie back in the day and written to Peter Mensch, recommending the band try me out. Then there was the young South African producer of *Highway to Hell* – Robert 'Mutt' Lange – who also knew of Geordie and had also mentioned me to Angus and Malcolm. And I learned later that Bon had also told them about me after our Torquay adventure.

The other question at the top of my mind was whether Angus and Malcolm and the other lads would even *want* to continue without Bon. Again, it would take a while before I learned the full story, but the answer might have been 'no' – at least right then – if it hadn't been for Bon's parents, Isa and Chick (Chick was short for Charles). They told Angus and Malcolm that Bon would have wanted

AC/DC to keep going and finish the album that they'd just started work on. At the very least, they thought it would be a welcome distraction for the band – something to give them a bit of comfort and help them deal with their grief.

As for me – my mind was racing by the time I got off the phone with Olga.

I mean, I was flattered and excited to get the call, of course. It almost didn't feel real, auditioning for a band that was so well known around the world. But I also knew that there'd be dozens of other contenders all vying for the same gig, and I wasn't sure that I had the heart to go through all the anticipation and disappointment, especially since my little band was doing so well.

Hang on Brian, get yourself together. Get the facts straight. You're thirty-two, living with your mother and father. You've got a successful little business and a successful little band. You're happy with your girlfriend, you've got your two lovely daughters, you can afford things for them – everything's going great. Why would you do this? I'll tell you why – I fucking *have* to.

But first, how the fuck do I get down to London on such short notice?

I'd have to cancel my vinyl jobs for that day. Meanwhile, Ken needed the Austin Maxi for the business – the week of the proposed audition was a particularly busy one – and my own car at the time was a wildly temperamental Jaguar XJ that had a mind of its own and could be very bad tempered.

'I think I'm going to have to say no,' I told Ken, after I'd explained what the call had been about.

'Oh, you've *got* to give it a shot, Brian,' he said.

'Look, I'm not going to get it, anyway,' I replied, already starting to talk myself out of it. 'They'll hire someone they already know, probably another Aussie.'

'Why don't you sleep on it?' suggested Ken.

Before I had a chance to call Olga from the Volga back with my answer, another call came out of the blue.

This time it was my old pal André Jacquemin. We'd kept in touch, and he'd gone on to found Redwood Studios in London.

'How would you like to earn £350?' he asked.

'Look, André, whatever it is you want me to do for that kind of money,' I said, 'the answer's yes.'

'Great,' he laughed. 'All you need to do is come down to London for a day and record a jingle for a Hoover advert. Now, I can't promise you that they'll use your take – you're up against a very large lady who sings gospel music – but you'll get paid regardless.'

The gearwheels in my mind had started to spin even before he'd finished his sentence.

'. . . and, er, *when* do you need me there?' I asked.

He named the day – and it was on the same day as the proposed AC/DC audition.

'Let me talk to my business partner,' I said, grinning. It wasn't just the AC/DC gig that I was pleased about. I'd also never done any kind of commercial work before – and I loved the idea of doing a session at a brand-new state-of-the-art studio like Redwood.

At which point, Ken walked in and saw the look on my face.

'What are you looking so pleased about?' he asked.

I told him about the call.

'Brian, I think someone up there is trying to tell you something,' he grinned.

After debating how best to get to London, I decided to throw caution to the wind and take the Jag. Then off I went down the A1 to meet André at Redwood Studios.

After singing about the sucking power of a vacuum cleaner, I felt fucking fantastic. My contract even included *repeat fees*, a very alien concept to anyone who had worked in the 1970s rock'n'roll business.

Finally, at about 3.30 p.m., it was time to drive the three miles southwest across London to Pimlico – the journey took only about fifteen minutes in those days – where I'd been told that in the back of a commercial garage there was a rehearsal space and recording facility called Vanilla Studios. That's where I would be meeting the band for my audition.

By the time I'd got there and found a place to park, I was feeling pretty hungry – I'd been up since the crack of dawn and driven 300 miles – and there was still some time to kill before my 5 p.m. audition slot. So, I ducked into an old café, a real London before-the-war kinda place. I ordered a cup of tea and a meat pie. The woman behind the counter – at least I think it was a woman, the six o'clock shadow made it confusing – had a cigarette dangling from her lips, ash flying everywhere when she talked. It didn't bode well on the hygiene front. The fact that the pie crust wouldn't give way using tooth, knife or nail was an indication of its age and ancestry. So, in the name of health and safety, I got up from the table, put on my cap, and decided to face the unknown on the other side of the street instead.

It's a miracle I ever found the entrance to the studio, it was so hidden away.

But I did – and then suddenly I was inside and being welcomed by the AC/DC road crew, who were in the middle of a game of pool. Next thing I knew, I'd put a coin on the table, it was my turn to play, and we were having a great old natter and a laugh.

I'd just sort of assumed that the band were busy with something and would come and get me, but no, they were in the rehearsal room, looking at their watches, wondering where the fuck the guy from Newcastle was. Eventually, the band's tour manager, Ian Jeffery, was dispatched as a search party.

'Has anybody seen that Geordie lad?'

'Well, I'm a Geordie,' I said.

Shocked, the crew looked at me. 'Are *you* Brian?' I nodded. 'Oh, for fuck's sake, we've been waiting for you for an hour!'

Nobody had even thought to *ask* me, because I looked like a working boy.

If the lads were irritated, they kept it well hidden. In fact, they couldn't have made me feel more at home. 'I believe this is your local brew?' announced Malcolm, holding out a bottle of Newcastle Brown Ale for me. It was such a Malcolm thing to do.

'Oh, I could kill one of those,' I grinned. 'Thanks, mate.'

'What do you want to sing, mate?' asked Malcolm casually.

Oh, Jesus. What a question. I didn't want to launch straight into an AC/DC song because they'd know it by heart, and I'd be flailing around, which wouldn't exactly be a level playing field. So, I threw out 'Nutbush City Limits', the classic Tina Turner song. Angus – who hadn't said a word – looked a bit taken aback but seemed okay with it.

'Well, you passed the first test,' said Malcolm, deadpan.

'What's that then?' I asked.

'You didn't say "Smoke on the Water". Good song, "Nutbush",' he added. 'Everyone ready?'

'What key?' asked Angus, finally speaking up.

'I think it's A?' I replied.

Malcolm looked at me and he said, 'A? Are you sure?'

'Yeah.'

You see, A is the high rock'n'roll key – it's Robert Plant area. *The* rock'n'roll key of rock'n'roll keys.

And then Malcolm said, 'Hang on, I think I've got it.'

Then, before you knew it, Phil and Cliff joined in, Angus was there, heads started rocking and off we went. I started coming in and they were waiting to hear this voice, to see whether it was worth their while, and it was the most electric moment of my life.

I mean, I played with a good little band, but nothing prepared me for that sound. It was just the best thing I'd ever felt and heard, and I started singing like my life depended on it.

'That was a lot of fun,' I said after, almost welling up, because it really had been just magic, for me anyway.

But then came the real test.

'Can you have a go at something of ours now?' asked Malcolm. 'Just name a song, any song . . .'

I didn't even have to think.

'"Whole Lotta Rosie",' I said.

No matter how good it had felt to play 'Nutbush', 'Whole Lotta Rosie' was almost an out-of-body experience. As soon as we got into it, I started to get these weird tingles and shivers. I felt like Bon was right there in the room with us, smiling and sipping on his rum and Coke. He'd been gone barely a month, you've got to remember. And there I was, in that tiny room, singing his signature song, with Angus next to me, this absolute force of nature. When he tore into the solo, it was so loud, and proud, the hairs on my arms were standing on end. Every member in the band playing like their life depended on it. It was the AC/DC way. It sounded so right. This was rock'n'roll. This was how it was all meant to be.

Then suddenly it was over and I was walking out of the room.

'Thanks, lads,' I said, because I thought that was it. 'The boys back home will *never* believe that I did this. I can't wait to tell them . . .'

A young guy followed me out, introducing himself as Peter Mensch. He was all bushy eyebrows, ruffled hair and New York accent – he couldn't have been more than twenty-seven at the time. He seemed like a very cool, easygoing kind of guy for a music manager.

'Hey, Brian – where are you going?' he asked.

'Oh, I've gotta drive back home,' I told him. 'I've got three Ford Cortinas and a Datsun Cherry waiting for me in the shop, and they all needed vinyl roofs on them yesterday.'

'No, no, no,' said Peter, 'the boys would love you to stay . . .'

'Ah, I wish I could,' I said. 'But I'm the only one who can fit the roofs, so I've really got to get going.'

It was about 8.30 p.m. by now. I couldn't believe how quickly the time had passed.

'Well, at least come back inside and have one more of those Newcastle Browns before you go.'

'Mate, it's a five-hour drive back up the A1, so I'm not going to get back until 1.30 a.m. as it is – and I've got to open up the shop at nine. Then I've got a show tomorrow night . . .'

Peter threw up his hands, giving me a disappointed look.

'Can I at least give you a ring when you get back?' he asked.

'Any time,' I told him.

That's the last I'll ever hear from that guy, I thought.

19

Grand National Day

I didn't so much drive back to Newcastle as float. It wasn't that I thought that I'd got the job. Quite the opposite. I was more convinced than ever that the job was a fairy tale – I was too old, too short, and definitely not Australian enough. But none of that mattered. I was just on a high from the once-in-a-lifetime experience of singing with a band as good as AC/DC – and, of course, I had a cheque for £350 in my pocket, with the promise of 'repeat fees' and more work from André to come.

Life was good.

In fact . . . it had never been better.

I couldn't wait to tell the lads in the band about my wild experience in London. Since the audition was already over – and clearly wouldn't lead to anything – they'd have no reason to worry that it would affect the band or the album we'd started to make.

But when I walked into the shop the next morning, the phone was already ringing.

'Hello?'

'Ze Peter Mensch vood lick to talk from you.'

Olga. The very last person I'd been expecting to hear from. Especially at this hour.

'Er . . . okay then,' I said. 'When would be a good time?'

'Remain on ze line.'

Then: 'Hey . . . good morning, Brian – it's Peter.'

'Oh, hello Peter,' I said. 'Look, I just want to thank you for last night, that was one of the greatest experiences of my life, would you please thank the lads? They really couldn't have been nicer.'

Peter chuckled down the line. 'You'll get used to Angus – he's a man of few words,' he said.

'The Brown Ale was a lovely touch,' I told him.

'Listen, we'd like you to come back,' he said.

Oh, shit . . .

The flat-out rejection that I'd been expecting would have been far easier to handle than a second audition, which meant more nerves, more raised hopes and more uncertainty. And, as usual, the logistics would be a nightmare. We now had a serious backlog of vinyl jobs. I'd promised Joanne and Kala that I'd take them out at the weekend. And I had a show that night – this would have been a Tuesday or a Wednesday – followed by gigs all weekend. We even had a gig lined up for Monday at Heaton Buffs – and that was going to be a big one, with a crowd of 300 to 400 people.

'Okay,' I said, desperately trying to think of how I could make yet another midweek drive to London work – but this time without the convenient cover story of needing to record a jingle for a Hoover advert. 'How about, er . . . next Wednesday?'

'We were thinking tomorrow,' said Peter. 'We can fly you down if that helps?'

I was sweating now. This was all moving so fast – and I hated the feeling of losing control.

'Oh no, no, no,' I told Peter. 'I'll drive – I like to drive.' Which of course meant: if I drive, I'll be in control. I can just jump in my car at any moment and take off.

'Fair enough,' said Peter, 'but we insist on paying for your petrol and all your other expenses.'

'That's very good of you.'

'Just one more thing,' he added.

Oh, shit, here comes the catch.

'Can you learn "Highway to Hell" before you get here?'

I grinned.

That wasn't much of a catch. I loved that song.

If you'd have been driving down the A1 to London the following day, you might have passed a thirty-two-year-old Geordie in a cloth cap driving a borrowed Toyota Crown at seventy-plus, singing his head off to a cassette of 'Highway to Hell'. A friend of mine had insisted on lending me the Toyota – Simon Robinson was his name, he ran a rustproofing business around the corner from the vinyl shop – because he was convinced that the Jag wouldn't survive a second round-trip to London.* As for the cassette, it belonged to another friend, who'd given me the third degree when I'd asked if I could borrow it for a day. 'What d'you need that for?' he'd demanded to know. 'That's my favourite album that is! You can't fucking lose it!' In the end, I'd had to lie and say that we were thinking of adding some of the songs to Geordie II's set list.

Once again, I'd been told to head to Vanilla Studios, where Malcolm, Angus, Cliff and Phil would be waiting. But this time, there was no messing around with rounds of pool or bottles of Newcastle Brown Ale. It was straight to business.

* Ironically enough, one of the Toyota's tyres blew just outside of Newcastle, so I had to spend half an hour kneeling by the side of the car in the mud and drizzle, changing the wheel. Not ideal when you've got a five-hour drive and a big job interview ahead.

First, we ran through 'Highway to Hell' a couple of times – which felt just as good as I'd hoped it would – then Malcolm announced that they'd been working on the title track for the new album.

'It's a tribute to Bon,' he said. 'About death, but not in a morbid way or anything. More of a celebration – with some rock'n'roll swagger. It's called . . . "Back in Black".'

'Are there any words?' I asked, hardly able to believe that I was actually a part of this, you have to understand.

'No words, mate. No melody. Right now, it's just a riff that goes round and round. Angus, play Jonna the—'

It was so loud, I almost ducked.

'Hey Jonna,' called out Malcolm, as Angus repeated the riff, still at nosebleed volume. 'We'll just keep going with this, see what you can do over the top. Take your time . . .'

I nodded back.

But as Angus continued, I felt suddenly light-headed. *This was one of the best fucking riffs that I'd ever heard in my life.* And I was supposed to just . . . sing over it? Sing *what*? The title of the song? And what about the tune? – without thinking, I just opened my mouth and I screamed.

'BACK IN BLACK!' the air just exploding out of my lungs, 'I HIT THE SACK!'

Oh, *fuck*, that might work!

I tried the 'Back in Black/I hit the sack' line again – it still sounded great – but I just had to keep singing the first thing out of my head stuff over the rest of the riff, because no more words were coming out of me. At least the melody had started to take shape, though – and for the briefest of moments, I felt a change in the room. People were appearing from behind mixing desks and amplifiers, people I hadn't noticed before. Eyes were moving. There was a buzz in the air. I mean, there's no mistaking the look on someone's face when they hear something for the first time that gives them chills. It's involuntary. Their ears send a message to the muscles in their face, and there's absolutely nothing that you can do about it. For the first time, I began to feel this sense of belonging, but it was gone as soon as I'd noticed it. And when I looked around again to try and gauge the band's reaction:

Nothing.

They were lost in the music.

Totally unreadable.

'Sorry, lads,' I said, when we finished the first 'Back in Black' session, 'I wish I had more than those two lines.'

'No worries,' said Malcolm.

'I know it's a bit straight and sudden,' I added, meaning the direct attack of the melody. 'It just popped into my head, so I sang it. I really hadn't expected it to come out that way . . .'

Looking back now, of course, I think the lads got their first glimpse of a way forward when they heard me improvise the opening line of that song. Even if it was just for a couple of seconds. Remember, they had to follow 'Highway to Hell', while respecting and building on Bon's legacy. But they couldn't just hire a Bon impersonator. They needed someone a bit different . . . but not *so* different that they ended up throwing away everything that they'd already built. The pressure on them was even greater than it was on me.

Unlike the first audition, when I drove straight home afterwards, I stayed overnight at a hotel near Lord's Cricket Ground. I don't remember the name of the place. I just remember thinking, what the fuck am I *doing* here? This is brilliant. But AC/DC were footing the bill, and it would have been rude for me to just insist on heading home.

Keeping me company at the hotel was a guy called Keith Evans, one of AC/DC's roadies. We'd get to know each other well over the years that followed, and we became great friends.

'I think you've got it, mate,' he kept telling me, which was nice of him, but I wished he'd shut up because it was making me so nervous, I didn't know what to do with myself. I'd sung enough with AC/DC by now to know that being their singer would be the greatest job in the world. Even though I'd taken a chance leaving Parsons with the first Geordie and that had ended badly, this made all of that go away.

'Actually,' I told Keith, 'I think they're still trying to make their minds up. This is *big* for them.'

'Nah,' he replied. 'They're dying to get back on the road, they're not going to waste any more time looking at other singers. I know these guys. I can tell what they're thinking – and they're thinking that with you, they've just found the missing piece.'

Later that night in the hotel, I was reading a copy of *Melody Maker* and saw a double-page spread about the band and that they were already in the studio, doing auditions while starting work on the new album. It was impossible to sleep – especially when I realized that I'd already forgotten the melody that I'd sung over the 'Back in Black' riff.

Great, I thought, that was the *one* thing that they liked . . . and I couldn't remember it.

I got back to Newcastle on the night before the Grand National, the big horse race.

The day of the race had always felt special to me, ever

since I'd bet my pocket money on Merryman II in 1960 and won enough money to buy a collection of toy cars and a model aeroplane. But this year's Grand National felt even more special because it was being held on 29 March, which also happened to be my old man's birthday. The plan was for the whole family to watch the race on television at home – it started just after three o'clock – then I'd give my dad his present, a bottle of Famous Grouse, his favourite whisky. After that, we'd have a celebration dinner.

That morning, I woke up late, wondering if I should place a bet, only to find Ken waiting for me when I came downstairs. My luck had apparently already run out in another, more important way. The papers were reporting that AC/DC had found a new singer . . . who obviously wasn't me. Instead, the lads had gone for one of their own – another Australian – as I'd predicted all along. In fact, they'd gone one better, because the guy they'd found – Allan Fryer, the lead singer of an Adelaide band called Fat Lip – had been born in Scotland, just like the Young brothers and Bon.

They really couldn't have asked for a better fit.

My reaction was just, 'Oh, well, there you go.'

The relief was greater than the disappointment, to be completely honest with you. I thought I was boxing well above my weight.

Besides, Allan Fryer was a great singer and a Scottish-born Aussie, so how could I argue with that?

Malcolm, Angus and the boys had done what they needed to do.

After passing on the news about Allan Fryer, Ken suggested that we walk up the hill to a pub called The Crowley for a beer. (It's now The Poacher's Cottage, I believe.) My ma was out somewhere and my dad had already gone off to his club, so I took Ken up on his offer and we shot a few games of pool, put some coins in the jukebox, and talked about how utterly surreal the last few weeks had been.

It was about 2 p.m. when I got back – and the house was still empty.

With an hour or so to kill before the race began, I made myself a cup of tea, raided the biscuit tin, and put my feet up. *Ahhhhhh*. It felt like *years* since I'd had a moment to rest . . .

The phone rang.

Oh, for God's sake.

I picked up the phone – and got the surprise of my life. It was Malcolm. Which made no sense at all. I mean, how had he got my home number? And was the guy *seriously* calling me at home to say, 'Thanks, mate, but hard luck, we hired someone else'?

'Hallow, Malcolm, my son.' I was feeling a lot more relaxed with him than I had been before, now that I knew for sure that I was out of the running. 'Are you doing alright?'

'Yeah, I'm alright,' he said.

'Glad to hear it. So, what's up?'

'Look, uh, Brian, we were just thinking . . . are you okay to come back down here and start working on more tracks for the new album? We really liked the way "Back in Black" was going.'

There was a long pause. I took the phone handset away from my ear and looked at it, thinking, either I'm hallucinating from the beers at The Crowley, or this guy's taking the piss.

'. . . what do you mean?' I asked.

'Well, we've got to make this new album, y'know.'

'Mate, I don't understand,' I said. 'I just read in the press that Allan Fryer is your new singer.'

'Oh, no, no no . . . they got that wrong, mate. Totally wrong. The guy didn't even audition.'

Suddenly my chest tightened.

'Are you trying to tell me . . . that I'm *in* the band?' I was hardly able to get the words out.

'Well, y'know . . .' Malcolm laughed softly, deflecting the question.

God bless him, but he was just as scared of getting burned as I was.

'Look, Malcolm,' I said, deciding to be bluntly honest, 'you're a good lad, I had a great time with you and the boys, but I'm having a hard time believing there's no bullshit going on here. So, I'm going to put the phone down. And if you're *really* serious, would you ring me back in ten minutes and tell me that news again. Because I'm confused, and I feel like I'm dreaming.'

'Okay, Brian,' said Malcolm, 'I understand. I'll call you back in ten minutes.'

Click.

I was frozen. I just sat there, staring into space, counting down the ten longest minutes of my life. If this was real, it meant that everything I'd been through for the last ten years had been worth it. Throwing myself out of the back of a plane for a P.A. system. Giving up a good career at Parsons for a band that had only one Top 10 hit. Slumming it on the road for months – no, *years* – at a time. Falling for every music-industry racket ever invented. Ending up so broke, I had to go to court to stop my house being repossessed. My marriage disintegrating. Moving back in with my parents. Dealing with all those pompous fucking working men's club concert chairmen with their rules and regulations and decibel meters and disciplinary tribunals—

'Alright Brian, it's Malcolm again – calling you back like I said I would. Look, we've got to leave town in a week or two to start recording the new album, so we need you to come down to the rehearsal studio tomorrow and start getting ready. So, if you're up for that . . .'

'So, I really *do* have the job?' I asked. 'I'm not just going to be the backup guy or something?'

There was a long pause. Malcolm took a deep breath. 'Well,' he said, with a hint of mischief in his voice, like he was enjoying keeping me in suspense. 'It's yours if you want it, mate.'

And with that, I went from being a vinyl roof fitter to the new lead singer of one of the most exciting bands in the world. It was . . . quite a moment. It left me totally paralysed, in fact.

'Brian?' said Malcolm, after a couple of moments had passed. 'You still there?'

'Aye,' I managed.

'And you're in?'

'OH, FUCK, YEAH!! Where do I sign?'

'You know you're going to have to take a fair bit of flak, right, mate? Because our band . . . they hate us. The critics. The establishment. And it's gonna take the fans a while to adjust. Are you sure you can take all that heat, Jonna?'

'No,' I grinned, 'but who gives a fuck? I'm in.'

20

Breaking Up

⚡

If there was ever a moment in my life when I wanted to share some good news with somebody, this was it. But there was no one to tell. Ken had long since gone home. My ma and dad were still out. It was unbearable. I felt like I was about to explode. There wasn't a drop of alcohol in the house, other than the bottle of Famous Grouse that I'd bought for my dad's birthday. And I could hardly drink that. Although . . . this *was* an emergency. And my old man would surely understand. Ah, fuck it, I thought, opening it up and taking a swig. Then I just stood there, looking around the room, thinking, here I am, thirty-two years old, living with my parents in the same council house that I grew up in, with the same view over the railway line to the power station and Vickers tank factory, and now I've just had a phone call that's going to change everything . . . maybe forever. The kind of phone call that never comes in most people's lives.

I took another swig . . . then another . . .

In came my dad from his club. My ma close behind.

'Happy birthday, Dad,' I said, holding up the whisky. 'I got this for you.'

My dad gave me a funny look. 'Did you eat my cake too?'

'Oh, I'm sorry about that,' I said, realizing the bottle had been invaded. 'I'll buy you another one.'

'Bloody right you will.'

'It's just . . . I've been offered a job, Dad. A big one. So, I wanted to celebrate.'

'A job?' he said. 'With who?'

'AC/DC.'

My dad sat down on his chair with a groan. 'AC/DC, you say? Haven't they just been nationalized?'

I put my head in my hands. 'They're a rock band, Dad.'

'Oh . . . well, I've never heard of them.' In my dad's opinion, if he hadn't heard of a band, that meant they'd failed to achieve any kind of meaningful success whatsoever. Then again, The Beatles to him were a bit of a challenge.

Then in came my ma.

'I got a new job, Ma,' I told her, bursting with pride. 'I'm the new lead singer of AC/DC!'

'Oh, that's a-nice, son,' she said. 'Would you like a sandwich?'

It was impossible. It just meant nothing to them. Also, as far as they were concerned, turning professional with a band had been the cause of all my problems. So, the thought of me doing it again – and giving up my business – only confirmed their deepest fears that there was no hope for me.

At least Maurice understood. 'AC/DC?' he said, when I phoned him. 'They're canny good, them.'

When the Grand National was over – the winner was Ben Nevis, the horse my dad had backed – it was time for me to head over to Westerhope Comrades Club for Geordie II's show that night.

As usual, the place had sold out, with a queue out of the door and halfway down the street. (I still have the flyer somewhere – admission was 55p.) Also on the bill that night was Dave Black's band Goldie. And because Dave Robson's brother Geoff was also in Goldie, it felt like a very close-knit, family affair.

I remember just sitting there in the audience, listening to Goldie play their hit single, 'Making Up Again', and this girl came up to me and said, 'I heard that AC/DC got a new singer, but it should have been you, you'd have been perfect for that.' And I just smiled and nodded, feeling like I was in one of those scenes in a movie where everything goes quiet around you because you know that something huge is about to happen, but you can't breathe a word about it.

All I could think was – how am I going to get out of this life that I've built for myself here? I'm going to kill my band-mates' dreams. I'm going to break my girlfriend's heart. I'm going to put good-hearted Ken out of a job. And there's always a chance that it will all go tits up.

What I couldn't have known, of course, was that in just a few years' time, the golden age of the working men's clubs would be over, and they'd all start to close down. Meanwhile, the vinyl roof craze would also end just as quickly as it had started. Staying in Newcastle, in other words, would have been a far greater risk than joining AC/DC.

But on that night at Westerhope Comrades Club, I felt like I'd planted a bomb that was going to hurt everyone around me when it went off. And all I could do was sit there, rehearsing what I was going to say, how to explain why being excited and sad at the same time does really tear you up.

The day before I set off for London to start my new job was about as rough as you'd imagine.

My appointment still hadn't been made official, but at this stage, I had to come clean to those closest to me.

Telling my girlfriend was the worst part. She knew

immediately that she'd lost me, she just knew. Not because I
didn't want to be with her anymore, but because she wanted
to settle down, and that would be impossible if I was in a
band. She was devastated. 'Please,' she said, 'I don't want to
lose you.' It was the saddest thing, it really was. I mean, she
was stunning and classy – we could have had a beautiful life
together. But I'd given up on having a normal life when I'd
left Parsons.

Then it was time to go and tell Ken. I said to him, 'Look,
it's going to take a couple of months to record this album
and see how it does, and if I don't come back, the business is
yours.' He seemed happy about that, but of course I was
worried that it would all fall apart as soon I was gone – after
all, the main reason that we were doing well was the quality
of our work, but I was the one who did most of the fitting.

Finally, I had to call for a band meeting at the pub with the
two Daves and Derek in Geordie II.

They were in shock, of course. 'Look,' I said, 'I've been
offered this job, but it hasn't been announced yet and I don't
know what's going to happen, but it seems real, and I'm off
to London tomorrow to start working on the new album. I
just need a bit of time.'

It was like a funeral, the mood was so grim.

'Jesus, I really thought we were going to make it,' said
Davy, staring into his pint.

'So, Heaton Buffs is off?' asked Derek.

'Everything's off . . . for now,' I said – and I could see the
horrible realization on everyone's face that all the gigs would
now be gone. It was the worst feeling, knowing that I was
responsible for that. 'Look, if it doesn't work out, lads,' I
added, 'we can get back together. But I have to try this.'

Once the news had sunk in, though, the lads couldn't have

been nicer or more generous about it. They knew that no man could have turned it down. They were just the greatest guys, they really were. In fact, it's no exaggeration to say that some of the best times of my life were shared with Geordie II.

On that day I should have been playing at the social club in Heaton Buffs again – Monday, 31 March – but instead I was at E-Zee Hire rehearsal rooms in King's Cross for a meeting with Peter and the band. He told me that I'd be paid the same as the rest of the band, and given 'per diems' whenever the band took me away from home. I had no idea what a per diem was, having never been paid one before – but Peter explained that it was cash-in-hand that I'd be given every day on the road to cover 'incidental expenses'.

All I could think was, there must be a catch. But this time, amazingly, there wasn't. I was playing in a different league now.

Then Peter asked me if there were any other 'loose ends' that needed to be tied up.

I told him about Red Bus, and he made a note to find out what the terms of my contract were.*

'So, what else, aside from Red Bus?' asked Peter. 'Do you have a mortgage?'

'Yes, I do, on a house that I don't even live in,' I told him.

'What's the balance?'

'I dunno. It cost £11,000 and I've been paying £70 a month under a court settlement.'

'Which bank is it with?'

'Well, it's a building society, not a bank – and it's Leeds Permanent.'

---

* I'd later have to borrow £30,000 against my earnings to buy myself out.

'Okay, I'll call them and pay it off.'

'What? Are you *serious*?'

'Of course. Anything else we should know about?'

I was in shock at this point, but I remembered the previous night with the lads from Geordie II. I told Peter that I felt really bad about them, because we'd had to cancel a month's worth of gigs, and they were all hard-working guys who could do with the money. I told him that I would love to use some of my salary to reimburse them for the month of April, which would at least soften the blow while they found a new singer.

'Would £2,000 be enough?' asked Peter.

I almost fell off my chair. He wasn't kidding, either – he later gave me the cash in a brown envelope, and I took the lads out to an Indian restaurant and handed it out over dinner. I couldn't have been happier to help them out after leaving the band so suddenly.

'One last thing,' said Peter. 'The boys want to make you a full member of AC/DC. I know you were just an employee with Geordie, but this time we're looking for a total commitment.'

'So . . . what does that mean?'

'It means you don't just get a salary. You get a fifth of the profits.'

'There's *profits*?' This was a foreign language to me.

'Not yet, no,' Peter replied.

'Oh,' I said. 'Well, never mind. Maybe if the new album does well . . .'

'Well, that seems fair enough.'

The announcement that I'd been hired as AC/DC's new singer came the next morning – April Fool's Day – by which time we were already rehearsing the new album, which we were going to record at Polar Studios in Sweden.

After my business meeting with Peter, Malcolm had handed me one of those yellow, wide-ruled legal pads and asked if I wanted to have a go at writing lyrics for one of the riffs. Now, my memory as to *when* exactly this happened is a little hazy, given how quickly things were moving – but most of the photographs taken of me at E-Zee Hire show me holding the pad, so I probably put pen to paper for the first time there, even though most of the writing happened later.

It was just a few lines, that's all Malcolm wanted at first. But, of course, at this point in my career, I'd only ever written a couple of songs for Geordie. What's more, given how strong the riff in question was, I was going to have to come up with something pretty special.

Trying to live up to Bon's songwriting legacy was the hardest part of it all. Bon had been the ultimate working-class wordsmith, from the non-stop double-entendres of 'Big Balls' to his joyful and downright hilarious account of a one-night-stand with a nineteen-stone Tasmanian woman in 'Whole Lotta Rosie'. While he was alive, of course, the critics had sort of missed the whole point of his lyrics – but after his death, they'd suddenly developed a newfound respect for his wonderful way with words. Not that Bon had ever given a shit what they said. The sneers of the establishment were probably a badge of honour to him.

I had no idea if I was capable of writing anything even one per cent as good as Bon's best songs. So, the second that I was given the legal pad and instructed to get something down on paper, I decided that I needed to find somewhere quiet where I could put my brain to work. But, of course, I was in a rehearsal room at King's Cross, leaving me with very few options for peace and quiet.

Write about what you know, Brian, I kept telling myself. But, of course, cars were the only thing I knew about. Well, cars and women. Actually . . . hang on a minute, I was getting an idea . . . 'She was a fast machine,' I wrote, 'She kept her motor clean.' Then a moment later, I added, 'She was the best damn woman that I ever seen.'

I was pretty chuffed with my effort. Now all I had to do was write another two verses, and a chorus . . .

During the week of those E-Zee Hire sessions, I was put up at the Holiday Inn, Swiss Cottage – which felt dead posh to me at the time. The only other member of the band staying there was Phil because everyone else had their own flat.

After each long day of rehearsals and writing, Phil and I would go back to the hotel and grab a quick bite to eat and a couple of beers. But I quickly realized that, unlike me, Phil wasn't much of a talker, so as soon as we were finished with dinner, we'd head back up to our rooms. It was unnerving. I started to wonder if he knew something that I didn't . . . like maybe that the band were having second thoughts.

One night, Phil must have noticed the look of concern on my face as we got into the lift.

'Hey Jonna,' he said, 'don't worry – we love you, mate.' Then he grinned and said, 'You'll be fine, mate.'

The relief was overwhelming because inside I really didn't know. So, God bless you, Phil, for saying that. It meant the world to me.

The weirdest part of joining AC/DC was suddenly being part of a social circle where it was entirely normal to hang out with other musicians – and not just any, but *heroes* of mine.

On our second day at E-Zee Hire, for example, in walked Ozzy Osbourne, the guy I'd listened to obsessively during my lunch breaks at Parsons. I couldn't believe it. And the crazy thing was, he walked right over to me, shook my hand, and wished me all the best in my new job. What made Ozzy's words even more touching was that he'd been a friend of Bon's. It was a really big moment for me – thank you, Ozzy.

The next night, meanwhile, Malcolm invited me to a pub in Maida Vale – The Warrington, next to a big roundabout – and it was packed with musicians. So, I went over there and had a pint with Malcolm and Cliff, and next thing I knew, Les Gray from Mud was sitting at our table, and he was going, 'Hello Brian, congrats on the gig.'

It was too much. It was a complete whirl.

Another night, I went over to Malcolm's flat, and this fab-ulous bearded American guy came in, and Mal said, 'Meet Brian, he's our new singer.' I quickly ended up deep in con-versation with the guy, and it turned out that he'd survived a plane crash in Mississippi. That was when I realized that he was in Lynyrd Skynyrd. Half of the band had died in that crash, it was absolutely terrible. It must have been Gary Rossington. He was still having trouble with his arm and walking with a limp.

There were so many other moments like that. I wanted to write down every detail, so I'd never forget it – but of course, I did.

Towards the end of our time at E-Zee Hire, the band's favourite photographer – a guy called Robert Ellis – stopped by. He'd been asked by Atlantic to take some publicity shots for the new album. It felt like months had passed, but it was only 4 April, barely a week since I'd arrived in London, and only three days since my hiring had been announced.

Phil was nowhere to be found, so we ended up doing some shots without him. Malcolm took up Phil's position on the drum stool for one classic picture. In another one, I sat on the drum riser, wearing my '22' shirt, holding the writing pad. Then when Phil finally showed up, we went outside to do some shots against a brick wall.

When the second the photo shoot was over, though, Peter came over to deliver some disappointing news: Polar Studios in Stockholm was no longer available because ABBA had just booked it.

'So where are we going?' asked Malcolm.

'Compass Point,' shrugged Peter – to which everyone just nodded and went back to work.

I waited a moment; I was too embarrassed to put up my hand in front of the lads, then took Peter aside.

'Where's Compass Point?' I asked him. I mean, at this point in my life, my knowledge of North East working men's clubs was unrivalled by anyone, but when it came to the world's most expensive and far-flung recording studios, I was clueless.

'Well, I hate to be the bearer of bad news, Brian,' said Peter, looking very serious for a moment. 'But' – he broke into a grin – 'we're going to be dragging you to The Bahamas.'

21

Welcome to Paradise

✦

I wasn't even a week into my new job, and already I was being jetted away to a tropical island in the West Indies. I could get used to this, I thought.

Now, I should probably mention that Compass Point Studios in 1980 was nowhere near as famous as it would be later. It had been built just three years earlier by Chris Blackwell. He'd wanted it to be a place where musicians like Island's own Bob Marley could work without any of the distractions of a big city.

Meanwhile, we'd been told that we'd have to share part of the studio with a band from New York called Talking Heads.

Only two weeks earlier, I was on stage at Westerhope Club full of working men and women – and now there I was, flying to the same recording studio that The Rolling Stones had just used. It didn't feel real. And in a way, it *wasn't* real, because I still had to prove that in picking me for the job, Angus, Malcolm and the boys in the band had made the right decision.

At least one thing hadn't changed – our seats were still at the back of the plane, just as they had been when Geordie went to Australia all those years earlier.

It was strange suddenly being in such close proximity with the band for the first time. But Peter immediately broke the ice by producing a bag full of professional-grade Sony Walkmans – the posh ones that came in a special leather case – then handing them out. I felt like a kid on Christmas morning when I got mine. The Walkman had been out only about a year at this point. It was the most high-tech thing that I'd ever seen in my life – and when I put on the headphones and hit play, the sound quality was better than just about anything that I'd ever heard before. And, of course, the boys had brought along a cassette of the riff that they'd been working on, so I spent a part of the next six hours getting familiar with it, and thinking about what I could sing over the top, all while downing as many beers as the flight attendants would give me.

I didn't expect to sleep a wink during the entire 4,000-mile flight, but the booze kicked in, the lights went out, and my head went dead.

It was still daylight when we landed. I looked out of the window at palm trees and blue sea. It was paradise.

It took all of five minutes for us to run into some trouble once we were off the plane though.

The customs officers basically took one look at our long hair and denims and decided that they didn't want us on their island – so they pulled Malcolm and Angus aside and started to interrogate them about what was inside their guitar cases. It was the same power game played by people in uniform the world over. But what the customs officers didn't realize was that Malcolm and Angus were pretty good at playing the same game themselves – and they could out-intimidate just about anyone. So, this incredibly long and tense stand-off ensued, until eventually the lead officer snapped and declared that he was confiscating everything.

And that was that – our guitars were impounded – while Malcolm and Angus were dragged away for more questioning. It took hours. And even though the lads were eventually released, their gear wasn't, including the guitars – amongst them Malcolm's Gretsch and Angus's Gibson – that we needed to start making the album.

'Oh, don't worry about it, Brian,' said Peter, 'it's just the way it goes.'

Malcolm and Angus didn't like anyone in a uniform, Peter explained. They just got their hackles up if spoken to disrespectfully. At the first sign of trouble, they'd put up this shield of immediate and total resistance – and if they thought they were being picked on, they wouldn't give an inch.

As for my own suitcase, the customs officers couldn't confiscate it because I didn't have one. I just had a carrier bag containing two pairs of socks, three pairs of underpants, one pair of jeans, a denim jacket, three T-shirts – including the '22' one – and a cloth cap.* That was it.

We were put up in a guesthouse right where the jungle ended and the beach began – and when I say beach, I don't mean a beach like Whitley Bay in Newcastle, or even Bondi Beach in Sydney. No, this was a *proper beach*, a *Robinson Crusoe beach*, with powder-soft white sand, swaying palm trees, and water of the most perfect aquamarine blue – although our guesthouses, in contrast, were about as basic as you could get.

What surprised me the most when we arrived was that even though the studio was only about 150 yards away, we were advised by our very large and strict Bahamian landlady to use our Honda Civic rental car to get there and back or

---

* That '22' T-shirt deserves a posthumous medal for valiant service. Not only did I wear it *every day* in The Bahamas, but also in all six videos to promote the album. (They were recorded in one afternoon in Belgium when we got back – then played on MTV for the next twenty years.) Sadly, the T-shirt was declared missing in action in late 1980. Next of kin were informed.

jump on one of the studio's 50cc motorcycles – and if we insisted on walking, she said, to always go in a group, and *never* at night. We thought that she was just being overprotective – probably on the orders of Atlantic Records, which wouldn't want us wandering off and getting distracted. But we soon found out that she had every reason to worry.

The Bahamas were in the middle of a crime wave. All kinds of boats were disappearing off the coast, stolen for drug-running. And there were these illegal gangs living in the forest, and hiding from the law. Dangerous buggers.

Armed robberies were also becoming common – especially home invasions. The victims had included Robert Palmer, who then lived opposite the studio.* While he was in the studio one night, some guys broke into his home, shot his dog, and held his poor mum and dad at gunpoint – which had left everyone who worked at Compass Point a bit shaken.

Our landlady wasn't taking any chances. Before she even showed us to our rooms, she presented us each with a harpoon gun. They weren't for fishing, she explained – but in case any nasty lads broke into our rooms while we were there. Then this guy came in and gave us each a machete, as a backup in case the harpoon guns failed. During my entire stay, I kept my harpoon gun by the door, and the machete under my bed – fully expecting to have to use them both at some point.

As for my room . . . it wasn't really a room. It was more like a little hut, about twelve feet by twelve feet, with a single bed, a handbasin, a small writing desk and a toilet.

No AC and no television, obviously.

Meanwhile, it was so hot and so humid, I didn't know what to do with myself. And, of course, I hadn't brought any

* This was six years before 'Addicted to Love'.

shorts – never mind any swimming trunks – because the only shorts I had were for football, and they were back in Newcastle.

So, I just wore jeans, like everyone else in the band.

There was very little we could do for the first five days because of the impounded equipment, other than set up Phil's drums. I ended up just walking around the place, trying to find something to do, until I found a pool table and a foosball table in the studio's communal area. Then, just as I got some games going, the guys from Talking Heads appeared, taking a break from a session.

Great, I thought, some new people to talk to. David Byrne seemed confused by the pub etiquette of putting a coin on the side of the pool table. I must have explained it to him five times. But he kept looking at me like I was speaking a foreign language, which to be fair, to his ears, I probably was.

That said, we did end up getting along well with Tina Weymouth and her husband Chris Frantz – the bass player and drummer of Talking Heads. In fact, the two of them later helped us out by standing in for Phil and Cliff when they went missing out in the jungle one day.

While we were still waiting for our equipment, Malcolm woke up one morning to find all his money gone, so the police were called in, and there was an investigation that ended with the landlady going out on the beach with our tour manager Ian Jeffery, armed with their harpoon guns. They never did find the culprit – probably just as well because I didn't much fancy their chances against any of the local criminals.

Just as we were starting to think that our gear would *never* turn up, Keith Emerson appeared and invited us out on his boat. Keith was great. He had this incredibly cool little

303

speedboat with a cassette player built into the dashboard, which I thought was just the best thing ever. On a later fishing trip, Cliff managed to catch this massive tuna, which was a cause of great celebration – until it was established that none of us had the first idea how to cook the bloody thing because the only tuna that we'd ever seen before had come out of cans.

Cliff ended up cutting the giant creature into steaks, each about three or four inches thick, then he put them in the fridge in the guesthouse's kitchen. But that night there was a power cut, and when we went in there the next morning, it looked like the scene of a murder. Because of the heat and humidity, the fridge had basically turned into an oven, and the tuna had gone off – spectacularly – with the blood seeping out all over the linoleum floor. It smelled like a fart past its sell-by date in there. So, we left the landlady to fumigate the premises, and relocated to a more fragrant room – where we were relieved to hear that our gear had finally cleared customs.

At last, we could get on with what we'd come here to do.

And I was straining at the leash to get started.

This would probably be a good moment to mention the guy who'd been hired by the band to produce the album – Mutt Lange, teamed up on this occasion with the sound engineer Tony Platt. I'd met both of them when I was at E-Zee Hire in London, but to me they were just two of many, many faces that had stopped by during the auditions.

At the time, of course, Mutt wasn't really a well-known guy. Born in Zambia and raised in South Africa, he'd been in a few bands around Johannesburg, so he knew his stuff, and it was the record company that noticed he was a bloody good producer. That's when they cut him in to produce *Highway to Hell* for AC/DC, and the boys liked what they heard.

One of the first things I learned about Mutt when I got to know him in The Bahamas – aside from his work ethic – was that he shared Malcolm's gift for near-superhuman hearing.

During one session, I remember we were listening to a playback of one of the songs and Malcolm went, 'What's that noise?' None of us could hear anything out of place at all, of course, even after listening to it three or four more times. But then Mutt came in and immediately picked up on the same noise. So, he went through each track – bass, vocals, guitars, drums – turning them down in turn, until finally, there it was, a noise on one of the drum tracks like a tiny pair of castanets. But, of course, that begged the question, *what* was causing it? We just about turned the studio upside down to get to the bottom of it – and low and behold, it turned out that a crab had wandered in from the beach and was making the unwanted noise with its pincers in the corner of the room and getting picked up by the drum mics. How Malcolm or Mutt had managed to hear that over Angus's guitar was beyond me.

My other early impressions of Mutt were pretty limited – mainly because on the morning after our gear arrived and we started working on the album, Malcolm came into my room with a request that made it hard to concentrate on anything else.

'Hey Brian,' he said, 'how did it go with those lyrics that you were writing?'

'Oh, pretty good . . . I think,' I said, remembering the lines I'd written about the 'fast machine' who 'kept her motor clean' – which was now almost a complete song.

'Good to hear,' said Malcolm. 'Can you keep going and write the rest of the album?'

For a moment, I thought he was kidding.

But no – he wasn't kidding.

22

Rolling Thunder

⚡

It didn't take long for us to establish a kind of production line for the album.

Every night, Malcolm and Angus would choose which of the riffs they wanted to work on the next day, then they'd hand me a cassette of it, with the song title scribbled in pencil on the label. I still had my Walkman from the plane, so I'd just listen to the tape, over and over, while trying to come up with some words and phrases that would do the music justice. Some of the cassettes were literally just a beat track with fragments of Malcolm's guitar here and there. 'Well, Jonna, it's not all there quite yet,' Malcolm would say, 'but see if you can have a go at figuring something out . . .' Then we'd count out the beats together, and he'd tell me the moment when he thought the vocal line should come in. After that, I was on my own.

From then until the next morning, I'd be in my little hut of a room, sitting on the bed, writing away, and thinking.

I should probably take this opportunity to put some of the rumours about the writing of the *Back in Black* lyrics to bed. The conspiracy theories are legion – usually started by people who think they know what happened but weren't there. That includes one journalist in Australia who claimed that Bon Scott had already scribbled most of the words to the album in one of his notebooks before he died. But no – it was *me* at the end of the pen, writing every night and every morning, with only the title to work with. That's what happened. That's the truth and I really hope that settles it.

That said, there were a few moments – like at my first audition – when I really did feel as though Bon was looking over me. When I finished the lyrics to 'You Shook Me', I remember just instinctively looking up and saying, 'Thanks, mate.' I can't explain that. In that sense, Bon had a huge influence on the album. We all felt his presence.

It was usually around 11 a.m. when I finally took whatever I'd written over to Mutt in the studio and said, 'Right Mutt, I've got it.' As much as the pressure was on, it was exciting – and full on. With the amount of words that I had in my head, I could barely even think about the singing that would come later in the day. Mutt would photocopy my notes, give a copy to Tony, we'd listen to the riff, I'd sing out the words, then he'd ask me a few questions – 'What do you mean here?' – and after I'd explained what I was trying to get at, he'd make a note in the margins. And that was that. The song was ready.

What makes me smile the most when I look back is just how immediate it all was. Every line and word on that album was written with an overnight deadline. There was no time to second-guess anything. It just *had* to be done. I mean, with songs like 'Have a Drink on Me', everything just felt so good, and it all just seemed to flow so easily – the riffs, the tunes, the words. 'Whisky, gin and brandy, with a glass I'm pretty handy, oh I'm tryin' to walk a straight line, on sour mash and cheap wine . . .'

With anyone other than Mutt, the pressure might have been too much. But Mutt was such a gentleman, you knew right off the bat that it was okay to make mistakes in front of him – that if you took risks, he'd help you get it right. He's just one of those rare individuals in the music business who you can instantly trust – and the album would not have been the same without him.

Meanwhile, the boys would be arriving with their guitars as I was presenting my lyrics to Mutt. They'd go through some riffs, have a cup of tea, then Mutt would basically tell me to get out of the studio. 'Stay away, Brian,' he'd say, 'I want you fresh. I want you here after lunch, at about 2:30 p.m., can you do that? Then I'll need you until 4.30 p.m. or 5 p.m. at the very latest.'

To me, of course, that seemed like a ridiculously cushy schedule. I mean, I was used to working from the crack of dawn until the end of the day, and then going out and doing a gig, or even *two* gigs. And, of course, it was hot and sunny outside with the beach and the North Atlantic right there – I ended up buying myself a pair of swimming trunks from one of the local shops eventually – so I felt like I was on holiday.

'But I can do more!' I kept protesting at the end of each session.

'No, Brian,' would come the firm reply, in Mutt's unmistakable and somehow very reassuring Rhodesian accent, 'We're good for today.'

Whenever we were recording the vocals, the control room – in fact, the entire studio – would be empty. Mutt never let anything else happen during my sessions, so there were no distractions. I mean, Tony Platt would be there, of course, along with Benji Armbrister, the second engineer. Benji was a big part of making that record because he was around the entire time. Everybody liked him, and he could jump in and help with anything – he just kept the pace flowing. Benji looked very serious most of the time, but when he did smile, it was dazzling, and then you smiled – it was infectious. And he was the undisputed king of the Compass Point foosball table. Tony was also a bit of an unsung hero. A very quiet man, very together – and a great sounding board for Mutt. I mean, Mutt always made his own mind up, but he really listened to Tony. And when we weren't in the studio working, Tony was great company and a great drinking buddy.

Now, normally when you're recording a brand-new song, you have a guide track with a rough take of the vocals, to give you the structure. But there were no guide vocals for the songs on *Back in Black* – we just hadn't had the time to get them ready. So, all I could hear was the backing track that the lads had finished between 11 a.m. and 2.30 p.m. As for the melodies, I just had to come up with whatever worked on the spot. But strangely enough, that part came very naturally. I mean, I'd already written the words and had a good idea of how the vocals would go, so it was all very second-nature. I didn't even really psych myself before each session. I just walked into the studio, screamed a bit to loosen up – then did it.

Mal and Angus always had a rough idea of how they wanted the chorus sung, then we'd give it a shot in the studio, and it worked every time.

When I sang, meanwhile, I wore headphones and stood behind a screen in the studio – the technology wasn't good enough back then to sing without headphones in the control room, like I do today. And there was no echo or other aids when I was doing the takes, so it sounded very dry. This was the way Mutt liked it, but it was a bit unnerving because a dry vocal can sound lifeless when you hear it on its own. But it also made for a lovely surprise when I heard it played back later with all the atmosphere added in.

Mutt spent most of our early sessions trying to get me to sing higher. I honestly had no idea that I could even make those noises. I thought it was impossible. But Mutt had a knack of making the impossible possible – and once he'd got me into that upper register, it was like being released from a straightjacket. Suddenly, I was like . . . holy shit, *this is fun*! From then on, I wanted to do it all the time.

'Shake a Leg' was the hardest of all the tracks to get right, for me.

Part of that was just Mutt's never-ending quest to get me into a higher key. But the timing was also bloody hard to nail down – I kept coming in too soon – so we ended up doing it without the music, with Mutt clapping his hands on the beats. The vocals you hear on the album ended up being stitched together from two separate takes.

'Shoot to Thrill' is another hard one. There's just no recovery time between the verses at all – you need a third lung. As Joe Elliott from Def Leppard later told me – he ended up working with Mutt on *Pyromania* – there are certain songs that you can put together in the studio, but when you rehearse for a tour, you've got to learn them again from scratch. 'Shake a Leg' and 'Shoot to Thrill' were definitely two of those.

Meanwhile, Mutt was so focused on what he was doing, the feedback from him was minimal.

'That was fine, Brian,' he'd say after a take.

'Should I do it again?' I'd ask – wondering exactly where 'fine' lay on the scale of crap to great.

'No,' Mutt would reply, not making things much clearer, 'I've got what I want . . . thank you.'

When I was leaving the studio at about 5 p.m., the lads would be coming back in. They'd work until about seven, then we'd all have dinner, which was usually in the guesthouse, with the landlady cooking. I loved every minute of being in The Bahamas, but those dinners were some of my favourite moments. Every night we got to try something new. Fried plantains. Coconut goat curry. Every kind of fish and tropical fruit that you could think of. Just the freshest, most delicious food that you could ever taste.

After dinner, Mutt would nearly always call one or more of us back to the studio for another hour or so of work – usually Angus, to add an extra solo on something.

Even though you could see Compass Point from the guesthouse at night – it was all lit up, a glowing oasis of safety – no one objected to taking the car. It wasn't just the drug gangs that we were worried about. The local wildlife also made us pretty nervous. One night, I was watching TV sitting on the floor of the only room with a TV when I saw something out of the corner of my eye. I froze. It looked a little like a tarantula in my panic-stricken mind. Then it crawled over my knee. I flicked it off only to watch a crab limp back out of the door. The worst it could have done was nip me to death. Still, it scared the shit out of me. Another night, Mutt got bitten by a centipede, which apparently hurts more than you'd think.

No one ever complained about the long hours. We all knew what had to be done, how much it mattered. But as much as Mutt kept us to a strict schedule – we must have worked every weekend during our time on the island – it wasn't frantic. Mutt and Tony put in longer hours than anyone, of course – they were always the last ones in the studio at night.

I have to say that I bet each of the lads remember it differently, from their own viewpoint. From solos, drums, bass riffs, time spent in the studio – it was a crazy ride. I'd often join whoever was going to the studio in the evening and just sit there quietly at the back of the control room, listening to what was going on, so I could feel like I was a part of it. It was on one of those nights that Malcolm and Mutt came up with the idea to turn Angus's and Malcolm's guitar cabinet towards the wall in the corridor, which helped create that epic sound you hear on the album. It was such a simple thing . . . but *so* effective.

I've heard stories from different bands over the years about people constantly coming in and out of the studio, offering their opinion on everything, having screaming arguments. But that just didn't happen with Mutt. I mean, he would always listen to Malcolm and Angus because they knew exactly what they wanted, and it was his job to make that happen. But in the studio, he was very much the guy in charge because he was so well respected.

The strangest part of those night-time sessions was hearing my own voice coming out of the speakers. I'd look over at Mutt, Malcolm and Angus, and they'd just be completely immersed in what they were listening to.

The attention to detail of those three – the levels of concentration they could keep up – was unreal. They were all built the same way. It was no wonder they got on so well.

Two weeks in, I got a little dead in the head.

The songs just never stopped coming. I'd finish one lyric, then, 'Here you go, Brian', I'd get another riff and a title . . . until one morning, I realized that I was really brain dead. The weather had also taken a sudden turn for the worse, with a strong wind blowing in off the ocean and all these black clouds forming.

I must have been running late that morning because I

remember Mutt coming over to my room at the guesthouse instead of me going to the studio. The moment I opened the door to him and he saw the look on my face, he could tell that something was up.

'What's the matter, Brian?' he asked, standing in the doorway.

'I'm struggling here, Mutt,' I told him.

'Are we giving you too much?'

'I've just got a bit of writer's block, that's all. It'll pass.'

Mutt thought for a moment. 'Are you stuck on anything in particular?' he asked.

'Yeah, this new riff that Malcolm just gave me,' I said. 'It's called "Hells Bells" . . .' What I didn't mention was that back in Dunston, 'Hell's bells and buckets of shit' is a common expression. It basically just means, 'Oh, bollocks.'

Maybe that's what had thrown me off.

At that moment, from somewhere behind Mutt, we heard a noise like a naval battle at sea, loud enough to make the whole guesthouse shake.

'That's rolling thunder,' said Mutt. Having grown up in Southern Africa, he was familiar with tropical storms. But I'd never heard the expression before – and Mutt immediately saw the light go on in my eyes. 'There you go,' he said, 'your first line . . .'

On cue, the heavens opened – a downpour the likes of which I'd never seen before.

'Pouring rain,' I said.

'And listen to that wind . . .' said Mutt.

'It's coming on like a hurricane!' I said.

I mean, okay, maybe the conversation didn't go *exactly* like that, but it was close. Suddenly Mutt and I found ourselves grinning at each other. Thanks to the weather report that we'd just given, the first three lines of 'Hells Bells' had been written. Then, of course, lightning flashed across the sky – that became the fourth line – and I started to think of Bon, the inspiration for the whole album. Before I knew it, my pen was moving across the page. 'You're only young, but you're going to die,' I wrote.

The rest of the lyrics to 'Hell's Bells' would be finished within a couple of hours – but by then, the storm would be right over us, and the power would go off, so we couldn't get anything down on tape.

Still, that song was a big turning point for us – the moment when everything started to click. And once the power had been restored and the vocals recorded, Malcolm, Angus and Mutt would get the brilliant idea to start the track with a tolling bell, and make it the opener for the whole album, which quickly escalated into an even more outlandish plan to commission a foundry in Britain to cast a real one-ton bronze AC/DC bell . . . which we could carry around the world, with yours truly getting to ring it every night with a Thor-like metal sledgehammer.

'Yeah lads, great idea, great idea,' I said to them when they first explained it all to me.

It didn't occur to me for one second that they were actually being serious.

A few days after 'Hells Bells' was done, some happy news arrived from England – Malcolm's wife, O'Linda, had given birth to a baby girl, Cara. To celebrate, we threw a big party at the studio, but of course by this time we were all starting to miss our families, and I couldn't help but think of Joanne and Kala back home, and how much I wanted to give them both a big hug. It was the longest I'd ever been away from my girls in my life, even counting my time in Geordie. And in those days, you couldn't just pick up the phone. International calls had to be booked in advance and cost an arm and a leg. Your only other way of communicating was via letters and postcards but, of course, anything posted in The Bahamas would take forever to reach Newcastle.

Cliff spent hours that day creating a massive, triple-pronged spliff that was such a work of art, no one wanted him to light it. But he did. Then of course came the toasts – even Angus had a swig, and he doesn't drink – and before long we were more than just a bit merry.

I had my first-ever hit on a joint that night. It was amazing that at the age of thirty-two, I was still a virgin of the ganja. It was also the first time that I'd ever listened to music while stoned. I remember at some point we all went back to the control room, and Mutt started playing a rough mix of 'You Shook Me'. I just sat there with this massive grin on my face. I couldn't stop smiling. It almost hurt. At some point, Malcolm noticed the look on my face and said, 'Are you alright there, Jonna?'

'That's one of the best rock songs I've ever heard in my life,' I said, high as a kite.

'Oh, you think so, do you?' laughed Malcolm.

'Aye, I do. Honestly Mal . . . I think itsh right up there with "Get Back" by The Beatles.'

That was when the conversation ended – or so I was told by the boys the next morning – because I slid down the back of the mixing desk and fell asleep on the studio floor.

The vocals for 'Back in Black' were one of the biggest challenges of the whole album for me. Not only was I desperate to remember how I'd sung those first two lines in the audition, but I also had to follow up on them with something just as good for the rest of the song. And not just the vocal line, but the words too. I had so much momentum at that point, though, that the words just poured out of me – and to this day, I'm particularly proud of lines like, 'I've got nine lives, cat's eyes, abusing every one of them and running wild.' It was just magical, the way that song came together.

Mutt was a bit confused when he first saw what I'd written. I mean, those first two lines, 'Back in black, I hit the sack', sound like the start of a rap song, but this was years before 'rock-rap' was ever a thing. Even *rap*-rap was still in its infancy. But when I explained the metre of it to Mutt, he thought about it for a moment, then went, 'Oh, okay, I get it, clever, clever.'

Later that day, when it came time to do the vocal take, it was like something took over me. I've no idea how I produced those spasms of energy, I really don't. I couldn't contain them. It was almost scary. It was like I had this demon inside of me, and I was going, where did *that* come from? And, of course, Mutt was going, 'Do you think you could get just a little higher there?' And I was looking at him, thinking, *Higher?* Are you fucking kidding me? But he ended up getting it out of me – and without the use of a nutcracker to the testicles, contrary to what some have since claimed.

I think Mutt's secret in the studio is, he understands. The guy can play and sing just about anything that you can.

On the few nights we had off during our time in The Bahamas, I became well acquainted with the bar down the street called Traveller's Rest. (I'm pretty sure it's still there today.)

It sold things like Bahama Mama cocktails, made with pineapple, coconut and rum. They didn't taste like alcohol, they tasted like fruit juice. We got absolutely rat-arsed on those things – they were delicious. One night, after a few too many Bahama Mamas, I had a memorable encounter with a girl who claimed to be a former Miss Bahamas. She was American, and we ended up skinny dipping in the sea and the other stuff.

Another night, towards the end of making the album, we all went out to dinner to celebrate everything coming together – but Malcolm stayed behind in the studio to work on the last song, which still needed a riff. When we returned, he presented us with the unforgettable hook of 'Rock and Roll Ain't Noise Pollution' – the title again inspired by Bon, who'd once told the boys about an argument that he'd had with his landlord over the volume of his music. The landlord had apparently threatened to report Bon to the police for 'noise pollution' – the whole neighbourhood had been complaining – to which Bon had shouted back, 'Rock'n'roll ain't noise pollution!' I couldn't believe what Malcolm had come up with in just a couple of hours. It's one of those stealth songs on the album that creeps up on you the more you listen to it.

Five weeks after I'd arrived in paradise, my work was done, which meant that it was time for me to fly home. That's how it worked with the album. As soon as someone was finished, they were just gone, saving money on the room and board and the per diems.

Phil had been the first to leave, I think. Then Cliff. Then it was my turn.

Malcolm and Angus would stay another week or two, adding a few solos and other finishing touches here and there, helping Mutt with the final mix – leaving only the small matters of artwork, mastering and presenting the album to Atlantic Records.

Although five weeks is an unbelievably short time to make such a monster of an album, I felt like I'd been there a lifetime. And the funny thing was, I'd only heard one single unfinished track.

I had no idea how good the record was. I just knew I was really happy with what we had done.

„AC - DC"
29/6/80
300 Fr.

01344

Palais des Expositions - NAMUR

AC - DC

+ SUPPORT

Dimanche 29 juin 1980 à 20 h 30

23

Back from Black

⚡

My plane landed at Heathrow on 5 May, a bank holiday Monday. I remember that because it was the same day the S.A.S. stormed the Iranian Embassy in London. REAGAN DID A DEAL AND THE IRANIANS FREED U.S. HOSTAGES IN TEHRAN. It was surreal to be suddenly back in the real world, with the BBC and ITV both running continuous footage of this life-and-death raid.

Our lives in The Bahamas had been a laid-back breath of fresh air, in spite of all the work. I don't think we'd seen a single TV news report or newspaper headline while we were making the album. And now suddenly, here I was, back in London, where everything and everybody had to be somewhere real quick. Not that I minded. It was grand to be back in Britain, with the album finally done – like being dropped into the home end of a football stadium just after your team has scored a goal.

I took a taxi straight from the airport to Peter Mensch's office in Earl's Court. He asked me how the recording had gone, and I told him the truth – I had no idea. He said he'd heard good things, but hadn't got any official word – and I was like, *join the club.*

That was when Peter went over to his safe and brought out the biggest wad of cash that I'd ever seen in my life. It was my salary for the rest of the month, plus five weeks' worth of per diems. It was fucking insanity. I mean, I'd just come back from five weeks in The Bahamas, having the time of my life – if anything, I felt like I should have been giving *him* money. It was so much cash, I had nowhere to put it. I was stuffing it into my carrier bag of dirty laundry from the trip – and into every pocket of my jeans and denim jacket that I could find – like I'd just robbed a bank.

'So, what are you going to do now?' he asked.

'Well, I'd better get myself back to Newcastle and check up on the business and the kids.'

'Good idea, Brian,' he said.

'How long before you need me again?' I asked.

'Maybe a month?'

Then he asked me how I was planning to get home. I told him that I'd take a cab to King's Cross and then jump on the train, hoping to see my brother – I was dying to tell him all about The Bahamas. (And this time, I could afford to buy my own first-class ticket.) He asked me if I could do him a big favour instead. He'd just leased a Mercedes-Benz for the company, he explained, but the car they'd sent him was a 'stick-shift' – meaning it had a manual transmission. And being American – or more to the point, a New Yorker – Peter had only ever driven automatics, so he was too scared to drive the thing. Instead, it had been parked illegally outside since the day he'd got it, the pile of tickets on its windscreen getting bigger every day.

With that, he walked me over to the window, and we looked down on this absolutely fabulous Mercedes-Benz – but it was a rather dodgy latrine yellow colour – the kind of car that only captains of industry or the directors of football clubs could afford to drive.

'Would you mind taking care of it for a while?' he asked,

handing me the keys. 'It's a got a full tank of petrol, fully insured, only a thousand miles on the clock.'

'Are you kidding me?'

'Look, I know it's a pain in the ass, but the parking tickets are costing me a fortune.'

'Well . . .'

'Please . . . would you mind? It would be a huge, huge help . . .'

'Okay then. If you *insist*.'

I drove back up the A1 to Newcastle wearing the biggest shit-eating grin you've ever seen in your life. The car was brand new. It still had the smell. Even the key fob was huge and heavy, made of the softest leather that I'd ever felt, with a three-pointed star on it. I drove like I stole it.

All I could think was, I can't *wait* to take my girls out in this and spoil them rotten. The hardest part of being away by far had been missing Joanne and Kala. And now I was coming home in a Mercedes, and I could afford to buy them whatever they wanted.

My dad was the first to see the car. He wasn't impressed.

'That's a German car,' he growled, after I pulled up outside No. 1 Beech Drive.

'No, Dad. It's, er . . . American.'

'It's bloody German.'

'Well, it was *given* to me by an American.'

He at least let me drive him to his club in it. There were still no guarantees about what the future would hold, of course – but in that moment, I felt like I'd 'made it'.

The next morning, I went to see Ken at the shop.

'Oh Brian, you're back,' he said.

'Is everything okay, Ken?' I asked.

'Oh, yes. Although it's been very quiet these last few weeks.' He pointed at the Mercedes. 'Do you want me to put a roof on that? Did one of the dealerships send it over?'

'Ken,' I said, 'that's *my* car.'

'What? *Really?*'

I grinned proudly.

'Well, would you like a roof on it?'

'Where's the Maxi?' I asked, suddenly noticing that it was gone.

'Oh . . .' said Ken, his face dropping.

'Oh what?'

'There was an accident.'

'What *kind* of accident?'

'It caught fire. With all our materials in it. That's probably why it's been so quiet . . .'

I put my head in my hands and groaned.

Several weeks passed in Newcastle. By which time, The Bahamas and the tropical storms were all starting to feel like a very distant memory. I did get one phone call from Olga from the Volga, but that was it.

It felt weirdly normal at home, like nothing had changed apart from the car parked outside.

My ma and dad still hadn't heard of AC/DC and were still worried that it would all come to nothing. But Maurice was excited.

But there was in fact a good reason for the silence from the band.

What I didn't realize was that aside from working on the mastering and artwork, Malcolm and Angus had been deadly serious about the idea of starting 'Hells Bells' with a real tolling bell, then commissioning AC/DC's very own bell to take on tour with us.

And all of this had taken a massive amount of work.

It was Tony Platt who'd scouted around to find the exact bell he wanted to record, eventually settling on the Denison Bell in the Carillon Tower at the Loughborough War Museum in Leicestershire. Then he'd rented a mobile recording unit and gone over there to get it on tape. But every time the bell was struck, all the birds in the tower flew out, ruining the recording. And there was too much time between each ring of the bell to stop the birds from coming back. In the end, Tony had to abandon the effort and just wait for the band's own bell to be made.

The John Taylor & Co Foundry – also in Loughborough – had been chosen to cast the bell. Weighing in at 2,000 pounds, or exactly one ton, it had the AC/DC logo and the song title stamped on the side. The bell was finished just in time to make Atlantic Records' deadline, but there was a problem: it was smaller than the Denison Bell, so the tone wasn't quite right. Being a technical genius, however, Tony quickly found a solution – he simply slowed the tape down to half speed, making it a perfect match. In a touching gesture, Tony also asked the craftsman who had cast the 'Hell's Bell' to ring it for the final recording that's still played all over the world today.

I later found out that while the Hell's Bell was still in the foundry, the workers hung it from the ceiling and tapped it with a forklift truck to signal when it was time for a tea break.

So, for a while there, AC/DC had basically commissioned the world's most expensive dinner gong.

Finally . . . a package arrived for me.

It was one of the very first pressings of *Back in Black*.

After pulling the LP out of the protective cardboard sleeve, I just held it in my hands, staring at it, for what felt like hours. The cover was all black, with the AC/DC logo in grey outline, and the title in faded capital letters underneath. It was so simple . . . and so *unbelievably* cool.

I was desperate to hear how it sounded – but I had nothing to play it on because my parents still only had their Rediffusion radio. So, I phoned the one guy I knew who had a decent system at home – Derek Rootham, the guitarist from Geordie.

'Oh, you're back, are you?' he said. 'What have you been doing all this time then?'

'Well, if I can come over and use your record player,' I told him, 'you can hear for yourself . . .'

A couple of hours later, I was in Derek's living room, with *Back in Black* on the turntable. The opening track was of course 'Hells Bells', which begins with the bell, then Malcolm's main riff, then builds very slowly with Phil's bass drum and cymbals until it finally gets going, with my vocals starting at about the minute-and-a-half mark. That's quite a while and, for a moment, I thought they'd forgotten me. And all the while, I'm thinking, *this sounds fucking fantastic.* I mean, I had chills. But then I looked over at Derek, and he was frowning and shaking his head – and when we reached the 'Won't take no prisoners' line, he let out a little gasp and said, 'Ooh Jonna, that's *way too* high. You're singing way too *high* man!'

'*What?*'

'*Way* too high. Come on, I'll take you for a pint.'

And with that little kick in the guts, off we went for a pint!

It was late June – almost two months after I'd returned from The Bahamas – when we began rehearsing for the *Back in*

Black Tour at the New Victoria Theatre, opposite Victoria station in London. (Today, it's the Apollo Victoria.) We had all of four days to get our shit together. After that, the plan was to do a 'warm-up tour' in just two countries – Belgium and The Netherlands – with the big North American tour to coincide with the album's release set to begin on 13 July in Edmonton, Canada.

The main point of the rehearsals was to break in the material, while also breaking in . . . *me*. After all, everybody in the band knew all of the old songs, they'd been playing them for years. But they were new to me – well, apart from 'Whole Lotta Rosie' and 'Highway to Hell'. It was a hell of an ask. With Geordie II, we'd add maybe one or two new songs every few weeks. But now I had to learn a set list made up of songs from the band's previous six albums, along with most of the new material on *Back in Black*, which I'd only ever sung in the studio before.

As the rehearsals went on, meanwhile, the crew began putting together our set, until finally a delivery crew arrived with the Hell's Bell – and oh, what a magnificent beast it was. I mean, when this thing spoke it was menacing and magical, and brutal and sexy. When it was hoisted into position in the middle of the lighting rig, it looked absolutely *sensational*. But we wouldn't see it again for a while. When the rehearsals were over, the bell would be shipped off to Canada for the beginning of the North America tour – while we stayed in Europe for the warm-up shows.

The very first show of the warm-up tour – and my very first show as the new lead singer of AC/DC – was in Namur, about an hour south-east of Brussels, on 29 June, 1980. The venue was one of the halls at the Palais des Expositions. We were

327

expecting only about 2,000 people because the show hadn't been widely advertised. And by not widely advertised, I mean they'd basically kept it a secret because we wanted to find our feet before playing in front of a proper arena-sized crowd.

I was trying to stay calm and take it all in, but I couldn't eat. I couldn't sit still. My heart was pounding. I constantly needed to pee.

We were supposed to go on at 8.30 p.m., but then Peter came in with Ian Jeffery, the tour manager, and told us, 'Hold on' – a thousand more people than expected had shown up, so they needed to add extra seats in the hall. This was easy to do in a convention centre like this because the walls could be moved.

Okay, Brian, take it easy son, plenty of time.

The rest of the lads didn't seem fazed at all. They just sat there chatting away, having a beer and saying 'Okay, Brian?' and me saying 'Yeah, yeah, fine', as my brain was crammed with new songs, new words and fear of a fuck up.

I just wanted to get out there and go over the top with the lads and charge. I'd thought this was supposed to be a small, low-key show, in case anything went wrong. But no, they were letting in the extra thousand people, so we had to wait. Then after half an hour had passed, Peter and Ian came back in to say that a couple *more* thousand people had arrived. Fuck. There must have been some kind of word-of-mouth thing going on. And, of course, Peter wanted to move the walls again. So, he did . . . just in time for the next wave of fans to arrive. Anyway, this went on for what felt like a school maths class on a sunny day, until finally – by now very, *very* late – it was time for the show.

We were basically going to be playing to a packed-to-capacity arena.

Angus ran out first – and the crowd let out such an almighty, guttural roar it sent shivers down my spine. It was absolutely deafening – and seemed to go on forever. And it was in that moment that the full weight of the job that I'd taken on hit me for the first time. Then I remembered standing in the door of the plane for my first jump, and how I'd felt when I stood there, and there I was again. Only this time, I was in no danger at all . . .

In my mind it all went silent. I could see the lights just like my first jump from that plane. I felt ready. There's my cue. I had to push myself out this time. I've never had a rush like it. Ever.

And the crowd, the music and the band were my parachute.

24

The Last Bit before the End

⚡

There's nothing much more to write about *Back in Black* that hasn't already been written. All I can say is that when I walked out on stage that night in Namur, the support from the audience was beyond overwhelming. Everywhere I looked, I could see banners and signs with messages like, 'R.I.P. Bon' *and* 'Good luck, Brian'. A part of me really had feared that the fans would never accept another singer in Bon's place. But there I was, being welcomed. I'll always be grateful to AC/DC's fans for that – for giving me a chance.

Thank you, thank you, thank you . . .

It's hard to believe when I look back – in fact, I had to double-check it – but that first show included no fewer than *seven* songs from *Back in Black*, an album that wouldn't see the light of day for another four or five weeks. After the midway point of 'Highway to Hell', we did four of those songs *in a row* – 'What Do You Do for Money Honey', 'Rock and Roll Ain't Noise Pollution', 'Shoot to Thrill' and 'Givin' the Dog a Bone'.

Like I said before – AC/DC has always been an all-or-nothing kind of band.

What's also incredible is that the crowd stayed put and listened, totally absorbing every note – and by the second chorus of 'Have a Drink on Me', they were singing it back to us. We all believed in the album, of course – but that was beyond anything that we'd ever expected. By the time we got to 'Whole Lotta Rosie', the chants of 'Angus' between the opening riffs were so loud you could feel the whole building shake. Then we finished with 'Rocker' – coming back for an encore of 'Shake a Leg', then 'Let There Be Rock'. It was the first and last time that we ever played 'Shake a Leg' live.

I did make one big fuck-up that night, mind you.

After the opener of 'Hells Bells' – played without the aid of the bell, which by then was on a container ship to Canada – we were set to play a couple of classics, 'Shot Down in Flames', then 'Hell Ain't a Bad Place to Be'. But I was so nervous, I launched into 'Hell Ain't a Bad Place to Be' first . . . while the band were playing 'Shot Down in Flames'. Thankfully, the band was so loud, no one could really hear me – apart from the fans in the first few rows, who were looking at me, like, *what the fuck are you doing*? But no one else seemed to care. And by the time 'Hell Ain't a Bad Place to Be' started for real, I'd already done one run-through – albeit to the wrong tune – so I just sang it again. And after that, everything was fine.

In the dressing room after the gig, meanwhile, none of us could find any words – and I mean that quite literally. We were all gasping for breath, sweat pouring down our faces. You can't even have a beer in that state, you'd just throw it right back up.

I remember Cliff sitting there – always the coolest guy in the room – smoking a tab, looking at me. 'You alright, Jonna?'

'Brilliant, mate,' I gasped.

Outside, we could hear the crowd still roaring and clapping for more.

There was no need for any more conversation.

The fans were saying everything that needed to be said. What a night it was.

The most satisfying part of *Back in Black*'s success was that it let me give back to the people who'd always been there for me – above all, my kids, my ma and dad, my brother Maurice, sister Julie and brother Victor.

When the royalty cheques started coming in I bought my parents a house of their own – halfway up Whickham Bank, next to Dunston, with lovely views over Newcastle. My dad was nervous about the idea, thinking the guys at his club would stop speaking to him if he wasn't paying rent to the council. But he eventually came around . . . and, of course, in the end his pals were happy for him.

A few years later, I was also able to help Maurice get a job as a chef. He'd been going through a rough time after his marriage ended, so I asked the boys if they'd consider giving him a month's trial. And, of course, the second he started, everyone fell in love with him, as they always do. He even went on to win the band's 'most valuable roadie' award. It was the least that I could do for Maurice, really. To this day, in fact, I still owe him a new cap after that show at Lobley Hill.

Australia was the toughest part of the *Back in Black Tour* for me, I'm not going to lie. Bon hadn't just been famous Down Under, after all. He'd been an icon – a national treasure. They'd grown up with him. First in The Valentines. Then in Fraternity.

Our first show was at the Entertainment Centre in Perth, one of the biggest arenas in the country. This was very much Bon territory, with his hometown of Fremantle just a few miles away. I was more than a bit anxious, to say the least. But no sooner had we landed than Peter was handed a message from a member of the crew that read, 'Mrs. Scott would really like to meet Brian.' As soon as I heard that, a wave of relief came over me, because I knew that AC/DC coming into town would remind Bon's mum of her loss, which must have been so hard. It had been only a year since Bon's death, almost to the day.

I ended up spending the afternoon drinking endless cups of tea with Mrs. Scott – or Isa – and Bon's brothers, Derek and Graeme.* She was just the most wonderful woman, still with her broad Scottish accent. I later learned that it was Malcolm who first called her with news of Bon's death because he feared that the British tabloids would get to her first. That was just so Malcolm. Such a class act. I mean, the guts that it must have taken to make that call . . .

The best part of my time with Isa was hearing her stories about Bon as a young lad. 'Aye, Ronald was a wee terror, he wouldn't wear shoes, he was always gettin' intae trouble, he was fearless,' she told me.

I thanked her, of course, but it didn't seem enough.

At some point, Derek and Graeme also dropped the bombshell that Bon had been the guy in Fang who I'd met during that freezing night in Torquay. I couldn't quite get my head around that. I still can't . . . But I'm so happy that I met Bon at least once – and that it meant enough for him to tell his family about it when he got home.

Anyway, after we'd talked and laughed some more, I had to go to the show – and Isa came along too. We dedicated 'High Voltage' to her, and the lads in the band felt 'it' that

---

* I don't remember Bon's dad Chick being there, but then again, it was all a blur. I certainly wouldn't have blamed him if he couldn't have faced it.

night. I'm not really sure what the 'it' was exactly – but it felt good.

I'll end with a moment that sums up everything about the insanity of the year that *Back in Black* came out.

It was 4 September, and we were playing Long Beach Arena, just outside of Los Angeles. It was probably one of the biggest venues that I'd ever played until that time, with a capacity of just under 15,000. There was a traffic jam of limos outside, a helicopter circling overhead with AC/DC lit up under it and, of course, the RMS *Queen Mary* moored right there on the waterfront, all lit up. Just the most exhilarating backdrop for a rock'n'roll show – and one of the first signs that the album was turning into something much, *much* bigger than any of us could have ever imagined.*

We were each given a limo of our own to take us to the show that night – just for the spectacle of it – and as I climbed into mine, I said hello to the driver and asked how he was doing.

'Aye, no' bad, thank ye very much.'

'You're an awful long way from home, aren't you?' I said to him, a bit taken aback.

'Aye, well,' he said, 'I came over with a band, and we're still trying tae get a deal, make things happen.'

'Well, I wish you the best of luck, mate,' I said.

There was a pause for a moment, then he said, 'Actually, I'm a singer just like yerself . . .'

'Really?' I said. 'What's your band called?'

'Marmalade,' he said.

---

* It would eventually become the second-bestselling album in music history, behind only Michael Jackson's *Thriller*.

'*What*?!!' I just couldn't believe it. Not only was I very familiar with Marmalade, but I knew *exactly* who their singer was. His name was Alan Whitehead. I mean, Marmalade weren't just some unsigned band with a couple of demo tapes. They'd been a *major act*, with a No. 1 in the U.K. charts. They'd been *everywhere* for a while. But, of course, all that had been – what? – about eleven years ago now.

'Alan??!' I said.

'Yeah!'

'Fuck me!'

'I'm just doin' this to pay the rent,' explained Alan. 'And at least I still get tae hang around musicians.'

'Well, you might not believe this,' I told him, 'but a few months ago, I was living with my parents and fitting vinyl car roofs for a living. So, *anything's* possible . . .'

We had good a laugh about that, then chatted non-stop all the way to the arena.

Never give up.

Epilogue

⚡

I came to in a hospital bed with tubes running out of my arms, feeling very tired and very hungry. For a moment, I had no idea where I was or why. Then a smiley-faced man appeared and asked me how I was doing – and I remembered that I'd just had the first operation to try and fix my hearing. I was in Sydney, Australia. It was October 2015.

The guy was a nurse, it turned out, and when we got chatting and he realized who I was, he told me something that left me reeling – Malcolm was a resident of the care facility just over the wall outside my window. That was where he was being treated for his early-onset dementia. I couldn't believe it. Not only was Malcolm just twenty yards from me, but this nurse also did shifts over there – and one of his jobs was to take him out for his daily exercise.

'Could I see him?' I asked. 'I would love to sit and have a chat with him, you know, see how he's doing.' The smiley-faced man stopped smiling and dropped his eyes. 'Sorry, mate, I can't do that. It's the family's wishes.'

I told him I understood. In the next building was the man who I'd shared a stage with for thirty-five years. The man who'd hired me as the lead singer of AC/DC. The man who'd cared about me so much, he once visited my hometown to meet my parents. He'd even taken my dad for a pint at his club – I mean, who does that?

But I couldn't see or talk to him. It was like he'd become the man in the iron mask.

It's a tough thing, to shed tears in front of a stranger.

I later learned that it was Malcolm's wife, O'Linda, who'd wanted him to be kept away from the world. She'd been told by the doctors that they still didn't know enough about dementia and Alzheimer's to be sure that the people who live with these terrible conditions are completely without memory. O'Linda knew how proud Malcolm was – we all did – and she feared that if I or anyone outside his immediate family went in to see him, he might be embarrassed about his condition. She didn't want to take that risk, especially given everything else that he was going through.

She was just looking out for her husband, like she always did.

Angus visited him, as did his grandchildren, who I'm told made him very happy.

But it broke my heart all the same.

The next day, the guy who'd operated on my ears – Dr. Chang – came to see me and got straight to the point.

'I've got good news and bad news,' he said. 'Which do you want first?'

'This sounds like the start of a joke,' I told him.

'There's no punchline, I'm afraid,' he said.

I asked him to start with the bad news, to get it over with.

'Okay,' began Dr. Chang, 'so we operated on your left ear, but as hard as we tried not to do any damage, you lost pretty much 100 per cent of your hearing in that ear. I'm sorry. We did everything we could.'

I closed my eyes and felt myself going numb.

Deaf in one ear.

Fuck, fuck, fuck . . .

'The good news is that we got to your right ear in time,' Dr. Chang went on, 'and we were able to retain about 50 per cent of your hearing in that one, which should be enough to stay on the tour. You'll just have to adjust the mix that you get in your earpiece monitor.'

This was a bigger deal than it sounded. For as long as I'd used an earpiece monitor, I'd never put it in my left ear. That was the ear I used to listen to the band, while the monitor went in my right ear, so I could hear my own voice. But now that I was deaf in my left ear, I wouldn't be able to hear the band, so I'd need to get a mix of both the band and my vocals in my earpiece – and all with just 50 percent of my hearing left in that ear. It would be a nightmare. But I'd have to find a way to make it work . . .

That was when it dawned on me that Dr. Chang had been trying to soften the blow.

There really hadn't been any good news at all.

Dr. Chang at least said I'd be okay to play the upcoming show at ANZ Stadium, right there in Sydney – as long as I promised him that I'd never fly again on the day of a show.

So, I pushed ahead . . . and I got through the show, followed by eight more in Australia, then another two in New Zealand. But it was tough going with just one 'good' ear.

Finally, after New Zealand, we had a four-month gap until the *Rock or Bust World Tour* moved to Europe – so I could get some proper rest and get myself back on track.

Then the phone rang. It was Tim, our tour manager.

'Hello Brian,' he said. 'I'm pleased to say the tour's been going so well, we're going to add twenty shows in America before we head to Europe. That okay with you?'

***

Telling my bandmates that I was deaf in one ear, half deaf in the other, and that I needed time to rest my ears and work with Dr. Chang was as difficult and embarrassing as I'd feared.

Everyone was sympathetic, of course. But the twenty new American shows had been locked in.

'What do you think, Jonna?' Angus asked me. 'Can you do it?'

'I'm not going to let anybody down,' I told him, 'but if my hearing gets any worse, I'll have to stop.'

It was a dreadful, desperate time. We at least got a long break for Christmas and the New Year, during which I made a couple of visits to a specialist hospital near my home in Sarasota, where doctors tried to strengthen what little hearing I had left ... by injecting steroids directly into my eardrum. Not a pleasant experience.

At the same time, back in Newcastle, my great friend Brendan Healy, the musician and comedian, was dying of cancer – and his condition had taken a turn for the worse. I'd known Brendan since I was in The Jasper Hart Band, and we'd both later become members of the same drinking society, The Legion of the Damned. Tragically, we'd lost another member, the guitarist Dave Black, just a few months earlier. He'd been found dead after being struck by a train. He was only sixty-two years old.

Because of the situation with my ears, the next chance I would get to fly back to see Brendan would be at the end of February. 'Brendan,' I pleaded with him on the telephone. 'Keep fighting, mate. I'll be there as fast as I can. Can you do that for me?'

'Well,' said Brendan, who never lost his sense of humour, 'if you insist...'

***

The American gigs that followed – Tacoma, Las Vegas, Denver, Fargo and St. Paul – were some of the most difficult of my life. They were all arenas, for a start, which are much louder than outdoor stadiums. Hardly able to hear the band through my earpiece, I had to watch Cliff's fingers on his bass to see where we were in each song. I was constantly looking over to the side of the stage to John, my sound man, going, 'Is this okay?'

Some of the songs were almost impossible.

One night, I had to do 'Highway to Hell' and couldn't for the life of me find the note. I just said to the audience, 'Come on, you're going to have to help me out here.' I had no idea what key I was in . . . thank God they did. I was mortified when I came off stage. I knew that I couldn't go on like this. It was crippling. Something had to give.

Then, just as we got to Chicago – three days before I was due to fly back to Newcastle – I got a call from Brendan's home number in Haydon Bridge. It was his son Jack with the news that I'd been dreading. Brendan hadn't been able to hold on any longer.

We'd lost him.

I felt so useless and empty after Brendan died. He was only fifty-nine years old, with so much life left to live. Everyone who knew him was devastated. I hate the C-word, but cancer really is a c * * *, it has taken far too many of my family members and friends.

There were four more AC/DC shows before Brendan's funeral, and they went by in a blur.

The last of them was at Sprint Center in Kansas City. The moment the show ended at 11 p.m., I rushed to the airport, took a jet to New York, then a long-haul flight to London, followed by another flight to Newcastle, arriving just as the service was starting.

Everyone who was anyone in Newcastle was there.

Except for Brendan, of course.

But true to form, he found a way to get a big laugh. At the end of the service, as his coffin was being moved into the crematorium incinerator and the curtain closed, there was a deafening roar as we all cheered and applauded the man we'd all loved.

'Actually,' coughed the priest, with a little smile, 'Brendan left instructions if this happened.'

Then he nodded his head, the curtains reopened, and out came Brendan's coffin again.

It was his final encore.

We all laughed hysterically and sobbed our hearts out at the same time – not an easy thing to do.

When I got back to America, everything was different.

I wasn't just struggling to hear any more.

I couldn't hear anything.

A murderous silence had descended, leaving me feeling trapped and very alone.

Whether it was the flights to the funeral that made it worse, or just the natural progression of my condition, the situation had become critical. When I phoned Dr. Chang in Australia to tell him, he ordered me to go immediately to a hearing institute near my home in Sarasota and get tests. So off I went – and the verdict wasn't good.

'Mr. Johnson,' said the doctor, 'your ears are an absolute mess. This is very serious. And I'm told that you're on tour. You're not doing any more shows are you?'

'Actually,' I admitted, 'I've got another show in Atlanta in two days' time.'

'No,' he said. 'Absolutely not. You cannot do it.'

'But I have to do it. I've got a contract.'

'Mr. Johnson, what you've just suffered is a temporary complete hearing loss. If it happens again, it could be permanent. You'd be completely deaf, and at that point, your only option would be implants. We'd have to put you under and make an incision from each ear all the way down to the back of your skull, and the implants would stick out, so the batteries could be changed. You could suffer nerve damage, balance problems, tinnitus, there are all kinds of risks. And your brain would have to relearn to hear, which could take months – and what you'd hear would be synthetic. So, I'll say this one last time. Stop now. Or risk never hearing and singing again.'

The message had finally got through.

I called Tim, the tour manager, on my mobile right there in the room to tell him that I just couldn't continue. It was one of the most difficult conversations of my life – the pain of it made worse over the weeks that followed when the tour simply went on without me.

When I had to leave AC/DC in February 2016, it was a sheer cliff. I didn't tumble down, I was in freefall.

For most people, hearing loss is slow and manageable – a normal part of getting older. Not for me. One minute, I'd been travelling the world with a rock'n'roll band, singing to millions at packed-out stadiums. The next, the world had fallen silent, and it was like I was looking out at my own life from behind soundproofed glass.

I'd always been told there's nothing you can do about your hearing going. It's like being shot on the battlefield – it's just your turn. But no one had ever warned me about the awkwardness of not being able to understand, the sense of futility as you try to overcome what is a very real physical disability, not to mention the crushing sense of loneliness you feel when you finally realize, fuck, this is how things are going to be from now on. As The Beatles' producer George Martin once put it, you find yourself becoming the nodding dog at the dinner table.

Part of the pain of it was that I blamed myself.

For most of my career, I'd been in the loudest band in the world. I'd flown constantly. I'd flown even when I knew I wasn't well . . .

For a while, people would ask me if I was depressed. But depression is treatable. My hearing loss wasn't. What I was feeling wasn't depression. It was something closer to despair.

In my situation, others might have turned to drugs – or worse, therapy. But neither of those things are my style. So, I just went into my office and buried my head in a bottle of whisky. And before you start worrying, don't – I made sure that it was the good stuff.

I was replaced for the rest of the *Rock or Bust World Tour* by Axl Rose. I'm told that he did a great job. But I just couldn't watch, especially when you've been doing it for thirty-five years. It's like finding a stranger in your house, sitting in your favourite chair. But I bear no grudges. It was a tough situation. Angus and the lads did what they felt they had to do.

That said, after the band released a statement confirming that I was leaving the tour and wishing me all the best for the future, I couldn't relax or concentrate on anything.

It was just always there.

Then the calls started coming in.

Joe Walsh from The Eagles was the first, God bless him. Then it was Billy Connolly . . . 'How ya doin' Brian, does this mean we're not going to hear those dulcet tones from you any more?' which made me smile for the first time. Then my pal Roger Daltrey, who I'd first met backstage at *Top of the Pops* – then Ozzy and Sharon Osbourne, sending me their love and support.

I suppose I shouldn't have been surprised, but most of them had hearing issues of their own. 'There are only five restaurants I go to in New York, because they're the only ones I can hear in,' said Sting, adding that he blamed 'cymbals, of all things'.

Then the letters came, and kept on coming, from all over the world. Sacks of them. They were from people wishing me well and hoping I would one day sing on stage again. These people were the fans and I have to say it helped me more than you'll ever know. I wrote back to as many as I could. It was heartfelt. Thank you all so much for the kind words. They got me through.

Meanwhile, I distracted myself by doing the other thing I've always loved: racing cars.

Funnily enough, I found myself winning more than usual. People would come up to me afterwards and say, 'Brian, you're fearless!' But I wasn't fearless. I just didn't fucking care any more. I'd always thought that the best way to go out would be at 180 mph, flat-out around a corner. You'd hit the wall and boom, it would be over, just like that.

Don't get me wrong, I didn't want to die . . .

I just wouldn't have minded all that much.

***

Then one day I was contacted by a wonderful man named Stephen Ambrose, an audio and hearing expert from Nashville who'd started making in-ear monitors back in the 1960s, when he was a teenager. When we first met up, he brought along this machine that looked like a car battery, and he hooked me up to it, then put me through all kinds of tests. The way he explained it, the earpiece part of it was a kind of prosthetic eardrum, using a tiny inflatable bubble to conduct the sound. At the time, he was still working on miniaturizing it, which he's since achieved.

Whatever magic he used, it worked. I could hear again – even in my deaf ear, meaning I was able to enjoy stereo for the first time since that flight to Vancouver in 2015.

Suddenly, I felt something that I hadn't felt in what seemed like an eternity.

Hope.

Four months after leaving the AC/DC tour, I flew back to Britain to see my family and some friends – but no sooner had I arrived in Newcastle with my wife Brenda than the phone rang.

'Hello Brian, it's Peter Mensch. I'm managing Muse now.'

It was great to hear Peter's voice after so many years. I told him I thought Muse were a really solid band.

'Well, they'll be glad to hear that . . . because they'd love you to sing "Back in Black" with them.'

'What? Really? When?'

'Tomorrow. At Glastonbury.'

Now, by this point my hearing had got a lot better, but I hadn't performed on stage since the AD/DC show in Kansas before I flew home for Brendan Healy's funeral. I looked over at my wife, Brenda, who'd overheard the conversation, and she gave me a 'just do it' look.

Next thing I knew, I was with the boys from Muse, running through the song behind a curtain at one of the backstage areas of the festival. But it was loud enough for people to overhear, and the second I walked out, there was a mob of promoters – a guy from Germany, in particular – all wanting to know what I was doing there. That was when I realized it would probably be a good idea to let AC/DC know what I was doing. So, I phoned George Fearon in New York, and he asked me if I could give him twenty minutes to talk to the band's lawyers to see if there'd be any legal issues. And, of course, this being the music business . . . there were legal issues.

Lots and lots – and lots – of legal issues.

I couldn't do it. I had to back out.

I felt terrible, especially after Peter and Muse had gone out of their way to ask me to sing.

'Well, how about Reading next year?' asked Peter. 'We'll sort out all the legal stuff by then.'

'If you remember . . . I'll do it,' I told him.

He did remember.

And although I was nervous before I went on, it was wonderful – and when we had finished Matt Bellamy came over and gave me a great hug on stage.

That's when it all came flooding back. The excitement. The fun. The noise. There's nothing like playing live rock'n'roll, and I got my life back – it just flew out there over all these kids in the audience, college-age kids who'd been singing along, because somehow they knew every word. My daughters were crying. My wife was crying. 'I wish all my sets were this short,' I told Matt, laughing with relief. It was only one song but after two years of silence, it felt like a victory.

A couple of months later we lost Malcolm. His funeral was at St. Mary's Cathedral in Sydney at the end of 2017.

He was just sixty-four when the dementia that he'd been battling for years finally got the better of him.

A truly awful day.

O'Linda his wife, Ross and Cara, his children, led the mourning. Malcolm's Gretsch guitar was next to his casket. And when the mass ended, the family followed the pallbearers out to the hearse. Out on the street were the massed band of Scottish pipes and drums. The cortege set off to the tune of 'Waltzing Matilda'. I hope you can imagine it. The crowds, the tears, the pride and the love for one man.

When Malcolm left AC/DC back in 2014, the heart of the band stopped beating. To this day, I miss him more than I could ever put into words. He never missed a trick, from a band member's performance to a crew member's well-being. I don't know how he did it. He had his demons, but he beat them, and he beat them good. His guitar playing was masterful. And behind that powerful sound, there was a subtlety that music critics could never understand. Standing to his right on stage, I could only ever marvel at the man. But I kept my admiration to myself for the most part because he wasn't the kind of guy who enjoyed taking a compliment.

It was hard to see Angus struggle with such grief.

He and Malcolm weren't twins, but they could have been.

And to have lost him so soon after George, his older brother – another icon – it was incredibly tough. But the band and his wife, Ella, were there to support him.

I was sitting next to Phil Rudd at the wake afterwards, and

he turned to me and asked, 'So which is your bad ear?' I pointed to my left eye and said, 'That one' – which broke the ice like nothing else. Tears and laughter, that strange combination again.

Then AC/DC's sound engineer Paul Boothroyd – a Scouse known for speaking his mind – piped up and said, 'So c'mon lads, when's the band getting back together then?'

The whole room fell silent. We all looked at each other.

'Just saying . . .'

George Fearon called me not long after.

'Angus wondered if you'd be interested in doing a new album,' he said.

'Yes,' I said, 'I would fucking love to.'

The following summer, we were on our way to Vancouver, Canada, to record *Power Up* – with Brendan O'Brien producing. I'd been scared to get too excited about it in case the lawyers reared their heads again and found a reason to stop it.

But as the date drew closer and closer, I realized . . . shit, we really are coming back.

It was exhilarating. And a little nerve-wracking, to put it mildly.

I mean, when I'd left the band, a lot of people had written me off. So, in a funny way, it felt like starting all over again . . . Going into the studio was just what I did. But this time it felt very special.

I'm sure Angus, Cliff and Phil were also feeling the same – not that we ever discuss such things. Angus no longer had his brother at his side. Cliff was coming out of a comfortable retirement. Phil had been through some truly crazy shit in New Zealand.

But there was defiance.

We all had a point to prove.

We were the originals. We wanted to show what we could do.

And now here we are, on the other side of a pandemic – I hope – with all the rules of life changed.

Power Up ended up being released during some of the darkest days of the lockdowns, reaching No. 1 in twenty-one countries, while doing something that absolutely no one had ever expected: making the critics happy. Well boys, it only took forty years!

I listened to the album again last night. It's a miracle that it ever happened. I couldn't be happier that it did, though, because singing in AC/DC is not like singing in any other band. There are no ballads. There's no saving your voice for the next song. Every moment, you're standing your ground. It's attack. Like singing with a fixed bayonet.

Like I said before, 'nine lives, cat's eyes, abusin' every one of them and running wild.'

⚡

I of course went on, after the success of *Back in Black*, to tour and record with AC/DC for many decades, but I will save all those stories for another time, another book . . .

A ROCK'N'ROLL FAMILY TREE

Toasty Folk Trio (1963/64)
Brian Johnson (Vocals)

Section 5 (1964)
Brian Johnson (Vocals)
Steve Chance (Bass)
Les Chance (Guitar)
Rob Conlin (Drums)
Trevor Macarthy (Guitar)

The Nine Pins (1965)
Brian Johnson (Vocals)
Steve Chance (Bass)
Les Chance (Guitar)
Rob Conlin (Drums)

**Gobi Desert Kanoe Klub #1
(April 1967 – October 1967)**
Brian Johnson (Vocals)
Steve Chance (Bass)
Dave Yarwood (Guitar)
Les Chance (Guitar)
Rob Conlin (Drums)

**Hannibal Kemp/Fresh #1
(June 1969 – Sept 1969)**
Brian Johnson (Vocals)
Phil Hildreth (Bass)
Peter Callard (Guitar)
Shrimp (Keyboards)
Bob (Drums)

Fresh #2 (October 1969)
Brian Johnson (Vocals)
Phil Hildreth (Bass)
Peter Callard (Guitar)
Shrimp (Keyboards)
David Gluyas (Drums)

**Jasper Hart Band #1
(October 1970 – November 1970)**
Brian Johnson (Vocals)]
Ken Brown (Guitar)
Fred Smith (Drums)
Steve Chance (Bass)

**Jasper Hart Band #2
(November 1970 – June 1971)**
Brian Johnson (Vocals)
Ken Brown (Guitar)
Fred Smith (Drums)
Steve Chance (Bass)
Alan Taylorson (Keyboards)

Jasper Hart Band #3 (June 1971)
Brian Johnson (Vocals)
Ken Brown (Guitar)
Fred Smith (Drums)
Les Connelly (Bass)

**Jasper Hart Band #4
(June 1971 – August 1971)**
Brian Johnson (Vocals)
Ken Brown (Guitar)
Tom Hill (Bass)
Fred Smith (Drums)

**Jasper Hart Band #5
(August 1971 – October 1971)**
Brian Johnson (Vocals)
Ken Brown (Guitar)
Brian Gibson (Drums)
Tom Hill (Bass)

Buffalo #1 (October 1971)
Brian Johnson (Vocals)
Ken Brown (Guitar)
Brian Gibson (Drums)
Tom Hill (Bass)

**Jasper Hart Band #6
(November 1971 – January 1972)**
Brian Johnson (Vocals)
Tom Hill (Bass)
Brian Gibson (Drums)
Ken Brown (Guitar)

**U.S.A. #1
(January 1972 – August 1972)**
Brian Johnson (Vocals)
Vic Malcolm (Guitar)
Brian Gibson (Drums)
Tom Hill (Bass)

**Geordie #1
(August 1972 – December 1974)**
Brian Johnson (Vocals)
Tom Hill (Bass)
Brian Gibson (Drums)
Vic Malcolm (Guitar)

**Geordie #2
(January 1975 – September 1975)**
Brian Johnson (Vocals)
Tom Hill (Bass)
Micky Bennison (Guitar)
Brian Gibson (Drums)

Geordie #3 (September 1975)
Brian Johnson (Vocals)
Tom Hill (Bass)
Micky Bennison (Guitar)
Allan Bradley (Drums)

**Brian Johnson (Solo Project)
(January 1976)**
Brian Johnson (Vocals)

**AC/DC #14
(May 1977 – February 1980)**
Bon Scott (Vocals)
Angus Young (Lead Guitar)
Malcolm Young (Rhythm Guitar)
Cliff Williams (Bass)
Phil Rudd (Drums)

THE LIVES OF BRIAN

Half Past Thirteen (1966 – 1967)
Ken Brown (Vocals/Guitar)
Fred Smith (Drums)
Charley Foskett (Bass)

Lusika State Group (1965/66)
Sharkey (Guitar)
Alan Taylorson (Keyboards)
Tom Hill (Bass)
Brian Gibson (Drums)

Vince King & The Stormers (1963)
Bob Jerry (Vocals)
Malcolm Hooper (Guitar)
Joe D'Ambrosie (Drums)
Vic Malcolm (Rhythm Guitar)
Micky Golden (Bass)
Dave Ditchburn (Vocals)

Crusade #3
(January 1969 – October 1970)
Ken Brown (Guitar)
Fred Smith (Drums)
Steve Chance (Bass)
Alan Taylorson (Keyboards)
Jim Snowdon (Vocals)

Sneeze #2 (1968 – 1969)
Ray Coulson (Guitar)
Pierre Pederson (Keyboards)
Tom Hill (Bass)
Brian Gibson (Drums)
Rod Foggon (Vocals)
Roger Smith (Sax)
Jim Hall (Flugelhorn)

Gobi Desert Kanoe Klub #2
(October 1967 – August 1968)
Brian Johnson (Vocals)
Dave Yarwood (Guitar)
Ken Brown (Guitar)
Fred Smith (Drums)
Steve Chance (Bass)

Yellow #2
(August 1970 – June 1971)
Kenny Mountain (Vocals/Guitar)
Tom Hill (Bass)
Keith Fisher (Drums)
Bob Barton (Guitar)
Pierre Pederson (Keyboards)

Yellow #1 (March 1970)
Kenny Mountain (Vocals/Guitar)
Tommy Sloan (Drums)
Joe D'Ambrosie (Bass)
Vic Malcolm (Guitar)

Blondie
(August 1969 – August 1970)
Tom Hill (Bass)
Keith Fisher (Drums)
Bob Barton (Guitar)
Pierre Pederson (Keyboards)

Brass Alley (1972)
Franky Gibbon (Bass)
Barry Alton (Guitar)
Howard Martin (Drums)
Dave Ditchburn (Vocals)

Smoke Stack Crumble (1971)
Dave MacTavish (Vocals)
Vic Malcolm (Guitar)
Paul Thompson (Drums)

Sneeze #3 (1970 – 1971)
Rod Foggon (Vocals)
Brian Gibson (Drums)
Mick Balls (Guitar)
George Otigbah (Bass)
Roger Smith (Sax)
Jim Hall (Flugelhorn)

Geordie #4 (October 1976)
Brian Johnson (Vocals)
Dave Ditchburn (Vocals)
Vic Malcolm (Guitar)
Franky Gibbon (Bass)
Alan Clark (Keyboards)
George Defty (Drums)

Brass Alley #2 (1976)
Brian Johnson (Vocals)
Dave Ditchburn (Vocals)
Vic Malcolm (Guitar)
Franky Gibbon (Bass)
Alan Clark (Keyboards)
George Defty (Drums)

Fogg (1975)
Chris McPherson (Vocals)
Bob Porteus (Drums)
Derek Rootham (Guitar)
Dave Robson (Bass)

Geordie #5
(July 1977 – March 1980)
Brian Johnson (Vocals)
Dave Robson (Bass)
Derek Rootham (Guitar)
Davy Whittaker (Drums)

Geordie U.S.A. (May 1977)
Brian Johnson (Vocals)
Dave Robson (Bass)
Derek Rootham (Guitar)
Davy Whittaker (Drums)

U.S.A. #2 (April 1977)
Brian Johnson (Vocals)
Dave Robson (Bass)
Derek Rootham (Guitar)
Davy Whittaker (Drums)

AC/DC #15 (March 1980)
Brian Johnson (Vocals)
Angus Young (Lead Guitar)
Malcolm Young (Rhythm Guitar)
Cliff Williams (Bass)
Phil Rudd (Drums)

Acknowledgements

Brenda Johnson, for letting me do this.

Cliff, Angus, Malcolm and Phil.

Joanne and Kala, for always rooting for their dad.

Maurice Johnson, BS editor.

Victor, for being there at the beginning, and love to Julie for being the only girl of the bunch.

George Beveridge, Ken Walker, Vic Malcolm, Steve Chance & Phil Hildreth for reminding me of all the forgotten memories.

I would like to thank Darren Goulden for his unstinting work with all historical facts, dates and times of importance. Most of all his truly exceptional 'Family Tree'. Many thanks Daz.

Tarquin Gotch, my friend and manager.

Rowland White, my editor, for his belief.

Picture Permissions

⚡

Inset Images

All images courtesy of the author, except the below:
p.4, second row, Source Unknown
p.9, bottom left, BBC
p.10, middle, Source Unknown
p.10, bottom, Ian Dickson / Redferns via Getty
p.11, top, Courtesy of OVC Media and Eliot M. Cohen
p.11, bottom, The Hoover Company
p.13, bottom, Wikimedia commons
p.14, top, Blueee / Alamy Stock Photo
p.14, bottom right, Chris Walter / WireImage via Getty
p.15, top, Everett Collection
p.15, middle, Denis O'Regan / Getty Images
p.15, bottom right, ZUMA Press, Inc. / Alamy Stock Photo

Integrated Images

All images courtesy of the author, except the below:
p.x, Dana Zuk Photography
p.88, Records / Alamy Stock Photo
p.120, Jorgen Angel / Redferns via Getty
p.140, Wikimedia Commons
p.174, Gijsbert Hanekroot/Redferns via Getty

Index

⚡

'Shot Down in Flames'
(AC/DC) 332
Sinatra, Frank 249
Slade, Chris 6
Slade 186, 201, 213
Small Faces 176
Smith, Fred 129, 132, 156–7
Smith, Jimmy 145
Smith Patterson foundry 15–16
Smoke Stack Crumble 165, 353
Sneeze 164, 353
Sony Walkman 299–300
Springsteen, Bruce 245
Status Quo 158–60, 213
Stewart, Rod 176, 245
Sting (Gordon Sumner) 127, 345
Stirling, Corporal 162
Sunderland 173
Sunniside Working Men's
Club 105–7

Talking Heads 299, 303
Taylerson, Alan 157, 164
Taylor, Andy 251–2
Territorial Army 141–3, 153–4
basic training 143–6
German military exercise
160–64
parachute training 146–51
This Is It (Fogg) 242
Thompson, Chris 254
Thompson, Paul 165
Thriller (Michael Jackson) 335
'Thunderstruck' (AC/DC) 6
Toasty Folk Trio 105–6, 107, 352
Top of the Pops (BBC)

AC/DC 265
Geordie 181–5, 189–90
Torquay 197–200, 266, 334
'Touch Too Much'
(AC/DC) 265
Townshend, Pete 126, 192
Turner, Ike and Tina 126, 248
'Tutti Frutti' (Little Richard) 55–7
'Twist and Shout'
(The Beatles) 188
Tyne Tees Television 54–5,
78, 228

Udo, Mr 206
Underhill, Derek 241, 243, 256, 258
Uriah Heep 255
U.S.A. 165–72, 187, 352, 353
see also Geordie

'Vambo Marble Eye' (The
Sensational Alex Harvey
Band) 207
Vanilla Studios 269, 277
Vince King and the Stormers
168, 353

Walker, Ken 252, 254, 264,
267–9, 281–2, 290, 323–4
Walker, Newcastle 97, 98–9
Walker Boys' Club 107–110
Walsh, Joe 345
'We Are Sailing' (Rod Stewart) 245
Westerhope Comrades Club
288–9
Weymouth, Tina 303
Whale, James 210–211